THE
SECOND UNDERWATER
BOOK

Also edited by Kendall McDonald

THE UNDERWATER BOOK

THE SECOND UNDERWATER BOOK

Edited by Kendall McDonald
for the British Sub-Aqua Club

PELHAM BOOKS

First published in Great Britain by
PELHAM BOOKS LTD
52 Bedford Square
London, W.C.1
1970

7207 0013 2

Printed in Great Britain by
Ebenezer Baylis and Son Limited
The Trinity Press, Worcester, and London
in eleven on twelve point Baskerville and bound by
James Burn Ltd, Royal Mills, Esher, Surrey

Foreword

By Admiral of the Fleet the Earl Mountbatten
of Burma KG PC GCB OM GCSI GCIE GCVO DSO FRS

Honorary Life Member of the British Sub-Aqua Club

THE UNDERWATER BOOK published by the British Sub-Aqua Club in 1968, proved such a success that it is not surprising that the Club is publishing *The Second Underwater Book*.

I am glad to write the Foreward to this for two reasons.

Firstly as a man who served actively for half-a-century in the Royal Navy because the Navy is so strongly represented among the contributors.

Secondly because I spent most of my spare time, when in Command of the 1st Cruiser Squadron and later the Mediterranean Fleet, under the water using the Cousteau Aqualung. I had a very happy and thrilling time diving in many parts of the Mediterranean and Red Sea and since then I have dived in many more exotic waters, off Zanzibar, Ceylon, Singapore, Tahiti and the Bahamas. Each time has been a fresh thrill. I shall never forget my first encounter with a shark or killing a giant ray which weighed 40 lbs more than I did.

I found Chapter 3, "With all flags flying—200 feet down", very moving but Chapter 4 "Diving for the Weather" I thought the most fascinating. The author pays a well deserved tribute to Instructor Captain Graham Britton, who used to be my Fleet Meteorological Officer in the Mediterranean.

But every chapter will prove of real interest to the ever increasing thousands of Sub-Aqua enthusiasts, and I hope the book will entice people who have never dived to try their hand at this most satisfying and exciting sport.

Mountbatten of Burma

A. F.

CONTENTS

ILLUSTRATIONS

DIAGRAMS

INTRODUCTION

In *The Underwater Book*, the first volume in this series, the chapters and pictures were confined to the work being done by members of the British Sub-Aqua Club in the waters around the coasts of Great Britain.

But in this second book the British Sub-Aqua Club ranges farther afield. Not all the diving of the Club's members is confined to the waters around the British coasts—for holidays and work take British divers everywhere. Branches of the Club are world-wide. All do useful and interesting work in their own home waters.

We are particularly pleased that in this volume we have also been able to report on some of the diving done by the Royal Navy, who have always maintained the closest links with the Club and who have given us the benefit of their help and advice on many aspects of modern diving.

KENDALL McDONALD

"POOR ENGLAND HAS LOST SO MANY MEN"

by Richard Larn

A serving Chief Petty Officer in the Royal Navy, Richard Larn
has been an active diver for almost 18 years. As diving officer
of the Naval Air Command Sub-Aqua Club he was the in-
stigator of the successful search for H.M.S. *Association*. The
co-author of *Cornish Shipwrecks*, he has just completed a book
covering the wrecks of the Isles of Scilly.

THE western face of the Rock of Gibraltar echoed and re-echoed
the shrill commanding notes of bosuns' pipes as twenty-one
British men-o'-war prepared to sail. The date was 29 September, 1707, and a fleet of some forty vessels had laid at anchor
for weeks, preparing for this day, when half its number would
depart for England and home.

On board the flagship, H.M.S. *Association*, a ninety-gun,
second-rate ship-of-the-line, final preparations were being
made for sea. Her decks resounded with the noise of seamen
about their work, some of whom were on their knees, scouring
the upper deck with wet sand to remove the rust stains left
by the gunner's party. A large proportion of the warship's shot
and powder had been landed the previous day to stock the
newly constructed magazines ashore, and seemingly endless
rounds of ball, bar and grape had been slung outboard into
waiting boats.

In the great cabin aft, the nobility were being entertained
by Sir Cloudesley Shovell and his captain, Edmund Loades. It
was a farewell party, and many well-known names were
present, including Sir George Byng, Vice-Admiral of the Blue,
Sir John Norris, and Henry Trelawny, second son of the
Bishop of Winchester. The twitter of the pipes brought the
toasts and "*bon voyages*" to an end, and the gentlemen took their
leave. As the junior officers left via the ornate entrance port
and down the great steps attached to the exterior of the hull,

so their seniors were afforded the luxury of being lowered into their boats by chair, a mode of conveyance more suited to their portly figures and age.

As the various boats pulled smartly away from the flagship, oars dipping in perfect rhythm into a glittering sea, so the epauletted and bewigged officers turned for a last look at the huge, splendidly ornate vessel they had just left. None of them could have guessed that this fine ship and her entire crew were to be the centre-piece of the greatest maritime disaster England has ever known.

As the line of sail drew out towards the Straits of Gibraltar, so a lone vessel on the horizon drew closer. Soon the fleet was joined by the fifty-four-gunned *Panther*, from Tangiers, and they were complete, ready for passage to Portsmouth. The ships headed due west out into the open wastes of the Atlantic, their last sight of land being Cape Spartel. Lieutenant Jerome Barker of the *Panther* wrote in his log, "Spartel bore south-east, 5 leagues, at 8 in ye forenoon of 30 September".

All went well until the 14th of October by which time the fleet had reached a latitude of 47° north, and commenced the swing back east towards the English Channel. Then gales struck, first from the east, then north and finally north-west, so that by 22 October they were hopelessly lost, despite several noon observations that day. At about 11 a.m. (this was the time logged by the captain of the *Lennox*, although his lieutenants recorded 7 a.m. and 10 a.m., while the *Phoenix* recorded 8 a.m.) the lead ships, *Lennox*, *Phoenix*, and the French prize *La Valeur*, were detached to Falmouth for convoy duties, and *Association* assumed the van. A little before dark, at about 4 p.m., a meeting of the various sailing masters was convened on board the Admiral's ship, in order to establish their position. An almost unanimous decision put the fleet west of Ushant and at the mouth of the Channel, so sail was set and they continued on an easterly course before a favourable gale.

Between 7.30 and 8 p.m. the lead ships found themselves amongst rocks and fired cannon as a signal of distress. The *Association* struck the Gilstone ledges and went down with all hands save two, neither of whom lived for long. The *Eagle* and *Romney* struck either the Crebinnicks or Crim rocks and were lost, whilst a fireship, the *Firebrand*, which had followed the flagship on to the Gilstone but got off again, sank in deep water along the southern edge of the western rocks. From the four wrecks, there were less than twenty-six survivors, the Navy having lost almost 2,000 men in a single disaster. There was in fact a fifth wreck, the fireship *Phoenix*, one of the detached vessels, which also struck the western rocks and had been run ashore, half-full of water, between Trescoe and St. Martins. No wonder that John Ben of St. Hilary, in a letter dated 16 November, 1707, wrote, "—I am heartily sorry for the loss poor England has sustained of so many men". His letter was addressed to Sir Jonathon Trelawny, Bishop of Winchester, who had inquired as to the whereabouts of his son's body.

This was the basis of the information which eventually led divers of the Naval Air Command Sub-Aqua Club (B.S.A.C. Special Branch No. 66) to re-locate one of the wrecks in 1967. The expression re-locate is used in preference to discovered or found, since it is now obvious the wreck site was well known 250 years ago and has received the attention of many early divers. The most important aspect of the re-location was the fact it showed up the total inadequacies of our antiquated maritime laws regarding wreck and salvage; laws which were formulated to cover entirely different circumstances in a different age. Assuming the wreck is that of the *Association*, if it had to be sacrificed in order to bring these inadequacies to the attention of those who could change them—then all was not in vain. But it is now fairly certain that no changes in the Merchant Shipping Act will occur for some time, and that exactly the same situation might occur again. In order to understand the ridiculous situation which occurred over the Gilstone wreck, one which has been aptly summarized by Kendall McDonald as "the Scilly Shambles", one must know the full background story, which has its beginning in 1964.

In the spring of that year, the Naval Air Command Sub-Aqua Club planned an exploratory expedition to the Isles of Scilly. To date, there had been almost no serious underwater exploration of the area, and the intention was to commence a full-scale survey for future expeditions. Part of the preparatory work was the collection of wreck information relevant to the islands, and amongst the list of 500 or so ships the divers took with them appeared *Association, Eagle, Romney* and *Firebrand*. These were names that could be found in several reference books, there was no secret about them. But 1707 was over 250 years ago, and no one seriously anticipated that any part of a wooden ship with iron cannon would survive that long in British waters—and so the divers searched for more modern wrecks, and found most of them. Then, on 27 June, a single iron cannon was found, and from this insignificant and un-spectacular event grew the whole *Association* affair.

The cannon, a pretty poor and eroded specimen (now thought to have come from a transport lost in the 1680s) was found in ninety feet of water in a deep gulley, south-east of the Old Town Gilstone, off St. Mary's. In ignorance of the finer points of local geography, it was assumed it could possibly have come from one of Sir Cloudesley's ships, and interest ran high. Fur-ther exploration found an old anchor, nine foot in the shank, its wooden stock long eaten away, and the team felt sure they were on the right track. Only then was it realized that the islands have two Gilstones, one with "our cannon" and anchor close at hand, another six miles away to the west, close to the Bishop Rock. Time unfortunately was very short, in two days the expedition had to be back at the mainland, and weather conditions prevented any exploration of the "outer Gilstone", a very exposed location. The club departed in complete frus-tration, the divers scattering the length of the country to rejoin their various ships and air stations. All were firm in their reso-lution that the club would find the *Association* if anything remained, first on paper, and then in the sea. They little realized the situation which was to develop.

Over that winter, every possible source of local information was consulted and slowly a mass of data was accumulated. With it grew the realization that here was a wreck disaster of unprecedented magnitude, a disaster which in itself was of great interest, let alone the stories of vast treasure, murdered men, deathbed confessions and the like.

It was first necessary to prove which of the Gilstones had been the scene of the wrecks, since no one could be that certain. The most confusing aspect being the fact that Sir Cloudesley's body was washed ashore at Porthellick, a small cove on the south side of St. Mary's. Had the *Association* been wrecked on

Where a treasure ship lies. *Above*, an aerial view of the Gilstone rock just awash at high water. H.M.S. *Association* struck rocks close at hand off the Scilly Isles. This photograph, taken by Richard Larn, shows clearly that even on a calm day diving on the *Association* site is not for beginners. *Below*, an enlarged section of Admiralty Chart No. 34, showing the area where the ship sank and the approximate outline of the wreck site. Chart reproduced by permission the Hydrographic Department MOD(N). (See chapter 1)

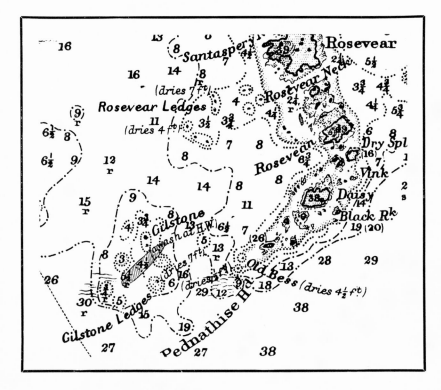

Above: Suddenly, and for no apparent reason, a giant wave would come out of nowhere and erupt across the Gilstone. Divers working on the *Association* wreck learned that these waves were a normal feature of the site and could usually be relied on to follow the same track. This would account for the complete unconcern of these divers anchored in an inflatable over the wreck. Picture by Paul Armiger of the *Daily Telegraph.* (See chapter 1)

Below: The first bronze cannon to be recovered from the wreck of H.M.S. *Association.* It weighed two-and-a-half tons, was of French origin and had been captured at the battle of Vigo Bay and kept on board the flagship. Notice the magnificent crests on the breech, the ornate lifting dolphins and the fleur-de-lis along the barrel. It is now in the Tower of London's collection of cannons. Paul Armiger picture. (See chapter 1)

the Old Town Gilstone then this was perfectly feasible, but was it possible for 2,000 men to drown so close to land and help? If on the other hand, the "outer Gilstone" was the site, then the death of that number of men was possible, but it was unlikely that the Admiral's body would come ashore seven miles away. Assuming that all the old records are accurate when they say Sir Cloudesley was alive when washed ashore, then he must have swum, drifted, or been rowed those seven miles, which would have taken him past St. Agnes light and its welcoming wood-fired beacon. Surely, anyone in distress would have made for the beacon and landed close at hand?

In order to resolve these arguments, two different lines of investigation were taken. The old records made mention of the wrecks occurring on the "Bishop and Clerks", a local geographical name fallen into disuse these past 150 years—so that needed clarification. Secondly, were there any log books at the National Maritime or Science museums in London from the surviving ships of the fleet? Although navigation was pretty inaccurate in the early 1700s, there must be some reference to the bearing of St. Agnes light when the wrecks occurred.

Investigation into the "Bishops and Clerks" revealed that the entire area west of Rosevean was once known by that name, which included the "outer Gilstone"—and a thousand other rocks! The origin of the expression, according to the Western Luminary of 17 April, 1821, dates back to the mid-1600s when, "a fleet of merchantmen coming from Spain were wrecked on them (the Bishop and Clerks) and only Miles Bishop and John and Henry Clerk were preserved on a fragment of mast". As for surviving logbooks, we were surprised to learn that no less than forty-four of them were available for study, all that remained of the original total of sixty-one from the various ships. It seems there was no single official log book for a ship, but rather each officer kept his own, which explains the large number involved. Details from these provided positive proof that the wrecks *must* have occurred on the "outer Gilstone".

The log, or journal, of Lieutenant Wiscard of the *St. George* states, "October 23—ye lighthouse of Silley bore ESE½S distant 6 miles". That of Lieutenant Field of the *Torbay*, "22 October at 9 ye light of Scilly bore E by S½S, about 3 miles" and

2

Captain Reddell of the yacht *Isabella*, "at 8 at nite saw ye light of Scilly bearing SE by S, distant per judgement about 4 miles". This confirmed the suspicion that at no time did the vessels pass south of St. Agnes, in which case the light would have had to bear due north at one point, changing to west.

The apparent discrepancy in the dates results from the fact that at sea a new day commenced at noon and not at midnight, so that at noon on the 22nd October the date became the 23rd. It must have led to great confusion, especially since the convention was not observed ashore. It is also worth noting that the wrecks did not occur on 22/23 October by our present calendar, but rather on 2/3 November. In 1707 the old calendar was still in use and it was not until 1752 that the present Gregorian system was adopted. In the change over (in its day as revolutionary as our decimalization), a period of eleven days had to be "lost", which led to civil demonstrations by people convinced the government had shortened their lives!

The following summer, 1965, a second expedition went to Scilly, the objectives being to find the *Association*, catch, tag and release as many crawfish as possible for the Ministry of Agriculture and Fisheries, and continue the general underwater survey. The "outer Gilstone" was still very much an unknown factor, and only experience would show up the conditions in which it was unsafe to dive. The skipper, Ted Barter, a retired naval lieutenant-commander, and his R.N.X.S. (Royal Naval Auxiliary Service) crew, drove the inshore minesweeper *Puttenham* around the western rocks as smoothly and unconcernedly as one would a car, if that were possible. Half way through the expedition the crew were amused, and not the least put out, to find the local fishermen were running a sweepstake—taking bets as to where the *Puttenham* was going ashore! They should have saved their money and run another sweepstake on some of the "sailors" who followed in the footsteps of N.A.C.S.-A.C. during 1967–8.

Knowing the course steered by Sir Cloudesley's fleet as they neared Scilly, it was taken for granted that the flagship would have struck the Gilstone from the south-west corner. For that reason the search was commenced from the Gilstone Ledges outwards. Looking back on events, the 1965 expedition missed the wreck site by yards, probably by the width of only two of the huge rock gullies that are a feature of the seabed. But, as any diver will tell you, miss a wreck by fifty feet, and you might as well be fifty miles away. Underwater, the reef is a mass of enormous boulders, interposed with these deep gullies or ravines which hide miniature caves and crevices, an area in which the remains of a dozen ships could lie hidden. Perhaps one of the divers did pass over the fringes of the wreck, missing the tell-tale line of a cannon or anchor. Be that as it may, the second expedition returned empty-handed, wiser in the ways of the "outer Gilstone", unanimous that the search should continue, knowing at least one area in which the wreck wasn't! That autumn, a decision was made by the central committee of the club that an application should be made to the Ministry of Defence (Navy) for permission to "search and salvage", in order to protect its interests in case the wreck was found. Unfortunately, the newspapers had by this time got their teeth well into the "treasure ship of Sir Cloudesley Shovell" aspect of the story, and brought the club's activities to the attention of others. As far as the services were concerned, the application for such permission was absolutely unique, since all the divers were serving members of the Royal Navy, and wanted to use a naval vessel to look for a naval wreck.

It took many weeks of consultation and patient waiting to produce that agreement, but eventually it arrived, and everyone was happy—all the club had to do now was find the thing! It was about this time that another diving team began to get newspaper publicity over the wreck of the *Association*, even proclaiming that they had found the wreck, first in 1964 and then again in 1965, but they were in fact only covering the old ground on the "inner Gilstone" and had found nothing new, and certainly not the *Association*.

During all this, the Navy team were complacent, secure in the knowledge, or so they thought, that their contract would prove a trump card if needed, but found, to their dismay, that at least one similar agreement had been signed, and yet a third was in the offing. However, at this stage there was no point in their getting unduly concerned, no one had found any of the four wrecks, and *Puttenham* was certainly the only diving vessel to appear at the "outer Gilstone". During 1966, a third expedition went to Scilly, but weather conditions could not have been worse. Torrential rain, gales, or fog—or a combination of all three, persisted for the entire period.

For days the minesweeper lay at anchor in the roads, absolutely fog-bound. To add to their troubles, one engine starter played up, the radar broke down and recording echo-sounder packed up. Luxury items one might say, but very necessary when navigating a vessel that size in places visited previously by nothing bigger than a motor boat. Only one dive was possible on the Gilstone, and that was made out of sheer bravado and frustration from a leaping, heaving Gemini inflatable boat in a force five, whilst off-shore the *Puttenham* literally rolled her gunwales under. That one dive cost the club a fortune in crockery, and their lunch, and the divers returned empty handed!

That winter a great deal of new research was undertaken, mostly outside Cornwall, in the Public Records Office, National Maritime, Science and War Museums, and similar institutions. The most significant find was the Grahame Spence chart of the Isles of Scilly, located in the archives of the Hydrographic Department of the Navy. It is a massive chart, hand drawn on linen, six feet square, and clearly showed that the rock now known as the Gilstone Ledge was once called the Shovel Rock. Without doubt, this was where the *Association* sank. Previously, a semi-pictorial map had been found in the Public Record Office which showed the stern of a ship in the area, and labelled "*Association* lost", but this was too general and small scaled to be accurate.

It was now common knowledge that the Ministry of Defence had handed out three "search and salvage" contracts for the same wrecks, and it looked as if anyone could have one for the asking. The three holders to date were, the Navy team, Mr. Roland Morris of Penzance, and the "Blue Seas Divers", and it looked as if others might well follow. Since the contracts were to "search for and salvage" the ships of Sir Cloudesley's fleet, one would assume the salvor, in return, would be required to make some sort of effort to do just that—but unfortunately this was not the case.

If fine weather could have been ordered in advance for the 1967 expedition to the Gilstone, the results could not have been improved upon. From the outset, the sun shone from a cloudless sky, flags hung limply from halyards and the sea round the western rocks was mirror smooth. It was obviously ideal Gilstone weather, and with the secret of the "Shovel Rock" in their possession, diving commenced on 2 July. The first day was spent to the west of the rock in fairly deep water, but showed a blank, as did the next day—but Tuesday, 4 July, was different. The result of that memorable dive was so startling, so spectacular and almost an anti-climax, because it was difficult to believe it was that easy. But then it wasn't easy at all really, this was the culmination of four years' work and planning. The divers landed smack down on top of cannon, and a quick reconnaissance showed not one or two others, but dozens—laid out in neat rows, upended in holes, clustered in groups or alone, the entire area was covered in cannon, and at least three of them were bronze. It was a team affair, no one individual seeking or deserving any publicity or credit for the event, but in answer to the bald question, "Who found the *Association*?" then the answer must be, Lieutenant-Commander Jack Gayton, the club's chairman.

From that moment on, the team and the R.N.X.S. crew worked like slaves, and deserve far more credit than they received. They were handicapped from the very beginning, in that their time in the islands was strictly limited, they couldn't hope to compete with the first civilian organization that turned up, and as always, the weather was completely unpredictable. By the end of the first week, a bronze signal cannon, two breech-loading cannon and several huge bronze wheels had been landed, also the first gold coin found in the wreck—a Portuguese 4,000 reis piece dated 1704, as well as many silver coins.

Attempts were made to lift the two-and-a-half-ton bronze cannon, but the team were ill-equipped to carry out heavy lifts. Even with eight, forty-gallon oil drums lashed to the barrel and filled with air, backed up with an assortment of kitbags, the weapon was only just neutrally buoyant, and had to be dumped in shallow water for the time being. Complete secrecy had been maintained, and outside of *Puttenham*, the world was in ignorance of what was going on around the Gilstone. The most pressing need was for more time—time to survey the site properly, to count the cannon and work out their various sizes, and to cover the entire area for loose artefacts.

When informed of the re-location, the Ministry of Defence (Navy) granted an immediate extension, but complications arose for the R.N.X.S. crew who were, after all, civilians with jobs from which none of them could have indefinite leave. So *Puttenham* returned to Penzance for some changes in personnel. Whilst there additional lifting gear was procured, since the recovery of the cannon left in shallow water was imperative. On the return passage to St. Mary's, a Breton fishing boat was sighted in distress, having yards of three-inch nylon rope round her propeller. Brian Lewis, one of the Navy divers, who left the Service to become a veteran oil rig man and who died in a tragic underwater incident in 1969, cleared it in mid-ocean in fifteen minutes, to the everlasting gratitude of the Frenchmen. They presented the team with a box of scampi, three huge fish, and five bottles of "plonk" for want of a better description. When the fish are described as huge, this is no idle exaggeration, just one of them fed twenty-eight people that evening!

On reaching the Scillies, bad weather kept the team fretting in harbour, but gave everyone time to repair battered diving equipment and make slings for the cannon. When finally the sea went down and the skies cleared, the first divers back on the Gilstone announced that the oil drums left on the bronze cannon were battered flat, and useless. They had, however, served a secondary purpose, since the cannon was now completely free of all marine growth and gleamed on the bottom. Aircraft lifting bags with a capacity of ten tons each were flown out from R.N.A.S. Culdrose, near Helston, Cornwall, and to the delight of everyone, *Puttenham* put into St. Mary's that evening, Monday, 10 July, with a magnificent trophy hanging over the stern. And the secret was out.

The cannon was highly ornamented, and the official description read as follows: "This piece of ordnance is 9' 7" from breech base ring to muzzle and weighs approximately three tons. It is a sixteen-pounder culverine of French origin, decorated with the crests of Old France and the House of Beaufort. It bears the inscription Le Duc de Beaufort, surmounted by the collars of the order of St. Michael and St. Espirit. It also bears an eight-pointed cross, which is the badge of St. Espirit, the Holy Ghost. The lifting rings have been cast as ornamental dolphins and the barrel forward of the trunnions is decorated with numerous fleur-de-lis and the letter L surmounted by a crown. Top centre and aft of the muzzle ring is a salamander, the touch hole being in the shape of a scallop shell. The remains of an iron ball was found in the breech."

The Duke of Beaufort was the last holder of the Office of Grand Maître de Navigation in France, and commanded the fleet for Louis XIV until he died in 1669. It is now certain the weapon was cast about 1652, and had been captured at the battle of Vigo Bay and kept on board the *Association* as a prize piece, along with other captured bronze guns, more ornamental than useful, but still part of the ship's main armament. There is a similar gun in the Musée de la Marine in Paris, found on the Moroccan coast near Ceuta.

After the first of the bronze cannon had been safely deposited in the "Queen's Warehouse" at Scilly, and a salvor's warrant duly completed, for everything had to be handed to the Receiver of Wreck, the team set about salvaging other items. Two hand-sounding leads, silver coins of William III dated 1696 to 1704, musket shot by the bucketful, lead bars from which shot was cast, lead pipes, wooden pulley sheaves, more bronze wheels and other items, they were all photographed and duly handed over. There was still not proof that this was the wreck of H.M.S. *Association*, although the evidence of the salvaged equipment pointed in that direction. Cannon balls and the bronze wheels, weighing 60 to 80 lbs. each, were stamped with the "broad arrow" symbol of the British government. The coins all pointed to a vessel sunk post 1704, and the number of cannon on the seabed pointed to it, having once been a ninety-gun ship, or more. Taking into account previous salvage work which managed to raise cannon, this could only be one very large ship, or two smaller vessels.

Regarding early salvage work, an old Scottish newspaper of 9th July, 1710, reported: "We hear from Scilly that the gentlemen concerned in the wreck of Sir Cloudesley Shovell have taken several iron cannon, seven brass guns with a cable, and have found the *Association* in four fathoms of water at low tide, the hull of the ship being intact, wherein there is vast treasure, the Queen's plate, several chests of money, besides ten chests of Sir Cloudesleys money, with great riches from the Grandees of Spain. The divers go down in a copper engine and continue underwater two hours, wherein they have also met with the fireship *Firebrand*."

It has been hinted that the Navy team "were sold up the river by their own publicity people", but this is unfair if one considers the circumstances. Despite what the average citizen might think of the Armed Services, the Navy especially are very time, money, and publicity conscious. The location of the wreck of H.M.S. *Association* was a unique situation, and if it should find its way to the front page of the dailies, then from the viewpoint of public relations, it was excellent—but for the divers it couldn't have been worse.

All the team were regular servicemen, who were unable to stay in the Scillies indefinitely. *Puttenham* was being run at public expense and had other commitments. It isn't every day that a "treasure ship" is found, and it is perfectly understandable that everyone was a little out of their depth. The simple matter was that the divers needed more time. To get it they had to state the reason why; to justify an extension; the M.O.D. (Navy) wanted to use the publicity, and so the wheel went full cycle.

Mr. Roland Morris, one of the other contract holders, was the first civilian organization on the scene, closely followed by the "Regency Divers", non-contract holders, followed by the "Blue Seas Divers" who did have a contract. Everyone waited expectantly, anticipating that someone, somewhere, would take charge of the almost ludicrous situation that had developed on the Gilstone—but officialdom remained quiet. The newspapers loved every minute of it, and each new gold coin, each piece of silver, each cannon, was treated as if absolutely unique. It's a pity some of the reporters had never paid a visit to the Tower of London or Woolwich Rotunda, where something like 250 similar bronze guns are on display, several of them having come from the sea.

At one time there were as many as five rival groups working the wreck, which became complicated when one appreciates the limited working area involved. But, in all fairness, they were "rivals" in name only. At no time was there any open conflict, verbal or otherwise, between the units, and sensibly everyone helped everyone else out. Even if the press preferred to anticipate an "underwater punch-up", quite the reverse occurred in fact, and equipment and advice were freely exchanged, even rival boats tying up to each other in mild tolerance.

It was a ridiculous situation indeed, but fortunately the divers were level-headed enough to realize they needed each other's support to avoid accidents. There wasn't a diver there who wouldn't have gone to the rescue of anyone in distress, regardless of which group they belonged to. Areas of the wreck became known by common names, and rival boats would motor up to each other and ask, "Which bit of the wreck are you working?" To which the reply might well be, "Cannon Gulley", "Death Gulch" or "Aladdin's Cave". The latter was the source of much newspaper drama which was mostly fiction. Two divers, working for Mr. Morris, found a hole which became known by this name, since something like 1,500 silver coins were taken out of it.

It was about this time that the word "explosives" was heard, since complaints had been made that underwater blasting was being carried out. The divers who weren't using the stuff said it was unfair, the armchair archaeologists said a valuable site was being destroyed, and the press played it all ends to the middle. Eventually, M.O.D. (Navy) issued a statement that any contract holder who used explosives would have their agreement revoked, but this unfortunately did not apply to non-contract holders who could blast as much as they liked. Had explosives not been used where necessary, then half the artefacts recovered would still be on the seabed.

In answer to the marine archaeologists—how many specialists were there capable of working on the Gilstone, and who would have financed them? It must be remembered that this site had become dubbed as a "treasure ship", and men will move mountains for less. Remember, too, that *one* gold coin from the wreck fetched £170 when sold legally at the July 1969 London auction. It is at least understandable then that archaeology went by the board at the Gilstone.

One thing is now very obvious, if Mr. Morris hadn't put his diving team in, and worked the wreck as he did, in all fairness, no one else would have taken the gamble and for that reason he deserves every praise. The divers who worked the wreck commercially, were very conscious of the value of the items they were recovering. On several occasions they worked for hours to recover the intact sole of a leather shoe, or a riding spur, or just a mangled "something" because it looked interesting. It would have been all too easy to have ploughed through everything with hammer and chisel to get at the specie.

Should the reader be perplexed by the reference to hammer and chisel, these are the tools necessary to recover coin. They lay, not scattered on the bottom like pebbles, but deep set in crevices, covered with 250 years of marine growth and underwater rubbish, set in a concretion as hard as cement. The most successful diver on the *Association* was the one prepared to work the hardest. Coins on the Gilstone are hard won, but the rewards are high.

In August of 1967, the Navy team returned for further diving, and put in something like 100 hours underwater in one week. As a result, ten gold and over one hundred silver coins were handed in, also the first of three gold wedding rings to be found. This particular one was engraved "God above increase our love". Also recovered was the largest of the ship's anchors, this being taken back to the Roads and dumped alongside Nut Rock, awaiting a decision on its future. A second bronze cannon was raised by the Navy, but not from the actual wreck site. It was found, quite by chance, whilst divers were searching the ring of rocks between Old Bess and Crebawethan, supporting the evidence already in hand that Rosevear was the base for the Herbert salvage operation of 1710.

This cannon, identical to the first raised, lay amongst weed in thirty feet of water, both lifting dolphins broken off. Although only supposition, the picture is fairly clear—the cannon was raised from the wreck, and when close to the salvage base the dolphins broke off, perhaps in a rough sea or as a result of damage in the actual wreck. Without eyes, it was almost impossible to re-sling, so was abandoned.

Two boats, and a considerable amount of diving equipment was lost as a result of the *Association*'s re-location. The converted American minesweeper *Regency* caught fire and sank off the Wolf Rock, and a landing craft, to be used by the Blue Seas Divers sank on its approach to the islands. The Scillies have probably benefited more than any one individual, for the wreck brought British and foreign newspaper men flocking over. Colour slides and photographs of the cannon were sold by the thousand, and the shops did a roaring trade in crowbars, jemmies, hammers and chisels. At one time it was impossible to purchase any tools of this nature in St. Mary's! The daily return of the diving teams brought the holidaymakers flocking to the end of the quay at Huth Town, to see "what sort of day they had had", and they were seldom disappointed. The new museum at Scilly put a number of the artefacts on display which were a great attraction, and by the end of 1967 there was hardly a person in the country who hadn't heard of Sir Cloudesley Shovell.

In the autumn of 1968, the Ministry of Defence announced that they were satisfied the wreck was that of the *Association*, and contract holders could retain anything salvaged which could be specifically identified as Naval property. Therefore, the Naval Air Command and Mr. Morris became the proud owners of five bronze cannon, worth £850 each in scrap metal alone. All the coins, wedding rings, plate, buttons, spurs, spoons, etc., were to be sold by public auction, after which the salvors would receive one-third of their sale value. In the meantime work continues, and coins can still be found, but not in any numbers. At the time I am writing, human bones in large quantities are being recovered, from which at least one intact skeleton has been re-assembled—complete even to a skull with teeth!

The final questions can only be, who were the losers, what went wrong on the Gilstone, why was this situation allowed to develop?

A professional team could have been sent to work the area, to salvage what they could for the nation, to whom, after all, the wreck rightly belonged. A comparable case occurred in the United States some years ago, when a team of divers found the Spanish Plate Fleet wrecks off Florida. They formed a company called the "Real Eight Co. Inc.", and as such approached the Trustees of the Florida Internal Improvement Fund, and did a straight deal, 75 per cent to the salvors and 25 per cent to the state. Since Florida had everything to gain, and nothing to lose, for the divers said no deal, no salvage, they waived the normal rules and signed the agreement, giving in return, complete legal protection to the salvors. When the coins were sold by auction, they were dribbled on the market in small lots —hence keeping up their price and value.

Why did the situation develop in the way it did in the Scillies? It was basically due to the fact no one seriously believed anything remained. This, coupled with the issue of non-exclusive contracts to more than one person for the same wreck and that no action outside the regulations was taken at Government level when the first coins appeared, all led to the "Scilly shambles".

It would be comforting to know the same thing couldn't happen again, but nothing has changed, and it will, unless the salvor is smart enough to get exclusive ownership in advance, or keep the find secret.

With thousands of unclaimed wrecks around our coastline, why not impose the following solution? A government committee to be formed to investigate and recommend changes in the Merchant Shipping Act relating to salvage. In the meantime, anyone owning, or claiming to own a wreck has one year in which to lodge title with the Board of Trade, after which all wreck becomes the property of the Crown.

At least, that way the record would be square regarding ownership of everything underwater, and wreck of a certain period could have additional protection from the historical point of view. Another change might well be a more realistic return for unclaimed wreck than the current 30 per cent, which does little to encourage honesty, and in many cases makes commercial salvage prohibitive.

SO YOU WANT TO RUN
A DIVING SCHOOL!

by Reg Vallintine

Reg Vallintine is the Director of the British Sub-Aqua Club.
He has thousands of hours underwater to his credit and has
taught would-be divers of all kinds, shapes and sizes from
1960–1963 at Giglio, Italy, and from 1964–1967 at Zembra,
Tunisia. Here he tells of the good times—and the bad—when
running diving schools in the Mediterranean.

ASK my advice on starting a diving school in the Mediterranean and I usually say "Don't!" This may seem an odd
reaction when you consider that I spent some of the happiest
years of my life doing just that. But the ambitious would-be
professional should know some of the facts before taking the
plunge.

Someone has likened diving and powerboat racing to tearing
up five-pound notes under a cold shower. This is particularly
true of diving schools. If you really want to get away from it
all and spend your summers in the sun, other watersports
might prove less complicated. Why not start a water ski-ing
school? Buy six pairs of waterskis, an inflatable dinghy, an
outboard motor, calculate the price of petrol and the attitude
of the natives, and you're in business. Start your own diving
school and you'll worry about everything from cylinders to
compressors, from diving boats to recompression chambers,
and from narcoses to spontaneous pneumothoraces!

If, in spite of all this, you feel that this is what you *must* do,
your reason will probably be that you have become a fanatic.
As all divers are fanatics during their holidays, this will help
you to succeed. British instructors have the highest reputation
in the Mediterranean countries; a product perhaps of their
training, experience and temperament. Make sure before you
leave that you have the necessary qualifications. A National
or B.S-A.C. Instructors' Certificate will not only give you added

confidence, but will provide proof of your ability to those who you will be teaching.

When I began my first diving school on an island called Giglio off the Tuscany coast, neither of these qualifications existed and I had a slender 42 dives to my credit. When I moved the school to Tunisia three years later, I had already completed well over a thousand. Experience comes quickly in the Mediterranean!

Some misguided people still think that diving in the "Med" is as easy and as safe as the deep end of a swimming pool. The truth is that the Mediterranean is unpredictable. It can change in a matter of minutes from a sunlit flat lake into a black and frightening maelstrom. Its subtle hazards include the false security engendered by good visibility and warmth which leads to diving to greater depths than you have ever done before—often without realizing that you are.

As the chief instructor of a diving school you may also suffer from the delusion that you are god-like, and your pupils, especially if they are beginners, do encourage your feeling of deification. It is difficult to resist the temptation of dogmatism and to keep an open mind. Experienced divers from your own Club quickly bring you back to earth. I soon found this out when the first party from my own Branch arrived on the island.

Accommodation was all arranged and a welcoming dinner was being prepared as the evening ferry arrived from the mainland. Familiar faces under unfamiliar headgear were pointing excitedly as the ferry swept in to the tiny harbour. The gangway descended and I waited for the first hairy figure to descend. I extended my hand in welcome. Then the first friendly words from my fellow divers floated down to me: "Don't just stand there with your mouth open. Where's the diving boat?" Divers are fanatics, and if you are a fanatic yourself your problems will be that much less.

Giglio was a beautiful island, some fifteen miles long and three miles wide with a population of two thousand of the friendliest Italians I have ever met. They are a small independent community of landowners, farmers and fishermen whose experience had been shaped by travel; most of the young men spend several years in the merchant marine before returning to settle into family life.

Beneath the surface of the sea, Giglio holds some of the most exciting diving in the Mediterranean. Vertical cliffs bear coral, gorgonians and lobsters. Rocky cathedrals shelter apprehensive groupers and, above all, the remains of another civilization is preserved as though in aspic on the gently sloping sand bottoms around the island. Rolling from our diving boat, *Sea Laird,* we sank effortlessly into the blue, banking and turning like dolphins, until the characteristic shapes of pieces of amphorae drew us down like magnets.

An amphora is a Roman or Greek two-handled vessel made of terracotta which was used for transporting wine, water, oil, grain or any cargo that would fit through their slender, graceful necks. The amphoras stood upright in the classical galleys, the jerrycans of the ancient world. The mention of the word in any Mediterranean language provokes an immediate reaction from the diver. Their acquisition has provided many mantelpieces with trophies, many recompression chambers with clients and underwater archaeology with its first scandals involving looted sites and freshly broken crockery. The diving accidents that they have caused are due mainly to the determination to surface with them combined with insufficient experience or equipment to do so. Only one other object excites such passion in the Mediterranean and causes so many accidents; the precious red coral *(Corallium rubrum).*

To be the first person to see a Roman wreck two thousand years afterwards is an unforgettable experience. Just outside the port of Giglio lies a rocky peninsula terminating in two tiny rocky islets. Its name according to our charts was "Le Scole". Early in 1961 I dived there with Sigi Koster and Franz Dobler of the Munich Underwater Club.

It was difficult to anchor the boat there because of the depth, so we swam out from the main island until there was nothing but mysterious blueness below us. We swallow-dived down into the blue with the columns of bubbles our only reference points back to the surface. Our gauges read a hundred feet as the bottom came into sight seventy feet below us. Clouds of black sea bream parted and sar slid into their rocky clefts as we flew down past great rock walls. The rocks ended and the gentle sand slope began. We raised dust trails over the sand as we bore downwards and soon all vegetation disappeared except for isolated shells and sponges. Down here, deep, on these flat shelving sea bottoms I always felt apprehension, never the symptoms of chronic euphoria so graphically described by French authors. Sinking effortlessly "into the blue" is to me the most relaxing and exhilarating feeling. Once you arrive on the dark sea bottom beyond the vegetation you feel instinctively that danger is present.

In the distance something was looming up, something huge and unnatural. We swam on and it gradually came into focus, a great mound of sand with masses of tiny tubes sticking out of it. We swam closer and, suddenly, our narcosis-sodden brains realized that we were looking at the wreck of a great Roman galley and that the "tubes" were the necks of hundreds of amphoras sticking out of the sand. Squeaking wildly into our mouthpieces and pointing, we thrashed around the wreck. Every amphora was complete and unbroken. Those on the top were covered with red, white and brown growths. In and out of the necks swam tiny pink fish (*Anthias anthias*). A moray momentarily poked out its head to check on the visitors to inner space. We felt as though we had found Atlantis.

During my first weeks at Giglio I was only keeping one step ahead of the divers for whom I was responsible. One afternoon they decided that we must try a night dive. I didn't dare to tell them that I had never done one myself!

At 10 p.m. all the preparations had been made. It was a moonless warm night in August and phosphorescence sparkled from the bow wave. Familiar land-marks disappeared and our boatman manœuvred us between dark rocks to the site. We anchored and the motor was turned off. All was silence for a moment and I briefed the first group, trying to appear as nonchalant as possible. I rinsed out my mask and was conscious of a flash of lights as I jumped with it firmly clutched in my hand, into the blackness. I surfaced again and waited for the first group to come in. With all torches on we swam gently down to 50 feet. Signalling "O.K.", I thought to myself how bad the underwater visibility was at night, as the divers appeared blurred in the torch beam. Suddenly I realized that I was still holding my mask in my hand! Putting it on and blowing out the water, I could suddenly see clearly!

After the diving the barbecue began, but I still had plenty

Everything had to be handed in to the Receiver of Wrecks. Items raised from the wreck of H.M.S. *Association* laid out in the Queens Warehouse, Isles of Scilly. Inspecting them is Bill Saunby, Receiver of Wrecks and Customs Officer. Paul Armiger picture. (See chapter 1)

Golden treasure from the sea. It was not long before the wreck of H.M.S. *Association* started giving up some of her secrets. *Above*, in close-up, gold Portuguese 4000 reis piece dated 1689. Notice the superb condition of these coins despite the length of time they had been under the sea. These coins were not uncommon on the wreck site. *Below*, a gold wedding ring from the wreck, one of three recovered. All carried some sort of inscription on the inside. This ring has "God above increase our love" inside it. Photographs by Jim Luke. (See chapter 1)

of air in my "twin set" and a dangerous feeling of over-confidence. I slipped quietly overboard without anyone noticing, and swam out from the boat until I knew that I was over deeper water. Then down the rocks to the beginning of the sand slope. I turned out my torch and feeling like a pilot flying on instruments, watched fascinated as my depth gauge crept round to 170 feet. I stopped gently on the sand at 200 feet blissfully unaware of the risks I was running. I switched on my torch. There in the beam sat a tiny pink scorpion fish too surprised to move. I swam quickly upwards through the darkness, thinking of Odysseus and his "wine, dark sea", and began to flatten out at 30 feet below the surface. As I drifted keeping my depth at 10 feet to decompress, I wondered idly how near I was to the boat. Ten minutes later I surfaced and swung round to look. After a moment I picked out the masthead light of the boat in the far distance! The sound of music came faintly across the surface as I swam back, an exhausted but wiser diver.

The dangers of deep diving are always present in the Mediterranean where, unless you are experienced, it is easy to find yourself at 100 feet or so before you remember to look at your depth gauge. Some of the more experienced British divers began to suffer from a new disease that became known as "rapture of the depth gauge". Groups were formed after the return to England. The "165 Group" of 1961 became the "200 Group" in 1962, each year demands were for deeper and deeper dives. We knew that we were on very dangerous ground because of the increasing risks from nitrogen narcosis and decompression sickness, and called a halt. Some experiences we had had during my first season at Giglio during the period when a recovery operation had necessitated a number of deep dives below the 200 feet mark had made me very aware of these risks.

Scoglio del Corvo means rock of the crow, and it is a wild and isolated rock off the south-west coast of Giglio. It looked an ideal diving site from the chart, but our young Italian crew were very anxious that we should never get there. The weather was always unsuitable and there were, so they assured us, strong currents, giant fish and rip tides. This only encouraged us to see for ourselves and, when it was clear that we intended to dive, they explained that the reason for their fear was that

two German divers had disappeared there one August afternoon in 1959.

We found Corvo to be an ideal but very deep site with great
rock clusters, bushes of crimson gorgonia, pale and fragile
"rose-de-mer" and, below 150 feet, crayfish and morays in
large numbers. Exploring a cliff face at 170 feet for crayfish
one day, we looked downwards and far below us could make
out two faint white patches on the sand bottom. The patches
intrigued me and a minute later their unnaturalness sank into
my mind. I checked with my companion that he had no narcosis symptoms and we continued down to 200 feet. From there
we could make out the shape of bones. I still didn't realize
what we had found, thinking that some animal had drowned
and sunk to the sea bed. At 220 feet an unforgettable sight
appeared. Two skeletons complete with aqualungs, weight
belts, fins and masks were lying on the sand. The missing
divers had been found.

The bodies were lying about ten feet apart with heads facing
down the gentle sand slope. It looked as though one had been
following the other. By the remains of the nearest body was a
still-loaded harpoon gun, heavily encrusted with marine
growth. I picked up a fin and we started upwards, our nitrogen
level high and our air low, to decompress under the boat.

The local Carabinieri were extremely interested in our find.
They arrived at our picnic site an hour later by speed boat.
Their first question was, "Can you bring the bodies up?" We
started the recovery operation several days later when I had
been joined by Roger Hale of Southsea Branch who was to
help me out as Instructor for the season. This time we arrived
at the head of a small flotilla of boats containing Georgio, the
mayor, Silvio, the Port Captain and Antonio, the police chief,
plus numerous assistants and, at the end, a grim reminder of
the job in hand, two coffins in a rowing boat.

Everyone was most anxious that the remains of the two
divers should not be mixed up. We therefore decided to use
two sacks, one marked with a distinctive red cross. The sacks
were paid out on separate lines from the boat and there was a
length of spare line beyond the sacks to tie on the respective
twin aqualungs.

Roger and I started down with our sacks at lunchtime on the

first day, but found ourselves swept out of course by a strong current. When we arrived at the bottom, we were unable to re-locate the skeletons. Towards teatime I made another attempt and managed to find the bodies beneath a great rock overhang that I had not remembered seeing before. Unfortunately the lines had got tangled on the rocks far above me and I was un- able to pull them as far as the remains.

The next morning we were again unable to find the bodies and I felt great anxiety and severe narcosis symptoms when I lost sight of Roger. By the time our nitrogen level had dropped in the afternoon, we tried again. Roger ensured that the lines were kept clear of the rocks and I managed to pull them, together with the sacks, to within sight of the bodies. We returned and the lines were left buoyed for the night.

By this time the Italian press had been informed and arrived in force. Sensational headlines greeted each of our efforts. All sorts of fantastic explanations were credited to us: "Huge fish were to blame . . . the divers had certainly been dragged down to this depth by a gigantic turtle!"

Next day we managed to complete the operation. In the morning we got the sacks as far as the bodies. We manhandled the first and better preserved skeleton into the first sack. Roger made fast the aqualung and I set off with the second line to the deeper body. I managed to get half of it into the sack before my decompression meter was into the red and air was getting low, necessitating a return. At four in the afternoon we dived again. While Roger hovered above me, checking that all was well, I finished packing the second skeleton and with great difficulty and much fumbling, managed to tie a knot on to the second aqualung. Noticing further white objects down the sand slope, I went to 250 feet where I collected grizzly souvenirs, pieces of bone and a Barakuda depth gauge with the needle jammed at 80 metres. Then I rejoined Roger and we swam upwards with a great feeling of satisfaction that the job was completed.

After our decompression stop, the police began to pull in the lines. Within a few moments the lines became snagged some- where beneath the surface. I jumped in clasping a single set which had been reserved to pass down to us if we had needed more air to decompress. At 150 feet I pulled the line out from under a ledge of rock and resurfaced. A few minutes later the lines stuck again. I was exasperated. The operation had already taken three days out of our holidaymakers' precious diving time. I plunged in again with the single set. The line wound down out of sight, clear of the shallower rocks. Only as my air became low and breathing difficult at 150 feet, I saw that one of the sacks had snagged on the bottom rock at about 200 feet. Relying on my reserve, which I had not yet pulled, I reached the sack, dislodged it, and was out of air. I pulled frantically at the reserve but got no relief and suddenly realized that the reserve lever had already been pulled on the surface as this was originally a spare set, and that I was without air at 200 feet. I gritted my teeth and set out for the surface, conscious that my return should not be too fast or I would have decompression problems. As I rose, lessening pressure enabled me to pull three or four wheezy breaths out of the bottle.

I hit the surface and called for another aqualung knowing that I probably had two minutes before bubbles might form inside me. Down again to 100 feet and a long inactive decompression as I watched the sacks being pulled up past me and knew that our problems were finally over. This last dive had been a valuable experience. I had learnt the dangers of diving alone and without some sort of reserve system. It had also given me the confidence that comes from knowing that, in emergency, one can get back to the surface even from considerable depths. The dives had also given us further insight into the dangers of nitrogen narcosis from which both Roger and I had suffered during all the deep dives.

The dead divers' aqualungs still had some air in them and they were sent back to Germany for analysis. Some time later I received a charming letter from the President of the German Underwater Federation who thanked us for our "fantastical work", but gave no news of the analysis of the air. Clues to the tragedy after several years were slight and it is now doubtful whether anybody will ever know what really happened on that sunny afternoon in 1959.

Life can be fun, though, with your own diving school. Underwater the Mediterranean teems with life of a million fascinating kinds. Our favourite pastime at Giglio was to collect and eat the delicious thorny oysters *(Spondylus gaederopus)* which grew on the rocks around the island. The late Maurizio Sarra, one of Italy's most brilliant underwater photographers, had shown me how to detect them in spite of their camouflage. A slight clamping movement as your hand approaches a rough nobbly rock was sometimes the only clue to their existence, although often they can be recognized by the red coloured growth on the upper surface of their shells. Opened with a diving knife and swallowed raw with a squeeze of lemon there is no delicacy to compare to them. The Italians swore that they held the secret of endless prodigious sexual feats, and we diving instructors were expected to be able to eat them underwater. This operation began with detaching the oyster from its concreted base. After having broken several diving knives, we found that the most suitable tool was a short hand pick used by the local land workers. You struck sharply into the edge of the base of the oyster, being careful not to hole it, and then levered it out. The next stage was to open the beast. You inserted the tip of your diving knife into the joint between the upper and lower valve, and worked it to and fro until you cut the muscle which held it together. When you had done this, it opened without difficulty.

Before carrying on with the most important part, you looked at the inside to make sure that all small fish, parasites, and marine worms had left "the sinking ship", then (we advised):

Take a deep breath.
Think of home.
Remove the mouthpiece.
Replace with oyster.
Swallow oyster.
Think of home.
Replace aqualung mouthpiece.
Breathe again.

The result was either ecstasy, or, alternatively, an emergency ascent!

Octopuses fascinated us, and we learnt much about them as the summers wore on. At first we had assaulted them with spears and harpoons, but we gradually realized how barbarous and unnecessary this was. Slowly we grew to admire their intelligence and sensitivity. We read all the books we could find on their habits, learning that they saw as clearly as we did through a mask and that their mating habits were legendary.

They were not often surprised in the open, and so we developed a method of getting them out of their holes. Many times it was necessary to work your way down through the writhing tentacles until you could get a firm grip with both hands around the body of the octopus. Then began a tug of war which fascinated watchers. There were variations which proved the intelligence of the animal. Wrestling a large octopus out of a cleft one afternoon, I suddenly felt a sharp pain across my hand. Could the octopus be using its beak I wondered? I had thought that they only used this for tearing their food. I looked into the hole. The octopus was pushing out half a beer bottle at me! Before I finally got him out he had pushed out the other half of the bottle and two sharp shells!

Once you got the octopus in open water, however, he was nearly defenceless and an ideal subject for underwater photography. Release your grip and they may not realize that they are free. Small octopuses have the habit of crawling under your bottles, where they feel safe until you climb out into the air. You could almost see the reproachful look in their eyes. I once thought that my exhaust valve had jammed until I discovered that the octopus I had been handling had wrapped himself around the regulator. Their colour changes also fascinated us. We let them go and watched them "jet-propel" themselves away, emitting puffs of ink. When they were settled on the bottom again we sailed down after them. Before we picked them up, they turned white with fear. The easiest way to make an octopus blush is to catch a "cigalle de mer" (*Scyllarides latus*), a type of Mediterranean crayfish whose antennae are modified into flat plates making them look like miniature prehistoric monsters. Octopuses love crayfish. We put the crayfish on a rock with the octopus nearby. The octopus pounced, shooting out a sucker-clad leg, and scooping the crayfish up. Move in and take the crayfish away, and the octopus will blush red with anger.

In 1964 came a mysterious invitation from Africa and the *Societé Tunisienne de Banque*. The bank had taken a lease on the island of Zembra which lay off the tip of Cape Bon and an embryo sailing school was already formed. Now they were thinking of diving. The conditions looked exciting and different, and I decided to move.

Zembra was a smaller island than Giglio and the only local

inhabitants were 46 boats and a dog called Sacapuces (flea bag). Shaped like an equilateral triangle, Zembra's sides measured 2 kilometres each. Rocky and mountainous, its peak rose to 1,300 feet and the only reasonable anchorage was on its South coast where a beautiful restaurant had been built over the sea together with twelve large bungalows on the hillside.

The fascination of Zembra underwater was its sea life. In Italy, unfortunately, spearfishing is allowed with the aqualung and anything that moves is considered fair game. No one I had ever heard of had dived at Zembra before, except for Rebikoff who had made a brief photographic excursion.

We soon found that the grouper *(Epinephalus Gigas)*, one of the largest and most impressive rock fishes in the Mediterranean could still be seen here swimming in groups and in open water away from the rocks. This was an ideal site for an underwater national park and after discussion with the Ministry concerned all was agreed.

We visited the best grouper site as often as possible and began to get to know each other well. The largest we christened "Oscar" and were sure that the others were his family. Whenever we approached, Oscar's first action was to chase his "wife" into their hole. After this he swam cautiously and almost motionlessly ahead of us.

In one of the training bays we fed the fish every day and they became so tame that we had only to sink through the surface and tiny black sea bream *(S. Cantarus)* and brilliantly coloured rainbow wrasse would peck at our masks. Their eyes bulged and rolled as they gobbled the pieces of sea urchin that we held out to them.

A group of dolphins seemed to pass the island occasionally at tea time and we soon got used to slipping quietly over the side while the boat was still moving to get a glimpse of them before they swam off. Although naturally curious and friendly, Mediterranean dolphins have had many unhappy encounters with man and only once did a small and exceptionally curious one (female?) stand on its tail and watch us.

One of the most impressive of our local inhabitants we called Boris. He was a giant, nine feet tall, weighing proportionately. He had an impressive moustache and liked girls. We first saw Boris in 1966 while climbing back into our auxiliary diving dinghy. A huge head with brown eyes reared up out of the sea. A twitch of whiskers and he was gone. The biggest seal we'd ever seen!

Mediterranean Monk seals *(Monachus albiventar)* are rarities these days, but two thousand years ago they were plentiful throughout the Mediterranean. Aristotle, Pliny, Plutarch and Homer all described them but the Newfoundlander, Abraham Kean, decimated them in the seventeenth century and boasted that he had killed a million. One of their last breeding grounds is the wild and isolated Galite Islands off the North coast of Tunisia. Boris, our Zembra seal, must have come from there.

We had heard about the harems that male seals formed and of their battles with the younger males for possession. Boris, we felt, must be an old rogue male. We next saw him in July. The Bay of Caves is a beautiful site for beginners—a sand-bottomed swimming pool thirty feet deep surrounded by grottoes and caves. As I was signalling to one of the girl divers, I suddenly saw a large white form weaving through the rocks at the limit of visibility. We followed, but he stayed always in the distance, diving and rolling warily.

Cousteau, I knew, had visited the seals of the Galite and was particularly impressed by a huge albino male. Could it have been Boris? Our next exciting encounters were in September. For the first time he approached us closely and we could see his whitish flanks speckled with dark spots, and his huge tattered tail. For fifteen minutes we followed him and then returned to the boat. Boris followed as if unwilling to say good-bye. We peered face to face at him across a rock while the rest of the divers looked down through masks from the surface.

At Zembra the school grew so that we were taking forty or so divers a day. This meant eight instructors. Our diving team consisted of British, Belgian, Turkish, French and Swedish instructors and we boasted of being able to give instruction in ten languages.

We were really put on our mettle when official trainees began to arrive from the Tunisian Navy, Army, Police and Fire Brigades. The Navy party were commanded by a C.P.O. who rejoiced in the name of "Turki". Turki had boundless energy and an air of command. He immediately took over the operation of our boat, shouting orders at the sailors. Turki, so

the others told us, was an ex-helmet diver. During my intro-
ductory lecture, I mentioned pressure on the ears underwater
and methods of clearing them. To my surprise a voice from the
back clearly said: "Nonsense!" Turki, it seemed, had no ear
problems—such difficulties he informed us, were all imagination. He would like to demonstrate a free dive to ten metres to
prove it. I agreed to watch.

The next morning after our first session we stopped at the
Bay of Caves and Turki jumped in feet first without any equipment at all. Peering through my mask, I saw him descending
motionless in the position of "attention", except for strange
whirling movements of his hands, which made him look rather
like an overweight humming bird. After a few seconds he
arrived, still at attention, on the bottom, whereupon he commenced the whirling hand movements in the opposite direction and popped importantly back to the surface. "Ears",
he said, "are no problem to the Navy." Our Doctor thrust his
spy glass into Turki's ears and informed us that he had drums
the size of a baby's.

Towards the end of their three-week course, we let the Navy
take it in turns to lead a dive under our watchful eyes. Turki
swam off at enormous speed downwards with scattered sailors
trailing behind clutching their ears. Omer, my Turkish instructor, guided them back, as I went after Turki. He was
resting by a rock at 160 feet eyeing me calmly as I approached
and made thoughtful "I am O.K." signals. When we got back
to the boat I told him in no uncertain terms how he might have
caused the death of his companions. "And a very good thing
for the Navy if I had," muttered Turki.

But beginners, whatever their size, shape, sex or nationality
are normally and naturally apprehensive. This natural fear
should never be singled out or referred to. The "hairy chested
school" of diving instructors whose declared intention was "to
separate the men from the boys" is now mercifully, no longer
with us.

Sometimes, however, when things go wrong one imagines
one can detect national traits. Many of the greatest divers I
know are Italians, but when an Italian beginner has trouble
it can be a real *catastrofo*, flailing arms, legs and rolling eye-
balls. The French are inclined to blame the equipment, and

their reproachful eyes imply a fiendish plot on the part of *les Anglais*. Englishmen on the whole are merely apologetic. Americans, always the most appreciative, are a very different proposition.

After a long talk in the bar one night an ageing American journalist decided that he was akin to a dolphin and I promised to take him just below the surface on the diving ladder the next morning. Next day we were surrounded as we made our way down the ladder by his young daughters who skin-dived effortlessly below us to 30 feet. The surface lapped calmly above us as we hung on to the bottom rung of the ladder at a depth of three feet six inches. White showed around the eye-balls of my companion and his clenched knuckles also showed white. Feeling disappointed I motioned for him to climb back up the ladder. "Anything wrong?" I inquired encouragingly. He looked at me a long time thinking deeply. "I think," he said, "what I feel is psychosomatic" . . .

Among Zembra's secrets were the giant sting-rays of the Dasyatis species. These measured a good six feet or so across their backs and lay like monstrous pancakes around a very beautiful islet called Lantorcho. Lantorcho (old Italian for lantern) is an islet standing on three legs through which huge bands of sunlight shone illuminating the vertical walls which were covered with yellow and orange cup corals. Swimming through the island underwater reminded me of a cathedral. Up in the top of the drowned arches were crayfish and "corbs" and tiny rock fish *(Serranus scriba)* that swam upside down in relation to the nearest rock surface.

The narrow rock plateau surrounding the islet attracted pelagic fish of all sizes. Huge amberjacks *(Seriola dumerili)* cruised past the striped groupers *(Epinephalus alexandrinus)* and circled curiously around us, their great eyes goggling.

The rays lay on their platform, huge and evil-looking with their spiracles, looking like eyes, moving in time to their breathing. Their tails stretched out like leather thongs for five feet or so straight out behind them. Half-way along the tail and almost invisible was the six-inch dagger which gave the sting-ray its name. It took a year for us to pluck up courage to the point where we took hold of the end of the tails. We felt sure that if you held the *end* of the tail, the ray could not operate his dagger defence, but we had no idea what they would do when we let go again! The tail itself was serrated and after suffering scratches, we found it better to use a sponge as a pad.

The first ray that I successfully gripped took off lazily from the bottom, pulling me effortlessly behind. He headed down the slope into deeper water. I dug my heels in, but could only stop him for a few seconds. He became more agitated as he realized I was still holding on and beat his wings furiously. At 150 feet I let go and the ray cruised on down into the distance. I relaxed as I saw that he had no intention of returning.

We met sharks too here for the first time. They were attracted to the island early in the year when the *Madrague* or giant tunny trap was operating a mile or so off Sidi Daoud on the mainland opposite Zembra. One day we visited the madrague and persuaded the Tunisian captain to allow us to dive in the nets before they were pulled up. It was an eerie feeling diving down the great wall of the net. Huge carcasses were entrapped in part of it—dead turtles, sharks and swordfish. Suddenly the tunny roared past us like midget submarines, smooth, powerful and perfectly in unison. After what seemed like only a few minutes, beating noises from the boat above brought us back to the surface. The Captain was worried because we were causing fish to jump out of the net.

In the afternoon we decided to dive on an isolated underwater island half way between Zembra and its sister island Zembretta. We were on the bottom at 100 feet photographing when I noticed a huge fish weaving across above us. I got a distinct view of a blunt shark-like head and notched tail before it became aware of our bubbles, turned a complete somersault and swam off the way it had come.

Our last and more impressionable encounter was in the Lantorcho. Stan Hayward, my companion, went in first, and I rolled off into the grotto putting on my mask as I sank. Clearing it, I saw the black form of a shark silhouetted against the blue background and turning into the grotto towards us. It was certainly unnerving, but I felt that I must warn Stan who was examining the growths on the walls and had not seen the shark. I swam down and grabbed his leg and pointed. Stan peered disbelievingly at the approaching monster and slowly drew his knife! The shark cruised out of sight again and we returned, reassuring ourselves with the thought that shark attack was practically unknown in these waters.

No description of our diving at Zembra would be complete without mention of our most important diving personality, "Sacapuces". One French writer described us as "the only diving school run by a dog" and Sacapuces, a Tunisian mongrel bitch and the island dog, took a very proprietary interest in the school. Every morning she was waiting on board for us to leave and once at sea would stand bravely, front legs braced on the gunwale as her eyes searched for distant signs of rabbits. One suspicious movement on the hillside and, whatever the distance from the shore or the size of the waves, she was gone with a great leap. We always continued on our course watching the pathetically small dark head as it moved slowly in towards the wave-beaten rocks. In fact, Sacapuces was something of a canine swimming champion, and it was impossible to keep up with her without using fins.

Perhaps her most famous exploit came during one of our night dives. Sacapuces' behaviour was no different at night and she would disappear into the darkness with the cries of worried holiday-makers echoing after her. Some ten minutes later we would arrive at our site, moor the boat and dive. Half an hour later someone would notice that the dog had swum up and was trying to climb the diving ladder. On one occasion she swam back with a rabbit in her mouth. If any dog deserved an aqualung this was the one.

This is the stuff that diving schools are made of. A mixture of dedication, excitement, poverty and exasperation. Responsibility that cannot be avoided and risks that are always present.

The rewards are there too. The look in the eyes of a beginner who sees his first fish eat out of his hand . . . the feeling that you are part of another world, a different never-ending life cycle that continues each day below that silver undulating curtain we call the surface.

WITH ALL FLAGS
FLYING—200 FEET DOWN

by Lieut.-Commander
D. P. R. Lermitte, R.N.

Lieutenant-Commander D. P. R. Lermitte, R.N., led his
diving team down to H.M.S. *Prince of Wales* and H.M.S.
Repulse where they lay on the seabed some 200 feet down. Those
divers reflew the great ships' Ensigns—underwater. Here
Lieutenant-Commander Lermitte, a member of the British
Sub-Aqua Club's executive committee, tells the story of the
sinking of the ships with the aid of eye-witness reports and
official war diaries, and of the diving operations which followed
years later.

It is impossible, if you have any imagination, not to be moved
by the stories of human courage that emerge as you set about
compiling the story of the dying moments of any ship. Often
the deeds of sacrifice and daring belong to long years ago and
the heroes of wrecks appear as shadowy figures behind documents written laboriously with quill pen in the great cabin
of some ancient flagship.

But this is not that kind of story. This is the story of men who
still live—or have died within the memory of many of us. This
is the story of the sinking of H.M.S. *Repulse* and H.M.S. *Prince
of Wales* and the Royal Navy's return to them as they lie on the
seabed some 45 miles NNE. of the island of Pulau Tioman, off
the East Coast of Malaya. The *Repulse* is 180 feet down and the
Prince of Wales, eight miles away to the east, is in 216 feet of
water.

To compile a report on such modern wrecks there is little
need to search deep in archives. Survivors live and thrive.
Newspapers, once the sense of national shock and the needs of
censorship had passed, were free to print their stories.

Sir Winston Churchill wrote about these ships. That great
war reporter, O. D. Gallagher, was on board *Repulse* and saw

it all. He continued taking notes as the ship sank under him and went on doing so until it was time for him, too, to swim clear. *The Official History of the Second World War* reports the facts in readable style. And finally, years later, Lieutenant-Commander David Lermitte took his diving team down to those two great ships on the sea floor and told the divers' story in his reports in the *Royal Navy Diving Magazine*. And told as well how his divers reflew their battle ensigns—underwater.

All those sources vouch for this story. All tell loud and clear that this was a day when the Royal Navy lived up to its greatest traditions.

*   *   *

Two days after Pearl Harbour at a meeting in the Cabinet War Room, Winston Churchill and his Naval chiefs pondered the consequences of the Japanese attack on Britain's own war strategy. We had lost command of every ocean except the Atlantic, Australian and New Zealand seas. Every island was open to attack. But the *Prince of Wales* and the *Repulse* had arrived in Singapore.

The *Prince of Wales*, a battleship of 35,000 tons, launched in 1939, was considered almost unsinkable. Her complement totalled 1,500 men. And her armament included ten 14-inch guns, sixteen 5·25-inch, five multiple pom-poms, which the crew called Chicago Pianos; she carried four catapult-launched aircraft and could speed through the sea at more than 30 knots.

But she was more than just a ship to the British people. She was symbol of their strength. She had carried Churchill to the Atlantic conference with Roosevelt and was in the action against the *Bismarck* in which *Hood* was sunk.

Repulse too was a mighty ship. Her complement was 1,200. A battle-cruiser of 32,000 tons, her armament included six 15-inch guns, twelve 4-inch guns, eight 4-inch anti-aircraft guns, four three-pounders and four aircraft.

What should they do after the Pearl Harbour attack? Churchill wrote that he, personally, thought they should go across the Pacific to join what was left of the American Fleet. The existence of such a fleet would be the best possible shield for Australasia. The meeting in the War Cabinet Room seemed

in favour, but as it was getting late they decided to sleep on it
and settle the next morning what to do with these two great
ships. But within two hours of the break-up of that meeting,
both were at the bottom of the sea.

*   *   *

What had happened during those hours is best told in the
Official History of the War and the words of the men who were
there.

"Force 'Z' consisting of the *Prince of Wales* and *Repulse*, the
destroyers *Electra, Express, Vampire* and *Tenedos* left Singapore at
5.35 p.m. on 8th December." During confused conditions
reports gave warning of the possible presence of two aircraft
carriers off Saigon and of Japanese bombers in south Indo-
China. Signals came in one after another—and one informed
Admiral Phillips that a Japanese landing had been reported at
Kuantan.

"It seemed to the Admiral improbable that the enemy would
expect his force, last seen steering to the northwards in the
latitude of Singora, to be as far south as Kuantan by daylight,"
continues the official history. "Kuantan, which he considered
to be of military importance, was not far off the return track
to Singapore and was 400 miles from the Japanese airfields in
Indo-China. On these grounds the Admiral thought surprise
possible and the risk justified and at 12.52 a.m. on the 10th he
altered course for Kuantan. He had however underrated
Japanese efficiency . . ." For the Japanese knew about *Prince
of Wales* and *Repulse* and at that moment their aircraft were
searching the sea for them.

*   *   *

On board *Repulse* war reporter O. D. Gallagher was quite
clear about the aim of Force "Z". He had the words of the
signal sent to all ships by the Commander-in-Chief Admiral
Sir Tom Phillips: "The enemy has made several landings on
the north coast of Malaya and has made local progress. Mean-
while fast transports lie off the coast. This is our opportunity
before the enemy can establish himself.

"We have made a wide circuit to avoid air reconnaissance,

and hope to surprise the enemy shortly after sunrise tomorrow. We may have the luck to try our metal against the old Jap battle-cruiser *Kongo* or against some Jap cruisers or destroyers in the Gulf of Siam. We are sure to get some useful practice with our high-angle armament, but whatever we meet I want to finish quickly and so get well clear to eastward before the Japanese can mass a too-formidable scale of air attack against us. So shoot to sink."

Repulse's captain, William Tennant, in his message to his officers and crew was more explicit. He said: "We are making for the nor'east coast of Malaya, and shall be off the nor'east corner at dawn. We shall be to seaward of Singora and Patani, where Japanese landings are taking place.

"Though we may, of course, run into Japanese forces anywhere during the day I think it is most probable that only submarines and aircraft are likely to be sighted. Some time at night and at dawn the fun may begin. We must be on the lookout for destroyer attack tonight.

"If we are lucky enough to bump into a Japanese convoy tomorrow, it will be of most invaluable service, and seriously upset their plans. Having stirred up the hornets' nest, we must be expecting plenty of bombing on our return tomorrow."

Action stations—aircraft—came that very evening. But it was hardly even a prelude to what was to come. They were being shadowed by enemy aircraft and now they knew it. But the call to real action did not come until the next day. Gallagher noted it all down: "At 11 a.m. a twin-masted single-funnel ship is sighted on the starboard bow. The force goes to investigate her. She carries no flag. I was looking at her through my telescope when the shock of an explosion made me jump so that I nearly poked out my right eye. It was 11.15 a.m. The explosion came from the *Prince of Wales*'s portside armament. She was firing at a single aircraft.

"We open fire. There are now about six aircraft. A three-quarter-inch screw falls on my tin hat from the bridge deck above from the shock of the explosion of the guns. 'The old tub's falling to bits,' observes the Yeoman of Signals.

"That was the beginning of a superb air attack by the Japanese, whose air force was an unknown quantity. It was most orthodox. They even came at us in formation, flying low

Among Zembra's secrets were the giant sting-rays. Reg Vallintine reports that they measure a good six feet across and lie on the bottom like monstrous pancakes. "It took a year," he writes, "for us to pluck up courage to the point where we took hold of the end of the tails." *Above*, the art of grabbing these fish is, of course, to avoid the sting. And *below*, that's better . . . Reg gives the diver's O.K. signal as the ray starts to take him for a ride. Pictures by Stan Hayward. (See chapter 2)

"The first ray that I successfully gripped took off lazily from the bottom, pulling me effortlessly behind. He headed down the slope into deeper water. I dug my heels in, but could only stop him for a few seconds. He became more agitated as he realized I was still holding on and beat his wings furiously. At 150 feet I let go and the ray cruised on down into the distance . . ." Stan Hayward picture. (See chapter 2)

and close. Aboard *Repulse* I found observers as qualified as anyone to estimate Jap flying abilities. They know from first-hand
experience what the R.A.F. and Luftwaffe are like. Their
verdict was: 'The Germans have never done anything like this
in the North Sea, Atlantic or anywhere else we have been.'

"They concentrated on the two capital ships, taking the
Prince of Wales first and *Repulse* second. The destroyer screen
they left completely alone except for damaged planes forced
to fly low over them when they dropped bombs defensively.
At 11.18 *Prince of Wales* opened a shattering barrage with
all her multiple pom-poms, or Chicago Pianos as they call
them.

"From the starboard side of the flag deck I could see two
torpedo bombers. No, they're bombers. Flying straight at us.
All our guns pour high-explosives at them, including shells so
delicately fused that they explode if they merely graze cloth
fabric. But they swing away, carrying out a high-powered
evasive action without dropping anything at all. I realize now
what the purpose of this action was. It was a diversion to
occupy all our guns and observers on the air defence platform
at the summit of the main mast.

"There is a heavy explosion and the *Repulse* rocks. Great
patches of paint fall from the funnel on to the flag deck. We all
gaze above our heads to see planes which during the action
against the low fliers were unnoticed. They are high-level
bombers. Seventeen thousand feet.

"The first bomb, the one that rocked us a moment ago,
scored a direct hit on the catapult deck through the one hangar
on the port side. I am standing behind a multiple Vickers gun,
one which fires 2,000 half-inch bullets per minute. It is at the
after-end of the flag deck. I see a cloud of smoke rising from the
place where the first bomb hit.

"Another comes down bang again from 17,000 feet. It explodes
in the sea, making a creamy blue and green patch 10 feet across.
Repulse rocks again. It was three fathoms from the port side. It
was a miss so no one bothers.

"Two planes can be seen coming at us. A spotter sees another
at a different angle, but much closer. Still blazing two-
pounders, the whole gun platform turns in a hail of death at
the single plane. It is some 1,000 yards away. I saw tracers rip

4

into its fuselage dead in the centre. Its fabric opened up like a rapidly spreading sore with red edges. It swept to the tail and in a moment stabilizer and rudder became a framework skeleton. Her nose dipped down and she went waterward. *Repulse* had got the first raider.

"For the first time since the action began we can hear a sound from the loud-speakers, which are on every deck at every action station. It is the sound of a bugle. Its first notes are somewhat tortured. The young bugler's lips and throat are obviously dry with excitement. It is the most sinister alarm of all for seamen: 'Fire'.

"Smoke from our catapult deck is thick now. Men in overalls, their faces hidden by a coat of soot, manhandle hoses along decks. Water fountains delicately from a rough patch made in one section by binding it with a white shirt. It sprays on the Vickers gunners who, in a momentary lull, lift faces, open mouths and put out tongues to catch the cool-looking jets. They quickly avert faces to spit—the water is salt and it is warm. It is sea water.

"The Chicago Pianos open up again with a suddenness that I am unable to refrain from flinching at, though once they get going with their erratic shell-pumping it is most reassuring.

"At 11.25 we see an enormous splash on the very edge of the horizon. The splash vanishes and a whitish cloud takes its place. A damaged enemy plane jettisoning its bombs or another enemy destroyed. A rapid Gallup Poll on the flag deck says: 'Another duck down'.

"Fire parties are still fighting the hangar outbreak, oblivious of any air attack used so far. Bomb splinters have torn three holes in the starboard side of the funnel on our flag deck. Gazing impotently with no more than fountain pen and notebook in my hands while gunners, signallers, surgeons and rangefinders worked, I found emotional release in shouting rather stupidly, I suppose, at the Japanese. I discovered depths of obscenity previously unknown, even to me.

"There is a short lull. The boys dig inside their overalls and pull out cigarettes. Then the loudspeaker voice: 'Enemy aircraft ahead'. Lighted ends are nipped off cigarettes. The ship's company goes into action again.

"'Twelve of them.' The flag deck boys whistle. Someone

counts them aloud: 'One, two, three, four, five, six, seven, eight, nine—yes, nine'. The flag deck wag, as he levels a signalling lamp at the *Prince of Wales*: 'Any advance on nine? Anybody? No? Well, here they come'.

"Now it is 12.10 p.m. They are all concentrating on *Prince of Wales*. They are after the big ships all right. A mass of water and smoke rises in a tree-like column from *Prince of Wales*'s stern. They've got her with a torpedo.

"A ragged-edged mass of flame from her Chicago Piano does not stop them, nor the heavy instant flashes from her high-angle secondary armament. She is listing to port—a bad list. We are about six cables from her. A snotty or midshipman, runs past, calls as he goes: '*Prince of Wales*'s stern gear gone'. It doesn't seem possible that those slight-looking planes could do that to her.

"The planes leave us, having apparently dropped all their bombs and torpedoes. I don't believe it's over, though. 'Look, look,' shouts someone, 'there's a line in the water right under our bows, growing longer on the starboard side. A torpedo that missed us. Wonder where it'll stop.' *Prince of Wales* signals us again asking if we've been torpedoed. Our Captain Tennant replies: 'Not yet. We've dodged nineteen'.

"*Prince of Wales*'s list is increasing. There is a great rattle of empty two-pounder cordite cases as Chicago Piano boys gather up the empties to stow them away and clear for further action.

"12.20 p.m. . . . The end is near, although I didn't know it. A new wave of planes appears, flying around us in formation and gradually coming nearer. *Prince of Wales* lies about ten cables astern of our portside. She is helpless. They are all making for her. I don't know how many. They are splitting up our guns as we realize they are after her, knowing she can't dodge their torpedoes. So we fire at them to defend *Prince of Wales* rather than attend to our own safety.

"The only analogy I can think of to give an impression of *Prince of Wales* in those last moments is of a mortally wounded tiger trying to beat off the *coup-de-grâce*. Her outline is hardly distinguishable in smoke and flame from all her guns except the 14-inchers.

"I can see one plane release a torpedo. It drops nose heavy into the sea and churns up a small wake as it drives straight at *Prince of Wales*. It explodes against her bows. A couple of seconds later another explodes amidships and another astern. Gazing at her turning over on the portside with her stern going under and with dots of men leaping from her, I was thrown against the bulkhead by a tremendous shock as *Repulse* takes a torpedo on her portside astern.

"With all others on the flag deck I am wondering where it came from when *Repulse* shudders gigantically. Another torpedo. Now men cheering with more abandon than at a Cup Final. What the heck is this? I wonder. Then I see it's another plane down. It hits the sea in flames also. There have been six so far as I know.

"My notebook, which I have got before me, is stained with oil and is ink blurred. It says: 'Third torp'. *Repulse* was now listing badly to port. The loud-speakers speak for the last time: 'Everybody on main deck'. We all troop down the ladders most orderly.

"It seemed slow going. Like all the others, I suppose, I was tempted to leap to the lower deck, but the calmness was catching. When we got to the main deck the list was so bad our shoed feet couldn't grip the steel deck. I kicked off my shoes and my damp, stockinged feet made for sure movement.

"Nervously opening my cigarette case I found I hadn't a match. I offered a cigarette to a man beside me. He said: 'Ta, want a match?' We both lit up and puffed once or twice. He said: 'We'll be seeing you, mate'. To which I replied: 'Hope so. Cheerio.'

"We were all able to walk down the ship's starboard side. She lay so much over to port it was rather steep, and I could easily walk upright. We all formed a line along a big protruding anti-torpedo blister, from where we had to jump some 12 feet. into a sea which was black—I discovered it was oil. I remember jamming my cap on my head, drawing a breath and leaping.

"Oh, I forgot—the last entry in my notebook was 'Sank about 12.20 p.m.' I made it before leaving the flag deck. In the water I glimpsed the *Prince of Wales*'s bows disappearing.

"Kicking with all my strength, I with hundreds of others tried to get away from the *Repulse* before she went under, and being afraid of getting drawn under in the whirlpool, I went in the wrong direction, straight into the still spreading oil patch which felt almost as thick as velvet.

"A wave hit me and swung me round so that I saw the last of the *Repulse*. Her underwater plates were painted a bright light red. Her bows rose high as the air trapped inside tried to escape from underwater forward regions, and there she hung for a second or two and easily slid out of sight."

Gallagher was saved. So was another journalist—Cecil Brown of the United States Columbia Broadcasting System. He heard Captain Tennant's last announcement to his crew: "All hands on deck. Prepare to abandon ship. God be with you." He too stresses the absence of any panic among the crew. He said: "I have seen British troops in actions in which they have displayed all the courage in the world, but the courage of the sailors aboard *Repulse* and *Prince of Wales* during the attacks was unparalleled.

"Seeing *Repulse* and *Prince of Wales* go down was one of the most tragic sights imaginable. When I was 50 feet away from *Repulse*, and being helped to safety, her stern rose into the air like an ugly red wound and quickly slid below the surface. . . . I saw the *Prince of Wales* lie over on her side and hover there for a few minutes. She then slid under, and the jagged bow rose into the air like the crippled limb of a giant and it too disappeared."

To both men, the loss of the two great ships was, of course, shocking, but their loss was no less a shock at long range.

*   *   *

Winston Churchill was opening his despatch boxes when the telephone at his bedside rang—"It was the First Sea Lord. His voice sounded odd. He gave a sort of cough and gulp, and at first I could not hear quite clearly: 'Prime Minister, I have to report to you that the *Prince of Wales* and the *Repulse* have both been sunk by the Japanese—we think by aircraft. Tom Phillips is drowned.' "

"Are you sure it's true?"

"There is no doubt at all."

Winston Churchill put the telephone down—"I was thankful to be alone. In all the war I never received a more direct shock."

*   *   *

Repulse had taken five torpedo and one bomb strikes. The *Prince of Wales* had taken a similar number of torpedoes (five or maybe six) and one bomb. The Japanese lost three aircraft. Out of the crew of 69 officers and 1,240 ratings of the *Repulse* 42 officers and 754 ratings were saved. Of the *Prince of Wales*'s crew of 110 officers and 1,502 ratings, 90 officers and 1,195 ratings were saved, but Admiral Sir Tom Phillips and her captain Captain J. C. Leach were both lost.

The ships had gone, but there is one more witness to the disaster, whose words deserve recalling. Though the Japanese did not interfere with the work of rescue, six tubby little Buffalo fighters—the only air cover that Singapore could spare—arrived over the scene and circled the oil and the survivors in the water.

Piloting the leading aircraft was Flight Lieutenant T. A. Vigors, the Officer Commanding 453 Squadron. He could do nothing except to let the men in the water see that no Jap planes would return to harass them. After an hour, he had to leave. He landed at the Australian Air Force Station at Sembawang and the next day, deeply moved by what he had seen, he sat down and wrote this letter to the Commander-in-Chief, Far Eastern Fleet:

"I had the privilege to be the first aircraft to reach the crews of the *Prince of Wales* and the *Repulse* after they had been sunk. I say the privilege, for during the next hour while I flew around low over them, I witnessed a show of that indomitable spirit for which the Royal Navy is famous.

"I have seen a show of spirit in this war over Dunkirk, during the Battle of Britain, and in the London night raids, but never before have I seen anything comparable with what I saw yesterday.

"I passed over thousands who had been through an ordeal the greatness of which they alone can understand, for it is impossible to pass on one's feelings in disaster to others. Even to an eye so inexperienced as mine it was obvious that the three destroyers were going to take hours to pick up those hundreds of men clinging to bits of wreckage and swimming around in the filthy oily water. Above all this the threat of another bombing and machine-gunning attack was imminent. Every one of those men must have realized that. Yet as I flew around every man waved and put his thumb up as I flew over him.

"After an hour lack of petrol forced me to leave, but during that hour I had seen many men in dire danger waving, cheering and joking as if they were holidaymakers at Brighton waving at a low-flying aircraft.

"It shook me, for here was something above human nature. I take off my hat to them, for in them I saw the spirit which wins wars. I apologize for taking up your valuable time, but I thought you should know of the incredible conduct of your men."

*　　　*　　　*

Beneath those men *Repulse* and *Prince of Wales* had reached their final resting places on the seabed. The years passed, the Navy took their revenge on the Japanese Navy, the war ended. And except for the occasional report from pilots who had flown over the spot and believed they could see the wrecks on the bottom through 200 feet of clear water, the ships, though not officially designated as such, became regarded as war graves and were left undisturbed.

Once after the war they became front-page news when there was some suggestion that they should be salvaged for the precious metal they contained, but the strong public reaction to the idea of a foreign firm being allowed to do this quickly put a stop to the idea.

In May 1965 and May 1966, however, the Royal Navy went back. Headed by Lieutenant-Commander David Lermitte, the Royal Navy's Far East Diving Team was granted permission to carry out brief diving surveys on the wrecks of both ships.

The *Royal Navy Diving Magazine* has given permission for the diving teams' reports, which first appeared in the magazine, to be used here:

H.M.S. *REPULSE*

Approval for this operation was granted on the grounds that it would be good training value as well as being of unusual interest. Although *Repulse* is not officially designated as a War Grave it is regarded as such and stress was placed on the requirement that the ship was not to be entered and nothing was to be disturbed externally. This trust was faithfully observed.

H.M.S. *Repulse* lies some 45 miles NNE. of the island of Pulau Tioman off the East coast of Malaya. Being so far from good navigational aids the initial location of the wreck had to be carried out by a suitably equipped frigate. H.M.A.S. *Yarra* was the one chosen for the task. Her mission was successfully carried out and a datum dan buoy was laid some three days before diving operations were scheduled to begin.

The location of this datum marker by H.M.S. *Barfoil* (acting as Diving Support Ship) and M.F.V. *164* (with the Diving Team embarked) was initially thwarted by rough seas and heavy rain and it was feared that the marker might have dragged well clear of the wreck or even have sunk.

Fortunately H.M.S. *Ajax* was in the area on her way back from Hong Kong and was able to assist. She located the marker and confirmed that it was still close to the wreck. By this time daylight was fading and the first day's work had been lost. However, *Barfoil* had laid a very accurate heavy marker alongside *Repulse* and diving was able to commence the following morning; which was, happily, a calm and clear one after the previous day's storm. Of the $5\frac{1}{2}$ days remaining one more was to be lost due to rough weather and, in the closing stages for no accountable reason, the tide changed its working pattern and ran more strongly, further hampering diving operations.

Diving conditions, generally, were excellent. The water was very clear and, needless to say, warm. In fact, underwater visibility was so good that the silvery shape of *Repulse* could be seen from the surface of the sea through a face-mask, before the sun rose too high and veiled her with the increased reflection from the mass of minute particles in the water.

Those that claim to have seen *Repulse* from the air and to have clearly seen her mast are mistaken and have in fact seen the shadow area cast by the bilge keel. For this majestic and awe-inspiring ship lies on the sea-bed almost completely capsized to port with her starboard bilge keel uppermost and her decks under-hanging the horizontal by about 30 degrees. She lies in a mean depth of 180 feet with the stern in slightly deeper water of 196 feet, perhaps caused by a tidal scour created over the years by prevailing ocean currents. The bows lie on a heading of 196 degrees (true) which, were one to extend it on a map, ironically passes through Singapore from whence this magnificent ship set out on her ill-fated mission 24 years ago this December.

The hull is in very good condition with remarkably little marine growth other than a scattering of sea eggs, a few anemones and small clams about 8 inches across. On the wooden decks which are bleached white and have lost their caulking, hang a mass of oysters. Fish life abounds and the first customers normally seen on the way down were large shoals of barracuda, static and staring with those big beady eyes. Highly coloured angel fish and parrot fish were always present around the wreck and also, occasionally, larger and more fearsome inhabitants in the form of big grouper (or jew fish) over 6 feet long, twice as broad as the average man and having a viciously spiked long dorsal fin. These parochial creatures were given a wide berth, needless to say.

The only sign of action damage was a large jagged hole some 20 feet aft of and slightly above the starboard bilge keel from which twisted pipes and machinery grotesquely protruded. The theory put forward that the 15-inch turrets fell out when the ship capsized is certainly not so in the case of "Y" turret, which was seen to be properly in place and trained aft.

It was our intention, had *Repulse* been upright and her mast intact, to replace her battle ensign prior to leaving the area. As this was not possible, a mast was made up of a 60-foot span of dan wire supported by three elliptical floats instead and this was "keel hauled" into position and secured to its own part round a propeller shaft. From this "mast" and immediately below it was sewn a six breadths White Ensign which was last seen proudly billowing out in the tide.

H.M.S. *PRINCE OF WALES*

The *Prince of Wales* was located on sonar and marked with two mooring buoys prior to the start of the operation.

The Far East Clearance Diving Team backed up by Clearance Divers from H.M.S. *Sheraton*, and the Royal Australian Navy's C.D.T.*1*, carried out the survey, involving six days on task, between April 25th and May 6th 1966. Diving was initially carried out from H.M.S. *Sheraton*, but halfway through the operation, she had to be withdrawn for another task, and the team transferred to H.M.S. *Barfoil* for the remainder of the operation.

A total of 64 dives were carried out between 160 and 180 feet involving an overall underwater time of 33 hours. Most of the dives were carried out in S.D.D.E. (Surface Demand Diving Equipment), but S.A.B.A. (Swimmers' Air Breathing Apparatus) was used on a few occasions, particularly for the towed diver searches from the Gemini Dinghy. The weather was fine but the ocean current, although not strong, was unpredictable and at times hindered the operation by making the positioning of the diving support ship above the wreck difficult.

The *Prince of Wales* lies on a heading of 020° and bar about 10° is completely capsized. The shallowest part of the ship is in the vicinity of her starboard bilge keel at a depth of 150 feet. The large flat expanse of the ship's bottom is remarkably free of marine growth and apart from the occasional sea egg, weed or small clam, is only covered with a fine layer of silt. However, the vertical surfaces and those in the dark underhanging part of the ship are well covered with small clams, weed and similar encrustation.

Owing to the vast size of this ship and the problems concerned with mooring the diving support ship above her, it was only possible, in the limited time available, to dive on three separate zones of the *Prince of Wales*, namely, amidships in the vicinity of the engine room, right forward on the stem and right aft in the vicinity of the propellers and rudders.

During the course of the survey the following evidence of war damage was seen:

(a) A large jagged hole about 20 feet in diameter in the forepeak passing right through the ship and in one place fracturing the stem post.

(b) The starboard outer shaft crosses over the starboard inner and its propeller is wedged between the inner shaft and the hull. There is a jagged hole some 6 feet in diameter slightly forward of where the two shafts cross over.

(c) The port outer propeller is missing entirely and the bare shaft has pulled away from the ship snapping the A-bracket in the process. A few feet forward of the A-bracket stub is a large hole about 12 feet in diameter with the shipside plating jaggedly bent inwards.

Diving conditions were generally good, with at best a maximum horizontal visibility of 40 feet on the wreck, but this would reduce to some 15 feet when the ocean currents stirred up the silt. The wreck abounds with marine life and one was constantly accompanied by shoals of fish of all varieties. Apart from one very large and lethargic whale shark, no other kinds of shark were seen, but large shoals of barracuda were frequently in attendance and on a few occasions, large grouper or jew fish were sighted.

As one ascends away from the wreck and out of the milky blanket that enshrouds this great ship in her rest, one comes into crystal clear water with visibility in excess of 120 feet. As you look down on this awesome sight, the full effect of the tragic saga becomes very near to one in the stillness of the underwater world. As with the *Repulse* the year before, our final task as a mark of respect to this great ship and those lost with her, was to rig the White Ensign on an 80-foot wire span, suspended there by three floats.

Whilst diving in the amidships section, scuttles (portholes) and escape hatches in the ship's side were found to be open. Here the underwater camera operated at the scuttle entrance, revealed information not visible to the diver's eye. The flashlight of the camera captured the internal picture which otherwise would remain a foreboding black aperture to the diver. Because the water inside is still and undisturbed by the ocean currents the pictures were clearer than many taken externally and free from small particles in suspension that reflect back the flashlight and thus mar the picture's clarity.

Because the ship lies capsized the deckhead (ceiling) becomes the deck and the pictures showed the hammock bars from which the sailors slung their hammocks, a light fitting, a ventilation shaft with its operating flat handle, some windscoops and a corroded mess bucket.

"It was somewhat amusing to find," says Lieutenant-Commander Lermitte commenting on his reports, "that after all the effort we took in the Navy to locate and mark these wrecks and moor our diving boat above them, the local fishermen knew their exact position and used to come out, as a regular feature, some 50 miles from shore without no doubt a compass between them in their open fishing boats straight to the position to lift fish traps which they had placed in the vicinity of the wrecks.

"Another small point of interest was that when we were diving on the *Prince of Wales* and we were tending the divers from the diving boat one would notice every minute or so little droplets of oil would break the surface and spread out on the sea. Oil fuel was still seeping away some 25 years after the sinking. One wonders how long this will continue."

But the divers were very aware of the men who had died in this wartime disaster. They did not enter the wreck as they had promised. But they had one sad ceremony of their own to perform. One of the diving team who had dived on *Repulse* the previous year was not there when the dives on the *Prince of Wales* took place. He had been killed in a car accident in Singapore some months before.

After his cremation his ashes were scattered at sea in true Naval tradition, but the casket, which had contained those ashes, was, with the permission of his widow, placed on the wreck of the *Prince of Wales* as a gesture of the diving team's affection and respect for their deceased comrade.

And so the Navy left those two great ships—their Ensigns flying once again. The flags are probably gone now, but from that day to this no one has dived down to the scene of one of Britain's greatest naval disasters. The *Prince of Wales* and the *Repulse* rest in peace.

DIVING FOR THE WEATHER

by Dr. John Woods

A British Sub-Aqua Club member employed by the Meteorological Office, John Woods explains how the weathermen
benefit from diving expeditions to the Mediterranean.

SOCIAL acquaintances who ask what I do for a living usually
give a double take when I tell them I work for the Meteorological Office as a diver. Their expression shows they suspect a
rather laborious leg-pull, yet it is quite true. I am now in a
second three-year contract with the Meteorological Office, with
the enviable task of spending several months each year abroad
diving in the warmest, clearest waters to be found. Most years
that means spending the summer months at Malta, but this
year for a change I'm trying the Bahamas which become suitable in early spring. In fact I'm writing this chapter in Miami,
a handy base for diving around the Bahamas.

Why does the Met. Office, whose main concern is weather
forecasting, sponsor such work? As often happens in research,
several apparently quite different answers can be found to this
64-dollar question. But they can be summarized as follows: the
original motivation was to exploit new dye techniques described
below to discover the types of motions that occur in the upper
layer of the ocean, which is sensitive to the weather. Meteorologists and oceanographers both need to know how the air and
sea interact with each other and one of the important factors in
this interaction is mixing in the ocean down to depths of a
hundred feet or so. Mixing, due to turbulent motions in the
sea, is a necessary factor in the equations used to describe air-
sea interaction, but virtually nothing is known about it. What
I set out to do was to search for these mixing motions and if
possible to measure them.

The long-term goal of the search is to produce a description of mixing in the sea that is sufficiently accurate to allow us to predict how the sea temperature changes and how ocean currents grow and decay in response to changes in the weather. Such predictions of "weather under the sea" or ocean forecasting, as it is sometimes called, could one day be as important as weather forecasting, which gives economic benefits (in aviation, agriculture, shipping and the building industry) estimated to exceed £20 for every £1 spent by the Met. Office.

Reliable ocean forecasting would not only directly help the submariner, fisherman and civil engineer, but it would also improve atmospheric weather forecasting. In fact it seems likely that meteorologists will provide the most urgent calls for better knowledge of oceanic mixing, as their giant computers begin to forecast further into the future. As a rough rule, we can safely ignore the interior of the oceans when forecasting for up to twenty-four hours ahead, but it becomes increasingly important when attempting to predict the movement of depressions and anticyclones for days ahead. Already several research groups are making forecasting models that include both the ocean and the atmosphere, but one of the serious oversimplifications made in all these models concerns oceanic mixing. The Meteorological Office interest in my work is that it may lead to a significant improvement in this aspect of the computer models and hence in the precision of their forecasts.

The research began in 1965 in a holiday atmosphere, when Instructor Commander Geoff Fosberry was given leave from the Admiralty to join my team to test the feasibility of using aviator's fluorescein dye packs to help visualize flow in the sea. These dye packets were provided by Geoff's boss, Captain Graham Britton, a 19th-century romantic, who followed the dying tradition of combining a naval career with a scientific interest in nature. Captain Britton's research, often carried out in the face of frustrating conflict with military expediency, defies the common belief that the day of the scientifically enlightened naturalist has disappeared with the arrival of the large research institutes. Even at the end of the 20th century, the gentleman scientist still has a role to play, and Captain Britton's role in our story was to use his position as Director of the Naval Weather Service to provide the essential facilities for our feasibility study in Malta.

Captain Britton's suggestion that we try following the small-scale patterns made by dye fitted in well with my own diving interests at the time. For several years I had been attempting to make a high resolution sonar for use as a surveying aid for divers. By the early sixties it had become clear that it would be possible to make an instrument with sufficient time resolution, but we were so ignorant of small-scale fluctuations of the sound speed in the sea that there would be an unacceptably large uncertainty in the range computed from the time interval between transmitting the pulse and receiving its echo. Clearly it would be necessary to investigate the small-scale variations in the sea's temperature and salinity, which control the speed of sound. The oceanographic textbooks and the experts I consulted at the National Institute of Oceanography all pointed out that these small fluctuations would depend critically on very short internal waves inside the sea and on the mixing processes. I learnt that virtually nothing was known of either factor, especially in the summer thermocline, where the temperature falls by as much as 10°C in 30 metres.

Geoff had a special interest in the summer thermocline and the irregular behaviour of sonar in this layer. He was commanding a small unit charged with developing methods for forecasting the depth of the thermocline, which Second World War submarines had found limited the range of sonar (then called ASDIC) used by submarine chasers. He too found that his main concern was with mixing and internal waves (like those shown in Fig. 1 on page 64). This and his experience as a naval ship's diving officer made him ideally qualified for the Malta project. The rest of our team comprised Frank Irving, a university lecturer in aeronautical engineering, Bob Ward, a chartered accountant, and Gill Yeates, a school teacher.

Each day in Malta during August 1965 we were taken out in a naval M.F.V. to our working site two miles out from Grand Harbour. The navigation was done by one of two midshipmen who joined us on alternate days from their frigate, in Malta for a few days while on passage to the U.K. from Singapore (the Suez Canal was still open in 1965). One of them, Nigel Weston, was also a ship's diving officer so he was able to help in the underwater work too. Strong competition followed Geoff's threat of a report on which midshipman was the better

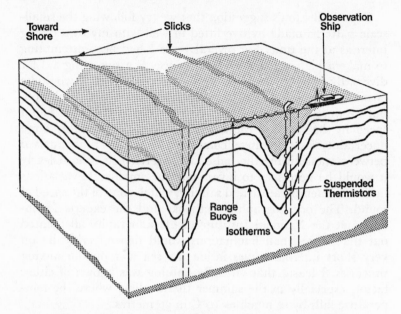

Fig. 1. This diagram shows an underwater or internal wave moving towards the shore, Internal waves can move the thermocline up and down by tens of metres without significant change at the sea surface. These waves exist because of the density step between warm light water over the thermocline and cold dense water below.

navigator, but Nigel's ability to dive finally led to proof that he was the better: on a well-remembered day, after anchoring, he reported we were "on precisely the same site as two days before, when he had noticed a white plastic bucket on the sea floor by the anchor". We were invited to check and there was indeed a white bucket by the anchor; confirmation was dismissed by our midshipman with a very naval "of course". Needless to say he never repeated the performance and the rest of us spend hours inventing ingenious ways by which he could have perpetrated a fraud.

Our first experiment consisted of tying a dye packet to the moving line of a conveniently sited navigational buoy, named "Congreve" on our charts, but bearing the painted letters

Now Reg Vallintine found an octopus and, as he says, they do make ideal subjects for underwater photographers . . .

. . . they'll even sit on your arms as though about to whirl into an eight-armed reel . . .

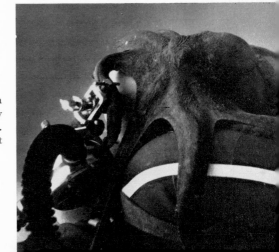

. . . But they can become a nuisance—especially if they start to clog up your air supply. Pictures by Tim Glover at Giglio. (See chapter 2)

The moment of discovery. Reg Vallintine describes it like this: "We swam closer and, suddenly, our narcosis-sodden brains realized that we were looking at the wrecks of a great Roman galley and the 'tubes' were the necks of hundreds of amphoras sticking out of the sand. Squeaking wildly into our mouthpieces and pointing, we thrashed around the wreck . . ." Picture taken 170 feet down off the island of Giglio by Sigi Koster. (See chapter 2)

CONGRIEVE. Naval humour, or Maltese spelling? We soon discovered that the patterns made by the dye as it flowed steadily from the packet depended on the depth of the packet. If we positioned it at the same depth as one of the sharp temperature steps familiar to all Mediterranean divers the dye flowed smoothly and spread across the current to form a thin, ever-widening sheet (Fig. 2 in plates opposite page 96). If, on the other hand, we placed the packet at a level where we could feel no temperature change, the dye flowed out in a turbulent plume, like smoke from a factory chimney (Fig. 3 in plates). Clearly the temperature steps were very important and we set about measuring the temperature difference across them by lowering down a temperature probe borrowed from the National Institute of Oceanography. It proved to be up to 1°C across the strongest steps, which we were soon calling "sheets", to distinguish them from the intervening "layers". When we looked very carefully at the strongest sheets (before dyeing them) we could detect a shimmering, like the interface between gin and tonic before they are stirred. Subsequently we found that the same effect had been described in 1954 by some Americans, diving off California, though they never followed up their discovery.

Because we were looking for mixing in midwater, we always injected the dye well above the sea floor. So we were invariably diving into the blue, with no frame of reference other than the dye. This took some getting used to at first—especially if we could see dye moving in different directions at different levels. Once we started following a meandering dye sheet we lost all sense of position; only the sun reminded us of direction (we had to keep the sun behind us for the best contrast in our dye photographs). After an hour watching the dye we were liable to surface up to a mile in any direction from the boat. So each diver was equipped with a Fenzy lifejacket and instructed not to attempt to swim back but wait to be collected by Zodiac. When working a long way from shore in deep water where the boat could not anchor we were also equipped with smoke flares and surfaced for a position fix after half an hour. These precautions worked well in practice, even if the Zodiac failed to cover the divers when their bubbles were confused with whitecaps. They gave us the confidence to carry out drift diving in deep water out of sight of land, a potentially hazardous procedure.

The second exciting discovery was that the dyed sheets were not smooth but they undulated in response to internal waves only a few metres long. Such short internal waves had been suspected but never before been detected. As we prepared to come home, we already knew that the dye method was capable of revealing internal waves and the difference in mixing at layers and sheets that could be detected by a thermometer. The feasibility study had been a success and we were already full of plans for more detailed investigation the following year.

Our 1965 results were so encouraging that both Geoff and I moved to new jobs where we could devote more time to the work. Geoff became the Mediterranean Fleet Meteorological Officer, based in Malta, and I started my first three-year term with the Meteorological Office. The first task in preparing the 1966 season was to design and make a new temperature probe to look at thermocline sheets and layers. With help from Captain Britton, we obtained the support of the Admiralty Research Laboratory (A.R.L.) at Teddington. The newly formed A.R.L. oceanographic group soon produced a probe that had two thermometers set 50 cm. apart in order to measure the rate at which the temperature was dropping at different levels in the thermocline. During July and August Geoff and I used this instrument to identify and measure the sheets before we went down to mark them with dye. This year we were joined by Roger Wiley and Trevor Sanderson from Imperial College, University of London and Gill Yeates, who had joined the Natural History Museum.

During the 1966 season we made a discovery which solved a problem that had been worrying me through the preceding winter. The problem arose from our observation in 1965 that the flow in the sheets appeared everywhere to be smooth (i.e. non-turbulent). This implied that heat was being conducted down through the sheets only by molecular agitation which is very ineffective compared with the turbulent mixing process assumed to be present and seen by us in the layers. My calculations showed that heat was getting through the sheets about thirty times faster than could be explained by molecular conduction. Our discovery in 1966 was that from time to time "apertures" form in the sheets where heat is pumped down-wards by turbulent mixing. Such an aperture is shown in Fig. 4 (in plates). It consists of several rows of billows on the crest of an internal wave travelling slowly along the sheet. We imme-diately concentrated our efforts on a hunt for more apertures. We wanted to see how large they were, and how frequent, what caused them and whether they always have the same form. So we devised a rig that would allow us to stain a greater area of a sheet by using ten dye packets on a horizontal line as shown in Fig. 2. After considerable manœuvring to make sure the packets lay across the current flow, we opened them (they last for over two hours) and started watching. Within an hour we hit lucky. I was able to photograph in close-up the billows shown in Fig. 5 (in plates). During the summer we found many more and gradually began to realize that the problem of heat trans-port through the sheets had been solved.

Next we turned to the layers between the sheets. In the previous season we had found that the flow from dye packets is too disturbed in the layers to reveal the details of the flow. Once it dawned on us that this was because the pattern in the wake of the packet had roughly the same size as the mixing elements in the layers we realized that we should use a much smaller dye source, with a tiny wake structure. We set about designing a suitable source, but soon found that it could not be completed until after the expedition was due to finish.

Furthermore, the weather was deteriorating and it seemed that whenever the weather improved the Navy needed their boats for other work with higher priority. Gradually a sense of gloom set on the expedition, things seemed to be getting bogged down. But after a fortnight of very little progress Geoff managed to convince the officer in charge of boats at H.M.S. *St. Angelo* (the headquarters of C.-in-C. Mediterranean, in Grand Har-bour) that we should be given the spare harbour ferry for a week. So for the next five days, the Grand Harbour ferry was seen drifting two miles out to sea, surrounded in bright green dye. We soon lost count of the number of boats that came to our unneeded aid; one glorious day we had the entire Medi-terranean fleet steam past us in line astern at half-mile inter-vals, with a friendly offer of help from each. Of course they knew we were all right, but that didn't stop Geoff and myself

having our legs thoroughly pulled in the Wardroom afterwards. But we had our revenge. Next week we were joined by a
senior officer who wanted to see whether a smoke flare he had
"borrowed" from army stores would mark the sea breeze for
his yachts. We steamed off to our normal site and let off the
smoke. I think it was rather more potent than our guest had
expected and it certainly lasted longer that he had planned.
Panic at H.M.S. *St. Angelo*, eighteen boats came to our rescue,
including the Admiral's barge lined with Maltese ratings
"presenting arms" with fire extinguishers and doing pretty
things with boat hooks. This time the laugh was on them—
especially as our guest, being the senior officer, was the one to
explain to Admiral Sir John Hamilton. (I still treasure a
printed invitation from C.-in-C. Mediterranean and Lady
Hamilton—sweet memories of Nelson.)

During this troubled week we finally hit on the solution to
our problem of staining the layers without disturbing them. One
day, as an emergency solution, we cut open a packet of dye
underwater, rolled some tiny pellets in our hands and dropped
them through the thermocline layers. The results were astound-
ing. As each pellet fell it left a dyed wake, which took up the
motion of the water at every level. Here was the answer to our
problem. We had been wrong in trying to design a modified
source to stain horizontal surface inside the layer, we could get
all the information we needed from vertical dye streaks. They
showed us that the current changes fairly smoothly in the layers
then jumps abruptly at the sheets. We were able to calculate
the current shear (i.e. the rate of change of current with depth)
by measuring a series of photographs of the same dye streak.
And we could tell from the way the dye spread whether the
flow was smooth or turbulent. As in the sheets, the flow in the
layers seemed to be mainly smooth, with occasional spots of
turbulence. But just as we were beginning to explore the layers
with this new technique the time came to go home, further dye
studies had to wait for next year.

Back at Bracknell that winter, I started work relating our
underwater observations to the background of theoretical fluid
dynamics. A discussion with some friends in the Applied Mathe-
matics department at Cambridge led me to read a recent
theory by Miles and Howard, which turned out to provide a

good description of the billows on the sheets. According to this theory, the spacing of such billows should be about $7\frac{1}{2}$ times the sheet thickness and they should only occur when the current difference across the sheet exceeds a critical value, dependent on the sheet thickness and the temperature difference. Our photographs and temperature soundings contained enough detail for me to show that the billows do indeed follow the Miles-Howard predictions rather accurately. This was, in fact, the first confirmation of their theory, though further support came soon afterwards from laboratory experiments performed at the National Institute of Oceanography by Dr. Steve Thorpe.

During the winter I wrote up this analysis for the *Journal of Fluid Mechanics* and another paper analysing aperture conduction for the *Meteorological Magazine*. These were the first of a series of papers describing various aspects of the Malta work. The conclusion in each was necessarily rather tentative as we were continuing to make new discoveries at Malta, but the delays involved in having a scientific paper published are often so long that one is forced to submit a tentative analysis and if necessary modify or supplement it later at proof stage. While this procedure may not be ideal it is often the most practical way of informing fellow workers of one's results as soon as possible. Another method is to give lectures and present papers at conferences and both Geoff and I were active in this field during the winter of 1966–67.

In the spring I was joined at the Meteorological Office by Stewart MacKenzie, a trained electronics technician who had also been an R.A.F. diving instructor in North Africa before joining the Met. Office. Stewart rapidly familiarized himself with the instrumentation required for the thermocline work and spent a week at the Admiralty Research Laboratory learning how to make oceanographic apparatus watertight. Soon he was working alongside Gordon Wearden, the A.R.L. experimental officer in charge of developing improved instruments for the 1967 expedition. As usual everything was completed in a mad rush only hours before the deadline for flying the apparatus to Malta.

In June, our team, comprising Stewart and Gordon, David Hebblethwaite (a Met. Office scientific assistant and trained meteorological observer) and two graduate students, Mike

Davis and Ray Pollard, joined Geoff Fosberry and his staff in
Malta for a further two months' diving. This year I was determined to overcome the boat problem suffered in 1966 so I had
arranged that whenever the navy boats became difficult we
should switch to Marsaxlokk, the South-east Malta base of an
R.A.F. air-sea rescue boat squadron. We had occasionally used
these boats in 1966 with great success; their high speed (up to
40 knots in an emergency) made it possible to work 60 miles out
to sea, where the 2-mile-deep water of the Eastern Mediterranean began, yet still return home for supper at a reasonable
hour. This "hit and run" method is becoming increasingly
popular amongst oceanographers, who traditionally spend
weeks at sea cruising in a large ship.

The fast boats allowed us to make the first measurements of
the horizontal extent of thermocline sheets and layers; we
made a series of microstructure soundings as fast as possible at
one-mile intervals along a straight line. While these soundings
were not simultaneous, or "synoptic" to use a meteorological
term, they were made every half-hour, which is a short interval
compared with the periods of 12 hours or so we expected for
changes in structure. The results of these soundings were
puzzling, sometimes the sheets could be followed for many
miles, then they would disappear to be replaced by others.
There seemed to be some larger structure on a scale of a few
miles that controlled the horizontal extent of the sheets and
layers. This scale in the sea corresponds to the synoptic-scale
features such as depressions and fronts in the atmosphere, so
we began to wonder whether oceanic fronts were to be found
off Malta. The Americans had found that such features could
be detected with a radiation thermometer fitted under an aircraft to measure the sea surface temperature. When he was at
the Admiralty Geoff had managed to borrow one of these instruments for trials in the Channel Approaches and subsequently
the Met. Office had bought and fitted one to its Varsity research
aircraft. It was too late to arrange anything for 1967, but I
resolved to have the Varsity in Malta the following year.

After we had completed the experiments on board the R.A.F.
high-speed launches we moved back to our old base at Manoel
Island (the Mediterranean Fleet Clearance Diving Centre),
where Lt.-Cdr. John Grattan provided boats, air and storage

space for our diving operations. We civilians were rather diffi-
dent about diving in front of the clearance divers, who made us
feel fumbling amateurs, but as in previous years they went out
of their way to be friendly and helpful. Each day throughout
August we went out to the Congreve buoy to record the patterns made by dye streaks from pellets of fluorescein moulded
by David Hebblethwaite and sealed like Aspro tablets in a
polythene strip. These pellets were a great improvement over
the rather haphazard ones used the previous year; in particular
they gave the regular wake pattern seen in Fig. 6 (in plates).

This year I had arranged for the Min. Tech. Central Unit of
Scientific Photography to make up a special 16-mm. motion
camera for filming these dye streaks and during August we
exposed some 4,000 feet of dye streak film for analysis during
the winter. The filming required a high order of teamwork
which took several weeks to develop. The following technique
proved successful. After examining the microstructure profile,
we selected the approximate range of depths for our experiment, then we dived down to about 10 feet above chosen level.
My companion would then cut open the polythene strip and
release one pellet. As the pellet fell leaving a dye streak I sank
alongside it watching carefully to get a feel for the type of
motions present at that level. Then I would signal to my companion to release a second pellet some twenty feet clear of the
first. After dropping the pellet he used his Fenzy buoyancy vest
to rise smoothly above the dye streak so as not to disturb it by
finning. When he was clear he would lower a 6-armed, one-
metre scale on the end of a cord until it coincided with the
centre of my camera's field of view. It was important that the
scale did not disturb the dye so it was moved very gently as
directed by my directions while I filmed the dye. After a while
we became quite expert at giving and responding to tiny "crane-
divers" signals of this kind. I usually started filming at a range
of about twenty feet (we did not attempt to film if the visibility
dropped below 100 feet) and then slowly swam towards the
dye. In practice it was possible to get to within a foot or two of
it without causing any immediate disturbance. However, such
close approaches, like archaeological excavation, eventually
caused a disturbance and were avoided whenever possible.

These films have given us the data to measure the rate of

mixing inside the thermocline layers and hence, in principle, to answer the original problem. But as soon as I began to make the necessary computations it became clear that the small spots of turbulence responsible for the mixing are unlike any motion previously studied by fluid dynamicists. A whole new theory must be produced and tested experimentally before we can be sure what is really happening inside the thermocline. So the feeling we had at the end of August 1967 that the problem was essentially solved was premature, further expeditions and several more years of theoretical work is still needed.

We spent the last few days in Malta, during September 1967, repeating the dye sheet experiments of the previous season. These led to a quite unexpected discovery which answered a frequently posed question: how does the cycle of daytime heating and night-time cooling affect the thermocline? What we found is a delayed response to the night cooling. During the morning, between 0900–1100 local time, the top sheet of the thermocline suddenly breaks up in spectacular wave breaking and billows. In less than half an hour the top sheet changed from a smooth, laminar flow to violent turbulence, then back to laminar flow. We saw this happen by chance a couple of times before the penny dropped and then we devoted a week to studying the spectacular phenomenon. By the fifth day we were convinced that its timing was a direct consequence of the previous night's cooling and we were able to support this conclusion with calculations based on our dye streak observations.

After another winter of analysing results and furiously building new apparatus, by July we were ready for Malta again, with a team consisting of Stewart, David, Roger Wiley, John Leslie (a Met. Office forecaster and enthusiastic diver) and Ted Whittaker (an experienced electronics officer who had just joined my staff). The highlight of the 1968 season was undoubtedly the combined operations between the Met. Office Varsity aircraft and a high-speed launch from R.A.F. Marsaxlokk. The plan was that the aircraft should spend an hour surveying the sea surface temperature (S.S.T.) in a selected 20-mile square while the boat got into position at the centre of the square. When the survey was finished Ivan Pothecary, Chief Scientist on the Varsity, prepared a rapid plot of the S.S.T. contours and radioed me on the boat to choose the best line for the series of microstructure soundings made for the boat. As soon as we had chosen the best path, the boat started the series of soundings while the aircraft repeated the survey.

By a miracle combination of luck and planning the experiment worked first time—everybody was delighted and we held a party that evening to celebrate. After repeating the experiment with various modifications each day during the rest of the week we felt that the feasibility study had proved worthwhile. However, improved navigation would be needed before we could combine the aircraft S.S.T. measurements and the boat soundings with sufficient precision to answer the key question, does the synoptic scale structure detected by the aircraft affect the sheets and layers found by the boat? [We repeated the experiment more accurately in 1969, after this chapter was written, and are now analysing the results.]

The few diving experiments carried out in 1968 virtually completed the initial exploratory stage of the underwater dye programme that Geoff Fosberry and I had started in 1965. What have the four expeditions achieved? After starting with effectively no knowledge of the thermocline's structure and mixing processes, we have now reached a stage where we know what kind of structure and motions exist and their approximate dimensions. We know for example that the temperature in the thermocline drops in steps and we know these steps are about $\frac{1}{4}$°C, 10–20 cm. thick and spaced every few metres. We know that most of the flow in the thermocline is smooth, with sharp changes at the sheets, but that small short-lived spots of turbulence, usually less than a metre thick fill about 10 per cent of the layers and 3 per cent of the sheets at any instant. Our examination of these spots of turbulence has shown that they are all very similar, but we need more careful measurements before we can calculate the rate at which they mix heat, salt and momentum. It seems likely that when we have these figures we shall be able to explain why the thermocline is divided up into layers.

The fun of exploration may be ended, but that doesn't mean that we shall stop diving. We are going back to Malta—this time to test two new instruments designed to give the quantitative data lacking in our earlier experiments. These instruments will fall slowly through the sea under gravity so that they can make fine measurements without disturbance from the surface. I know that we shall spend days diving with these instruments before they will perform correctly. So diving now becomes a support for the instruments rather than vice versa.

If we are to continue our role as underwater explorers we shall have to go deeper. For example, we should look at the main thermocline under the Sargasso Sea, where small-scale mixing plays an important part in the general circulation of the Atlantic Ocean, which means mainly, of course, the Gulf Stream. This will involve diving to 3,000 feet—in a research submarine. Two oceanographers, Dr. Claes Rooth and Dr. Stewart Turner, have twice been to these depths in the research submarine *Alvin* and filmed dye tracers similar to those we used at Malta. Unfortunately *Alvin* was accidentally dropped overboard last year and now sits on the seafloor 4,000 feet down awaiting recovery by the U.S. Navy.* But there are other submarines and I hope to spend some time in 1970 extending the Rooth-Turner search for mixing elements in the deep ocean.

I started this chapter with a brief apologia for the Malta Expedition—and it became apparent that any economic benefits were unlikely to come in the immediate future. I should like to close by describing a quite unexpected short-term benefit of the Malta research—the forecasting of currents for our Olympic yachtsmen in 1968. The Met. Office was asked to advise the British team after they returned from a pre-Olympic trial in 1967 with stories of light winds and fast, rapidly changing currents. David Houghton, a senior forecaster, was asked to act as consultant during the Olympics and before he left for Mexico we spent many hours discussing the currents which caused so much trouble in 1967.

It soon became clear that Acapulco provided an extreme example of the phenomena Geoff and I had been studying at Malta, where the surface waters are so hot that there is virtually no mixing and the wind can set the top few feet of the sea skimming along while deeper water is quite unaffected. I had previously coined the term "slippery sea" to describe this phenomenon and when David and I prepared a briefing for the yachtsmen we found the expression gave just the right impression.

* Alvin was recovered during 1969 and is now being refitted.

Before the Olympics proper started our team watched the motion of markers and learnt when and where to expect the currents to change. They became the only team who understood the currents and this proved crucial in the races, when they won an oustanding gold medal and a silver. The Press made a great fuss about the "Slippery Seas of Acapulco"; *Newsweek* described the combined efforts of yachtsmen, meteorologists and oceanographers as being "a rare and satisfying example of the direct application of fundamental research without going through technology".

If there is a lesson to be learnt from this it is that when science is ignorant it usually pays to go and have a look, and in oceanography that means diving . . .

(The Director-General of the Meteorological Office has given permission for the publication of this chapter)

A CHESTFUL OF SILVER

by Lieutenant-Commander Alan Bax, R.N.

In 1711 the great Dutch East Indiaman *Liefde* crashed into the cliffs of the Out Skerries. Alan Bax led one of the expeditions to the site. Here he tells how they found some of her treasure.

LIFE at sea in the late 17th century would have been no place for we spoiled moderns. We can today reach Batavia by air in 20 hours—about two days for the round trip. But the 150-foot-long sailing ship *Liefde* took two years to cover the same distance. And that was on her maiden voyage which began in October 1701 shortly after she was built for the Dutch East India Company.

Navigation, of course, was not the precise art it is today and the course of a vessel could be shaped only some 45 degrees either side of the wind. Wind speed and direction dominated the life of the ancient mariner—when a gale blew he could do little but take in most of the sail and run helplessly before it.

So it was with *Liefde*. On the night of 7/8 November, 1711, on her fourth voyage to the East, she was running before a southerly gale somewhere near the extreme north of Scotland. By all accounts it was not a wind of great severity, just an "ordinary gale" common to this part of Britain.

From her position it was clear that she was undoubtedly taking the long route round from Holland to the South, but there was a good reason for this.

At the time Britain and the Dutch were allied in one of their not uncommon struggles against the French and as a result the English Channel was not considered the healthiest route through which to send valuable merchantmen by the "Gentlemen Seventeen" as the directors of the Dutch East India Company were known.

It is impossible to say now how exactly 39-year-old Barent Muijkens, the master of *Liefde*, knew his position, but in all

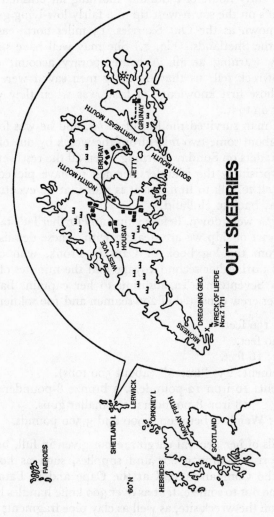

Fig. 7. The Out Skerries, showing their position in relation
to the Shetlands and the site of the wreck of the *Liefde*
in 1711.

probability he would not know his whereabouts to within 20 miles. And on this dark, cold and stormy night there was little he could have done in the teeth of the gale even if he had.

So in the early hours of a Sunday morning she crashed into the steep cliffs on the south-west tip of a fairly low-lying group of islands known as the Out Skerries, 15 miles north-east of Lerwick in the Shetlands. (Fig. 7.) She may well have struck without any warning at all. A contemporary account of a similar shipwreck tells us that the only men saved were the lookouts, whose first knowledge of land was when they were flung bodily on to it.

Only one man survived the loss of *Liefde*, and he was found wandering about some two miles from the wreck by one of the less holy islanders on Sunday morning when all the rest were in church. Surprisingly the islanders seemed to have picked up enough Dutch to talk to him and it is said that he eventually made his way back to Holland.

So the *Liefde* went down. Before going any further let's take a look at the sort of ship we are dealing with. These details are compiled from the log book of Captain Pronk, who commanded her during her second voyage and the minutes of the "Gentlemen Seventeen". In addition to her captain, Barent Muijkens, her crew consisted of 200 seamen and 100 soldiers.

Length: 150 feet.
Beam: 40 feet.
Draught: 16 feet.
Displacement: 250 "lasten" (about 500 tons).
Armament: 10 iron 12-pounders. 2 bronze 8-pounders.
            18 iron 8-pounders. 10 smaller guns.
Anchors: Weighed between 2,900 and 3,500 pounds.

The details of her general cargo are not given in full, but it would comprise trading goods and supplies, such as house-bricks, for the Company's staff at the Cape and in Batavia. (This is borne out to some extent as over 300 knife handles have been found on the wreck site, as well as clay pipe fragments and fruit stones, which may have formed part of a consignment with which to start the fruit farms of the Cape.)

Almost half her cargo space would have been taken up by beer, water and food, stowed as shown in Fig. 8. This would

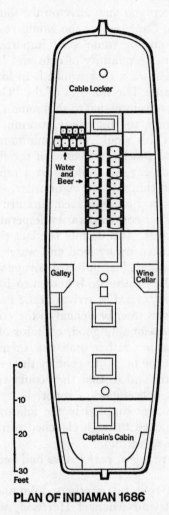

PLAN OF INDIAMAN 1686

Fig. 8. This plan of an Indiaman (1686) shows just how much room had to be taken up by provisions. However, these supplies had to keep about 300 men alive on the four-month passage to the Cape where she could re-provision in safety.

not appear to leave much space for other goods, but these supplies had to keep 300 men alive on the four-month passage from Texel to the Cape, where she would re-provision. It did leave enough room for some very important cargo. *Liefde* carried a considerable quantity of coin and bullion for use as wages and in other ways that would help forward the Company's eastern trade. The minutes of the "Gentlemen Seventeen" show that it was intended to ship some 1,850,000 guilders from Amsterdam in 10 ships that autumn. If split equally between the ships this would put a minimum of 185,000 in *Liefde*, but she was the largest vessel of the fleet, and records after the loss quote 227,000 guilders as a replacement figure, which seems to put things in the right order.

She was, then, a heavily-armed, mature and well-found vessel, but like all her contemporaries desperately overcrowded by modern standards. And despite the fact that over half her cargo space was taken up by food and water, conditions were not pleasant on passage. Her outward voyage would take about ten months and the death rate is known to have averaged 10 per cent on such voyages. On arrival in the East the delights of the shore might even then be denied to the crew. If the health on board looked reasonably good, captains often preferred to keep their crews at sea rather than risk them bring infection back on board. In the late 17th century they were experimenting with a seawater still so that they could remain at sea for longer periods! A contemporary report in 1705 describes the state of a ship's water supplies in the following words: "The water has to be sucked through clenched teeth to prevent the entrance of crawling vermin."

On that happy thought, perhaps we had better return to the 20th century . . .

In the spring of 1965 two brothers, John and Peter Bannon, together with a friend Michael Harrison, were watching a television programme in their flat at Ealing in West London. The programme was a film about the wrecks around the coasts of the United Kingdom. The three became very interested. However, only one of them—Peter Bannon—had any experience of aqualung diving, and none knew a great deal about the sea or boats. Though they talked of what they might do, they reached no firm decision.

H.M.S. *Prince of Wales*—180 feet down. These remarkable pictures were taken by divers who investigated the wreck of H.M.S. *Prince of Wales*. (See chapter 3). They show: *Left:* The ship's hawser reel on the starboard side above the engine room . . .

Above: View taken through ship's side scuttle of a compartment starboard side amidships. Buckets in the foreground. Windscoop on the left. Hammock bar also visible. Remember the ship is almost completely capsized. *Left:* Another view through a scuttle. Fan trunking with shut-off flap is shown in the right foreground and hammock bars nearby.

"A six-breadths White Ensign last seen proudly billowing out in the tide."
An historic picture—of the Ensign that the divers reflew from the wreck of
H.M.S. *Repulse* nearly 200 feet down. (See chapter 3)

There the matter rested, until a month later an article appeared in a weekly magazine. It included a colour map of treasure ships lost over the ages. This was the spur they needed. Dreams of exploring a treasure ship dominated all else and they set to work to find one. So enthusiastic were they that they decided to use all the spare money they had to select a site and make up a preliminary expedition that very year.

All the treasure wrecks on the map were considered and their history checked as far as possible in London. Finally out of all the possibilities they chose the Dutch East Indiaman *Kennermerlandt*—because her treasure seemed the most likely to have been unmolested over the centuries since her sinking in 1664.

That was the first problem solved, there remained two more equally daunting, but neither blunted the enthusiasm of the trio. First divers and equipment had to be found. Second they had to be transported to the Shetland Isles, some six hundred miles away—the equivalent of a journey to the South of France. John Bannon, however, had a friend in the underwater business, who knew a Naval Officer, keen on diving and more particularly marine archaeology. Which was where I came in. Would I take the expedition? "Delighted," I said. I had a diving friend, Malcolm Cavan, a Royal Marine Officer and so we formed a team of four with Peter Bannon and Mike Harrison.

Transport now remained as the only problem. How could we get this small team and their equipment to the Islands? A reasonable ferry service exists between Scotland and Lerwick, the main town of Shetland. But negotiations to hire a boat from Lerwick to the Out Skerries proved difficult and the hire of a local fishing boat expensive. We decided that we would have to provide our own boat. We were lucky. A suitable craft was found in a yard on the Thames, west of London—50 miles from the sea! Twenty-five foot long, she had a small petrol engine, a speed of six to seven knots and a fuel consumption of about one gallon per hour.

Now our plans leaped forward. Provisions and equipment were found and finally the boat was taken overland to Wroxham on the Norfolk Broads, some 20 miles inland from Yarmouth on the East Coast. On 8 August, 1965, we set sail in dull but calm weather. Relatively calm weather would perhaps be a better description for our little boat *Norfjord* seemed to have all

6

the qualities of a see-saw crossed with a particularly erratic roundabout.

The voyage north was uneventful except that the fuel consumption was 50 per cent higher than we had expected. Siphoning petrol from drums to fuel tank did not add to the joys of our stomachs. Four and a half days later, *Norfjord* passed through the southern entrance of the harbour in the Out Skerries and in the evening light berthed at the little pier that some of us were to learn to know well in the years to follow.

Our entrance caused something of a furore among the locals—they number about 100—who seldom get visitors, least of all direct from the south of England. However in their slow, quiet way, they made us more than welcome. In discussion that evening we learnt that a cannon had been lifted from the south-west corner of the Island the previous year by amateur divers—again from the south of England.

Next morning we made the two-mile journey from the harbour to the site accompanied by Gibby Johnson, a local lobster farmer, who was to help us considerably over the years. Gibby pointed out the spot where the cannon had been found. I then dived to start a towed search over the position. It was fruitless. The rocky seabed was completely obliterated by a carpet of kelp. Underwater visibility was in excess of 50 feet, although I found nothing, it was beautiful.

Then it was Malcolm's turn. Using his compass he dived on a course parallel to the cliffs while our boat followed his buoy marker. Two minutes later he surfaced, waving and making the most alarming noises. He didn't seem to be in trouble . . . We drew nearer . . . Then, muffled and distorted through full face mask came the words . . . "I've found it . . . I've found it . . ." In his hand he waved two silver coins!

So we found an ancient wreck. Not as it turned out the *Kennermerlandt*, but another Dutch East Indiaman *Liefde*, wrecked some 50 years later in the same area.

THE EXPEDITIONS

The expedition of 1965 was, as I have mentioned, not the first to search for the Indiaman. Salvage attempts began, of course, almost as soon as the wreck occurred. The earliest attempts on *Liefde* seem to have run true to the form of all salvage schemes that are spurred on by the lure of treasure—professional Dutch salvagemen and the Shetland amateurs were competing for the wreck at very much the same time.

In April, 1712, the Dutchman Luijtje Bontchoe reported that he "found only rigging" and in May another Dutch salvage expert, Wylie Wybrants, said that "he was unable to fish anything out". It would seem that either the Shetlanders had been too canny for their Dutch rivals, or that there was some collusion to the detriment of the Dutch East India Company, because some time that same year four Shetlanders are reported as having recovered chests of gold valued at £30,000!

The money was probably recovered soon after the wreck or some part of it was above or very near the surface. Two clefts in the area (in the Shetlands they call them "geos") are known as the "Dragging Geos" and they say that it was from these clefts or gullies that the gold was dragged out. Life and the law seem to have changed little for the four Shetlanders on admitting their recoveries to the local Crown official received 30 per cent of the value—from which they had to pay their salvage expenses!

The next reported expedition to the site took place between 1729 and 1735 when a "London Diver" worked on the wrecks of both the *Liefde* and the *Kennermerlandt*. He is said to have recovered some 2,000 ducatoons and 160 ducats. This seems a small sum for so long a labour, but this is, of course, only what he declared.

Then for some 229 years the wreck apparently remained untouched by man until 1964 when H.M.S. *Shoulton* with naval divers on board came to the site. Only two silver ducatoons were found and presented to Lerwick Museum. But they did find a cannon. Time did not permit raising it although an attempt was made. But the cannon was lifted in the end—by Mr. Eric Giles—and is now in Lerwick Museum.

So in 1965 came the expedition which I led. Time on the site was only four days and with two divers this allowed only the barest examination of the possibilities. We did recover a few coins. But if the expedition was short it did, however, lead to long hours of thought over the following winter and a new expedition in the summer of 1966.

This expedition, which consisted of about 12 people (not all divers) was there for eleven days. It included Ian Morrison, a lecturer at Edinburgh University, and Stephen Halliday, a professional underwater photographer. John Bannon and Owen Gander provided invaluable assistance in running the expedition and we gave the site a basic survey, carried out some tentative rock clearance with explosives, and made a visual diver search of an adjacent area.

The bonanza year was in 1967 when two expeditions recovered many artifacts, to say nothing of a chest of silver! The first diving took place in June when H.M.S. *Delight* paid a courtesy visit to Lerwick. By coincidence I was First Lieutenant and the Captain, Commander J. M. Child, R.N., permitted the landing of a 24-man 3-day expedition.

We tried elementary lifting methods to move some of the rocks which had fallen on to the site, after they had been broken up by explosives. Further survey work was carried out and we attempted a magnetometer search, but the results were inconclusive (the errors being more human than electronic). Then in August and September Owen Gander led another expedition. Financed by Scientific Surveys Ltd., it involved fifteen people for periods varying between two weeks and two months. The main work was that of excavation.

In 1968 there was yet another expedition—a more expensive affair than any of the others, again financed by Scientific Surveys. Work this time was directed by John Bannon and Owen Gander and I led the on-site work ably backed by Jim Gill. What was our work like? What sort of conditions did we dive under?

THE DIVING SITE

As sailing men will know an adverse wind can turn the gentlest of coastlines into a dreaded lee shore—from which there is no escape if the anchors fail to hold. The cliffs that *Liefde* struck were far from gentle, rising steeply and jaggedly from some 50 feet under the sea to 80 or 100 feet above it. Made of a form of granite known as gneiss—on the site it appears to be light yellow, brown or grey and has occasional streaks of pink—they are typical of the Islands, which are mainly made up of this rock with a thin covering of soil. Grass grows wherever there is soil and vegetables can be cultivated in the more sheltered valleys, but there are no trees. The wind and the ever-nibbling sheep see to that.

The climate tends to be windy with a great deal of grey skies. Air temperatures seldom exceed the middle sixties, though on one never-to-be-forgotten day in 1968 we were able to take off our shirts! It is, however, frequently quite humid and the damp makes it difficult to dry diving gear in the open. Orkney, Shetland, Fair Isle, Iceland are familiar names in the shipping forecasts and are usually associated with warnings of high wind forces.

Our luck with the weather on the site has varied. In 1966 we lost three days out of eight; in 1968 three days out of 42. The site is sheltered from northerly winds and it was found possible to dive from the 52-foot boat used in 1968 even in southerlies providing the sea height was not greater than five or six feet. Such diving was, of course, never comfortable, particularly on the surface, because we were only 50 feet from a stark lee shore. It was in fact only possible because we had laid a strong four-legged mooring.

The Islanders are reserved and equable in temperament, but are ever-helpful. They are not averse to the odd moment of "madness" for their wedding celebrations last days rather than hours. Their living stems mainly from the earnings of three fishing vessels and the unceasing work of the women who knit by hand the traditional Fair Isle patterns. The modern touch is given to this age-old tradition—the women can manage these complicated patterns, carry on a conversation and still watch TV! And in the winter when there is no fishing the men lend a hand with the knitting—by machine!

Below the surface we have found during our four years that the average sea temperature at all depths has been 52 degrees F.

The seabed in the vicinity of the main work area, which we nicknamed "Silver Gulley", is a jumble of boulders varying in size from one cubic foot to 250, and the whole area, particularly the reef, cliff face and larger boulders, is covered with a thick layer of kelp. This grows to a height of about three to four feet and extends down to a depth of 70 feet. And life abounds. Dog-fish, lobsters, crabs, sun stars, jellyfish and sponges are there in plenty. So are shoals of formation-flying tiddlers.

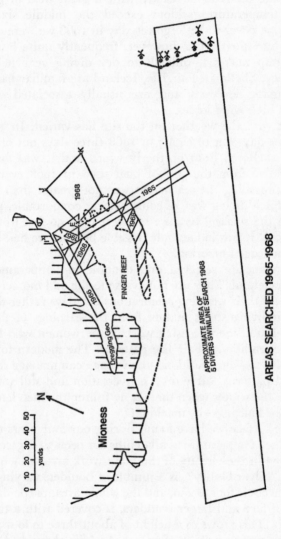

AREAS SEARCHED 1965-1968

Fig. 9. This plan shows the areas searched by the expeditions to the *Liefde* wreck site from 1965 to 1968.

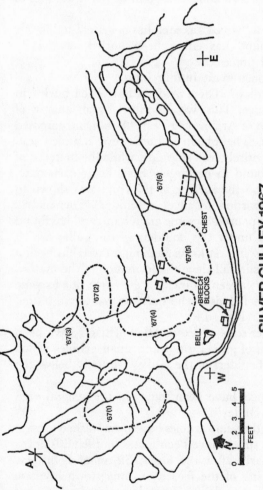

SILVER GULLEY 1967

Fig. 10. If a wreck site is being worked in a proper archaeological manner, everything must be recorded. Here, for example, is a plan of *Silver Gulley* on the site of the *Liefde* wreck as it was in 1967. The rocks with dotted outlines were removed in 1967, as were the small boulders and rock fragments in the blank areas of the plan. This removal revealed a mixture of sand, gravel, pebbles, coin, artifacts and some form of hard black oxide. The mixture filled in the spaces between boulders and formed the bottom in the blank areas. The attempt to blast and lift rock 67 (6), which had partially covered the chest, failed. Throughout the whole area coin, cannon balls and small objects of all kinds were found.

Visibility has seldom been less than 30 feet and often up to 50. The water is particularly clear in the bottom ten feet although we could detect no thermocline. Visibility higher up was often reduced by plankton. There is little tidal stream until the lower kelp line where one or two knots can often be felt according to the state of the tide.

The wreck? Well, a "wreck" as such has never existed in our time. Everything found has either been buried, or heavily disguised by natural processes.

Discoveries have been made in four ways.

First in "Silver Gulley". There artifacts have been buried in a hard black substance. This was described by an analyst of the London Institute of Archaeology as: "A matrix composed largely of sulphides. The black nodules were sampled and found to be almost entirely iron sulphide, while the material of "rust" colour was found to be largely basic ferric carbonate. The black material on the surface of the coins was shown to contain a high proportion of silver sulphide." This matrix appears to have been poured by some giant hand and has found its level around and under the boulders of the gulley which slopes from north to south. It looks as though there has been a minor, if not major, cliff fall since the formation of the matrix. The thickness varies between an inch on the north side to some 15"–18" against the reef. This is where a chest was found buried in it in August, 1967. (Fig. 10.)

Second. In a poorer state of preservation artifacts have been found in the mixture of gravel, sand and small pebbles which fills in between the boulders of the Gulley—usually below the black matrix.

Third. Other objects have been found in the general area surrounding "Silver Gulley".

And fourthly over the years articles have been washed ashore. Coin, both gold and silver, have been found on the cliffs north of the site, particularly after the Great Storm of February, 1900. I dread to think of the ferocity of any storm in these waters remembered that long. Tradition also has it that "many years ago" two Skerry lads hunting for limpets during an unusually low tide, found a bar of gold. Try as they might, goes the story, they could not free it from the rocks and the tide forced them back. And, so we are told, they never found it again. Perhaps though they had learnt from their ancestors' experience on *Liefde* and felt as many do today that a salvage award of 30 per cent is just not enough . . .

THE DIVING

A considerable amount of time has been spent underwater through the years, fortunately without incident—other than a few minor equipment malfunctions. The two main contributory factors to this record have been strict observation of the Royal Navy decompression tables, and a high proportion of experienced divers. Though 1968 saw 11-year-old Patrick Gill working on the bottom, and 15-year-old Douglas Young diving with the best of us.

From a mass of diving detail a few major points emerge:

Warmth

Again and again warmth, or rather the lack of it, emerges as the limiting factor on the diver's efficiency. It matters both above and below water. Although the water was not unduly cold—50 to 53 degrees F, old $\frac{3}{16}$th-inch suits do not permit prolonged static (60 to 90 minutes) work to be carried out with reasonable efficiency at the working depth of about 48 feet.

When the work is hard physically, and little thought is required it does not matter quite as much, but as soon as fine detail of thought and action are needed diver-comfort becomes of paramount importance. Attempts at writing by cold divers have been quite illegible. We learnt that every effort should be made to ensure that a diver is warm before entering the water, and that colds develop more quickly if he is unable to dry and warm himself after a dive. Obviously heated suits are beyond the pocket of this type of expedition, but it is thought that the simple facility to pour hot water over a wet-suited diver would be of considerable value both before and after diving. It was also found that the dry suit over wet suit combination worked well on static tasks, although clumsy.

Briefing

This was found to be a vital part of the expedition, for unless it was thorough and precise, the leader lost control of the work underwater, and "exploration" changed very rapidly to "scrabbling". It was found necessary to produce a small-scale map of the overall area to brief divers for search schemes, and a large-scale map of "Silver Gulley" to brief for recording and recovery.

The main brief was usually carried out towards the end of the evening—after supper was a good time—in the warmth and comfort of "home", when the past day's work, and theories, could also be discussed. On site, divers were given last-minute instructions depending on work progress and weather conditions from duplicate maps, either covered with thin polythene or drawn direct on plastic paper. This means of "instant" visual briefing proved invaluable, as it is sometimes difficult to "get through" to a diver who is kitted up, cold, and sitting in a boat whose motion is reminiscent of the funfair . . . Under these conditions there is a natural tendency to get underwater and do "something"—anything!—a tendency which the leader must combat.

Small reproductions of either of the two maps drawn on plastic paper were also found of great value underwater, and using the lines and tags of the marker system—the terrain did not warrant a true grid—divers were able to "mapread" their way to their work location with relative ease.

Equipment

Four different air compressors have been used at one time or another, and all have proved reliable. As to divers' personal gear, the cry of "standardization" shrieks out. How much simpler an expedition would be if weightbelts and weights alone, were similar—not to mention bottle pressures. The procedure of wrapping the pillar valve and "O" ring of charged sets with waterproof Sellotape was found to be most efficient. "O" rings stayed in, and there was no confusion between charged and uncharged sets. Finally an "airbank" provides by far the most efficient means of recharging on site, and if it permits the noisy compressor to be stowed in shelter below decks, it really is a winner.

Division of Responsibility

It has become clear over the years that the most efficient

expedition is one where some 25 to 30 per cent are non-divers. The brunt of the vital work of recording, cataloguing, photographic processing and logging, victualling and bottle charging can then be carried out by a standing shore party who have no other responsibility, and who are not subject to the rigours of work underwater. This is not to say that divers should not assist with these tasks, but their responsibility can be much reduced and the overall efficiency considerably increased.

WHERE WE SEARCHED

Initial location, normally a most difficult problem was quickly effected in 1965. However, little material was found, and the spread of the wreck was in no way determined. Our efforts since that time have been devoted to determining this spread, and exploring the area of initial discovery.

Exploration was relatively easy in as much that it entailed the recording and removal of rock, gravel, and artifacts from a relatively small area. Determination of spread was not quite so simple, visual methods only were available, for although a magnetometer was taken on more than one expedition it was not used effectively.

The use of such magnetic instruments must be carefully considered for they need a clear site, and during a short expedition the leader of it is probably loath to keep divers idle in good weather while the survey takes place. The choice of our search method was guided by three factors:

(a) The material state of the vessel when she struck
(b) subsequent break-up
(c) nature of the sea floor.

We felt it unlikely that the storm was strong enough to cause either the loss of *Liefde*'s masts and spars, or the need to jettison armament and cargo, furthermore it is likely that she hit the Skerries quite unexpectedly.

These surmises together with the knowledge that the Shetlanders recovered gold within a year of the disaster, and that a "London Diver" worked on the wreck until 1732 all point to the likelihood of heavy material remaining in the vicinity of the initial finds. This historical evidence is further backed by the present knowledge that the area is a "tidal backwater" with little stream at any time, and that the reef forms a natural trap for material.

It seemed sensible in view of this to search out from the cliffs to a ship's length (160 feet) plus an arbitrary allowance of say 40 feet, making a tidy 200 in all. As the seabed was mainly a jumble of boulders, and covered in a thick layer of kelp, the most careful and thorough visual search method was needed, and the jackstay type was chosen.

No method can be 100 per cent over this type of terrain. In this case the jackstay and swimline were frequently well above the diver, or out of sight because of boulders and kelp. It had, however, considerable overlap, which compensated to some extent for these difficulties. Experience showed that it was necessary to straighten out the swimline after each move, as it is very easily caught in the kelp or round a boulder. Unless this was done some areas were searched four or five times, and others not at all. It was also necessary to keep a record of where divers finished their search, and in which direction they were headed, otherwise the next pair could move to the wrong end of the swimline and again gaps would be left.

The terrain also affects the distance between the jackstays and limits the length of swimline to that which can easily be moved without snagging too many times—remembering that the more moves there are the less efficient the search—in our case this length was 60 to 70 feet.

In 1968 as there was more time and more divers, a leaf was borrowed from the "Blasket Sound" searchers, who had recently located the wreck of the Spanish Armada's *Santa Maria de la Rosa*, and a free swimline search of the area south of the kelp line was attempted. Our aim was to solve the cannon mystery. At our third attempt we successfully got a line of 5 divers 40 feet apart underway, but there was no sign of cannon and the mystery of the missing guns remains as deep as ever. One point of note during the successful search was a marked difference in tidal stream between the bottom (80 to 100 feet) and the surface. So much so that the snorkel cover had to swim in the opposite direction to the divers! (Fig. 9.)

KEEPING RECORDS

In the initial stages of our exploration the need for records was not fully appreciated. However, as the true extent of the site became clear we soon learned that if any attempt at reconstruction was to be made, full archaeological records should be kept. These developed along the following lines:

Diary

A diary of all events of interest, work, weather, personnel, plans, health, etc. . . . Illustrated with sketches and diagrams wherever possible, and cross referring to photographs and plans.

Small-scale Plan

A plan of the whole work area kept up to date with all new finds and areas searched.

Large-scale Plan

A plan of Silver Gulley redrawn after each explosion indicating the development of clearance and the position of finds.

Finds List

A daily list and description of finds.

These four types of record were backed by photographs and sketches wherever possible—it was even found of value to keep a running total of minutes spent underwater. In particular the plan of Silver Gulley was backed in 1968 by a simple photomosaic taken with a Nikonos camera at a height of 7–10 feet above the seabed by one diver in half an hour. The result was surprisingly effective, and was of great assistance in the initial drawing of the plan. The mosaic, and both plans were also used continually at the evening briefings.

Both the plans were drawn using basic techniques of triangulation. At first, difficulty was encountered in anchoring the two base points in the "gneiss"—masonry pins and very large nails bent with great ease. The problem was eventually solved by Jim Gill who dreamed up the simple expedient of hammering a hole with a star drill, plugging it with lead, then screwing in a brass cuphook. The result was a permanent mark to which a tape and marker buoy were easily attached.

The main finds were in Silver Gulley where exploration generally followed the same pattern. We set the minimum explosive necessary to loosen and/or break up large buried rocks. Then lifted all loose rock clear by winch and hand. Then surveyed the area, i.e. drew an accurate plan of all visible artifacts and half-buried rock. When this was done we photographed items of interest and carefully raised recorded artifacts. All sand, gravel, small stones, and the very small artifacts mixed with them were raised by hand and airlift—to be sifted through in the boat. Then we set more explosive, and so on . . .

The use of explosive was necessary as there appeared to be no other way of prizing out the larger rocks which were solidly jammed in position. Although at one stage in order to avoid its use, we set up an elaborate method of moving the rocks using the boat's power. Regrettably we only succeeded in parting the wire rope, causing the boat to accelerate somewhat faster than at any other time!

The removal of the "small stuff" provided us with one of the most interesting problems. Recording of the larger visible finds —cannon balls, barshot, etc.—was relatively easy using the triangulation techniques already mentioned. Incidentally, for the sake of speed and consistency this work was always carried out by the same small (3-man) team. But the smaller finds were thoroughly mixed with sand and gravel, and tended to be the same colour, which meant that plotting their individual positions would be extremely difficult, and time-consuming. It was, however, appreciated that for archaeological purposes their relative grouping rather than their positional accuracy told the story.

Having made this appreciation it was necessary to brief the changing team of divers fully enough for them to understand, and be interested in the work required. The plans and photomosaic were invaluable for they enabled the leader and divers to discuss the next day's work almost as though on site, and be quite certain that they both visualized the same area—bitter experience had shown that this was not always necessarily true!

As no fragile finds were made it was decided that diver time could best be utilized in recording and clearing this valuable mixture by bringing it to the surface from selected small areas. Sieving, separating, and listing could then be carried out in comparative comfort on deck. As long as the areas were kept small enough, the grouping of artifacts would then be known. Two methods of clearing the small stuff were used, one, a $2\frac{1}{2}$-inch airlift, the other, hand filling a fisherman's basket lined with sacking. On days when weather and equipment were with us the methods were used simultaneously.

It was possible to restrict the day's work by each method to just one of the small areas, so that there was no question of the material on deck being from one or other of the two working areas of the day—provided the divers worked accurately.

DAILY LIST OF ARTIFACTS RECOVERED BETWEEN 7 and 31 AUGUST, 1968

7th
3 Ducatoons
2 Pieces pewter plate
1 Small pewter spoon
9 Pieces knife handle
1 Knife handle complete
6 Fruit stones
1 Square wrought iron nail
  $\frac{1}{2}'' \times 4''$ (slightly bent)
1 Square wrought iron nail
  $\frac{1}{4}'' \times 2''$
1 Square wrought iron nail
  $\frac{1}{4}'' \times 1\frac{1}{4}''$
3 Beads—$\frac{1}{4}''$ diameter
7 Small pieces of Brass
Various small pieces of pipe stem, glass, wood, pottery, metal and canvas.

8th
2 Ducatoons
1 Piece of wood and canvas
  $8'' \times 4''$
1 Brass ring
1 Small piece of a padlock
2 Wrought iron nails
1 Piece of Brass drawer handle.

9th
3 Ducatoons
3 Knife handles

1 Thimble
1 Piece of padlock
1 Piece of wrought iron nail
  square $2'' \times \frac{1}{2}''$
Various small pieces of green glass, wood, metal, pipe stem and bowl.

10th
4 Ducatoons
1 Knife handle
1 Lead bottle or cask seal
2 Small pieces of padlock
1 Piece canvas
1 Small pewter spoon
3 Small wrought iron nails
1 Piece of cannon ball
Various small pieces green glass, pipe stem, wood, metal, and some tiny strips of lead.

12th
8 Ducatoons
1 Small piece of a gold coin
16 Knife handles
1 Small piece of bell
1 Lead stopper
1 Wrought iron nail $3''$ long
2 Fruit stones
Various small pieces pipe stem, glass, pottery, canvas, metal, and brass lock.

13th

19 Ducatoons
½ Cannon Ball
1 Piece of string
1 Musket Ball
1 Small pewter spoon (in half)
2 Small wrought iron nails
1 Piece of knife handle
4 Small brass pieces
1 Small piece of lead
Various pieces pottery, wood,
metal, and bar shot.

14th

14 Ducatoons
1 Thimble
1 Small piece copper
3 Small wrought iron nails
2 Knife handles
1 Brass pin
Various pieces wood, pottery,
and pipe stem.

15th

4 Ducatoons
13 Knife handles
12 Small nails
1 Piece canvas
1 Piece string
Various small pieces pipe stem,
glass, pottery, and wood.

16th

12 Ducatoons (Bad Condition)

1 ¾ Cannon Ball—from East
end of Gulley
1 Large square wrought iron
nail 6″ × ½″
3 Pieces pipe stem.
From "Hole 1"—see large plan
1 Piece of Brass 3″ × 1½″ × ¼″

17th

6 Ducatoons

18th

27 Ducatoons
½ Knife handle
Various pieces of pipe stem.

19th

14 Ducatoons
1 Ship's Sounding Lead

25th/26th

1 Lead seal or stamp, 3″ diam.
circular head, 4½″ stem
head inscribed 1711
3 Pieces of white cup with
blue decorations, one piece
included handle
1 3½″ Cannon Ball
1 Knife handle
23 Ducatoons
Some beads.

27th

27 Ducatoons

THE MISSING CANNON

Sieving the small stuff and listing finds were jobs which always went on long after the boat berthed for the last time each evening—though perhaps not quite as long as the refilling of tanks. The type of material recovered has grouped itself fairly naturally into the remains of the armament, ship fittings, trading goods, and valuables.

So far only one cannon has been found on the *Liefde* site, this was blown clear of the encrustation which bound it to the rocks

Left: Fig. 2. The dye flows smoothly in a thin sheet when the dye packet happens to be tied at the same depth as a temperature step. This is an elaborate rig with ten dye packets designed to stain a layer area of a thermocline "sheet". *Right:* Fig. 3. The flow in the wake of a dye packet is strongly turbulent in the thermocline "layers".

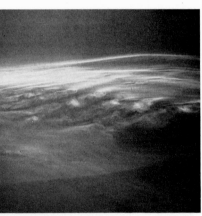

Fig. 4. A patch of billows on a thermocline sheet, triggered by the longer wave seen on the horizon. The spacing of the billows is about two feet.

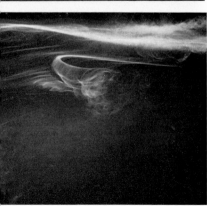

Left: Fig. 5. Close-up of a thermocline billow about nine inches high. *Right:* Fig. 6. The dye streak left behind a falling dye pellet has a regular pattern due to eddy shedding in the pellet's wake.

(See chapter 4)

The *Liefde* was well armed. We found bar shot as well as cannon balls.

We found the breeches of her four-pounders, but where were the rest of her cannon?

The ship's bell, almost complete.

Some of the wood of the treasure chest was quite sound. (See chapter 5)

with explosive, by divers from H.M.S. *Shoulton* in 1964, and later lifted by Eric Giles and the Islanders. It was a 12-pounder found SE. of "Silver Gulley" and was at one time thought to have been part of the ballast. However, in 1968 during the course of a "rest day"—when we all went diving in the vicinity of what we had determined as the *Kennermerlandt* site—the original target of the 1965 Expedition—we found another cannon, possibly an 8-pounder. It too was in an advanced state of decay, so corroded at the muzzle end that the barrel had disintegrated on one side revealing the bore.

Where then, are *Liefde*'s other 39 cannon?—have they corroded away as the *Kennermerlandt* find may indicate? This is unlikely as cannon of greater age have survived all round our coast. In any case two of *Liefde*'s cannon are known to have been bronze.* It also seems too much to expect that the only cannon found from two heavily armed vessels were ballast.

Jettisoning we have ruled out in earlier discussion. Attention should, I feel, be focused on the "London Diver" who worked on both ships from 1729 to 1735. He is certainly quoted as having found coin, and cannon would certainly not have been beyond his lifting ability—as work on the Swedish *Vasa* in 1648 indicates. Perhaps the work of this man is the key to the whole mystery of the cannon, as it may well be to that of the anchors! An authoritative work† indicates that a vessel of *Liefde*'s size would normally carry about 8 anchors, 5 of which would weigh in excess of $1\frac{1}{2}$ tons, and the others about $\frac{1}{2}$ ton. The same authority states that the length of the largest would probably be about 2/5ths that of the ship, some 16 feet; but so far we have found no trace of any. But we have found much other material connected with the armament. The bar shot were of two different types, probably for the eight-pounders. Single cannon balls have been found for all sizes of gun (4-, 8-, and 12-pounders), although actual weights have been up to one pound less. The smallest guns were breech loading, an interesting fact revealed by the find of four of the breeches consecutively numbered and stamped quite clearly with the initials of the Company "VOC"—"Verenigde Oostindische Compagnie".

---

* Logbook of Captain Pronk, Captain during her second voyage.
† Pieter van Dam, "Beschrijvinge van de Oostindische Compagnie".

THE TREASURE

Few ship's fittings have been recovered, the most interesting being the shroud plate, the ship's sounding lead, and, most fascinating of all, almost enough pieces to reconstruct the whole of the bell.

The trading goods she carried are difficult to distinguish from what must be personal possessions. The conjecture they arouse is almost limitless. For instance the thimbles we found can also be associated with two pins identical with those in use today, and as both seem too delicate for use by seamen, the finds raise the question: were there women passengers?

To me the similarity of some of these small finds with their modern equivalents is one of the most interesting aspects of the whole story. Were the small fruit stones part of a much larger shipment destined to continue the work of planting out the vast farms we know today in South Africa?

Finally, we come to the subject which has already, and I fear will always make archaeological recovery difficult because of its infectious urgency—treasure.

The vast majority of coins recovered have been silver "ducatoons", minted between 1632 and 1711. Most have been in good condition, having been preserved in the matrix described previously. The most exciting find was that in 1967 of a whole chest! It was buried in the matrix, and the wood remaining was in as good a condition as on that fateful day 258 years ago.

What of the future? What remains beneath those tons of rock? So far as each succeeding layer has been removed, more artifacts and coin have been revealed, and we do not feel that even in the lowest point of "Silver Gulley" we have found bedrock proper.

There may well be more to come . . . But much depends on the efficiency of those first Shetland salvors, and the six years' work of that gentleman whom we only know as a "London Diver" . . .

FIRST FILL YOUR VIEWFINDER WITH SHARK

by Colin Doeg

Colin Doeg is a recent holder of the title of British Underwater
Photographer of the Year as well as having won gold medals
for his pictures in many international competitions. He is a
member of London Branch of the British Sub-Aqua Club and
chairman of the British Society of Underwater Photographers.
Here he writes of the triumphs and disasters that swim into the
sights of a diving-photographer.

THE June sky was a blue dome. No clouds. Just the sun
burning down. The cliffs of Devon were a low smudge far
away on the horizon. The sea heaved and rolled around me
and the not-yet-warm water stung my face as I watched the
triangular fin of the shark slash through the wave-tops
towards me.

I dipped my face mask into the sea and stared through the
black-green water trying to see the fish before it saw me. But
it was still invisible amid the clouds of bright yellow and green
plankton. Yet when I looked up again across the waves, the fin
was still knifing its inexorable course towards me.

How big would it be? How big would it be? This question
kept hammering at me as I checked the camera settings for the
hundredth time. The shark had looked too big for comfort
when it was wallowing alongside the diving boat a few minutes
earlier. Now, because of the effects of refraction, when I saw it
underwater it was going to look even bigger—a third longer
than its 16 feet or a third nearer, whichever way you preferred
to look at it.

On the surface the fin was still cutting through the wave-
crests, heading directly towards me. The sea was so cold that
my face and hands were beginning to feel numb. I took a last
hurried glance at the high sun and then the shark was upon me.

The huge, gaping mouth loomed out of the plankton, its jaws straining open wider and wider as it swung from side to side seeking its prey. The maw looked enormous. Big enough to swallow a man. Big enough to back a mini-car into. The opening was at least six or seven feet high.

I swam away from those straining jaws as fast as I could, fins flailing as I worked the Nikonos underwater camera with desperate speed. The shark filled the viewfinder. First from nose to tail. Then the huge mouth on its own. Then the side of it began to slide by as I got out of its path. The shark took about a year to pass. Its body seemed as long as a train. The mighty tail swept to and fro in muscled grace, thrusting the vast body through the water with indolent ease. And then, as suddenly as it had appeared, the shark vanished into the banks of plankton. The fin sailed on, charting its unfaltering course.

I had seen my first shark . . . and was alive to develop the film! I checked the exposure again, taking a meter reading off the palm of my hand and the black sleeve of my wet suit and averaging them. The camera settings were O.K. But what about the composition of the shots? Did I frame them correctly as I finned out of the shark's path? I needed more pictures at different angles and camera settings before I would feel happy.

It was all very well thinking I had got some promising shots. But the camera lens can only "see" about half the distance underwater of a human eye so it is easy to be misled and think you have something good when really you should be much closer. Maybe, at the next attempt, I would be able to pluck up enough courage to go nearer. After all, it was only a *basking* shark . . . but, to me, it was as awe-inspiring as a famished man-eater.

During the next hour Brian Booth, Alex Double and I got closer to the shark. At first we had scrambled aboard our Zodiac inflatable each time the shark passed and then Roy Howkins would send the boat leaping ahead of the creature for us to roll into the sea in front of it once again.

Brian was taking pictures as well, and both he and Alex touched the shark's dorsal fin in a burst of bravery I couldn't match. I stayed further away, assuring myself it was only in order that I could include both divers and fish in the same photograph! But the one thing I did have to do during those memorable 60 minutes in the water was to call upon every scrap of experience I had ever gained at taking picures under-water.

All the classic problems were to be found in that small area of the English Channel. Visibility was poor—there was so much plankton suspended in the water that at times it was like trying to take pictures in a snow storm. The sunlight was strong but the surface of the sea wasn't smooth. The waves were a couple of feet high and this prevented the light rays penetrating as strongly or as deeply as they would have done if the surface had been calmer.

Furthermore, because the seabed was 180 feet below, none of the rays was reflected upwards again to illuminate the shark's belly—you get better light over sand or light-coloured rocks because they reflect some of the sunshine up again. To add to everything else, the fish was blue-black. Black-and-white film would see little difference between the colour of the fish and the water. Colour film would register even less contrast.

You can boost the contrast of monochrome film by extending the development time. That would help. The other thing was to ensure that the subject was as big as possible on the negative. This doesn't seem important until you have a negative you want to enlarge and then, if you want a print 12 inches by 15 inches for a competition such as the International Festival of Underwater Film at Brighton, you will find that it has to be enlarged at least 100 times.

With this magnification every little flaw and imperfection becomes that much more obvious. To get the best possible result you must get the minimum of water between your camera lens and the subject because water is not clear, especi-ally when silt, plankton and other foreign bodies are suspended in it. Consequently, when photographs are taken through this "veil", the detail of the subject will be broken up and appear to be slightly "fuzzy". The most dramatic example I have ever seen of the importance of getting close was a transparency of a diver taken in murky water with a camera fitted with a fish-eye lens. The lens was held about a foot from the diver and the detail and colour of his suit and other equipment was as good as if the picture had been taken in air. Taken with a normal lens from a distance of 3 feet or 4 feet the picture would have had a yellowish cast because of the dirty water and the diver would have come out only as a faint shape.

But back to the shark. Roy realized that it didn't like the noise of the 30 h.p. outboard on the boat and so was able to use this to herd the shark towards us. It worked like a charm. We edged the fish into water with less plankton and also made it head into the sun so that the vast mouth was better illuminated.

At last we were able to introduce some control into the situation. This is something which is usually difficult to achieve underwater because you are working in a constantly changing and developing situation. Also, if you are photographing people, there is the problem of communication.

Most of the time the underwater photographer has to seize his opportunities as they occur. Certainly this is the case in British waters, where there is less certainty of finding any particular subject on a specific dive. In warmer seas the problem is often one of selection when photographing fish because you have such a wide choice.

But, whatever the subject and in whichever waters it may be, you should begin taking pictures as you approach a promising situation. You should move in closer taking more shots, and then move round the subject taking further pictures. Many people wonder how you compose a picture correctly. The answer is that no photographer ever consciously composes his picture as if he were an art critic. However, he does press the shutter release when he likes what he sees in his viewfinder. This moment establishes the composition of his shots and his style of photography.

In addition to taking a series of pictures of your subject, it is also sensible to vary the exposure settings when there is any doubt. Even when using a meter it can be worthwhile. If you are estimating the settings it is essential. Estimating settings is done by finding the exposure recommended by the film manufacturer for the surface conditions and then opening up one stop for every ten feet you go down.

As far as the shark was concerned I wanted to play safe by taking a lot of alternative shots at various settings. Then I could be sure that some of them would work. I was lucky. I was able to expose one complete cassette of Tri-X and part of another one, as well as a few frames of High Speed Ektachrome.

In most circumstances I would have had the colour developed first because you cannot exercise as much control over it as you can over black-and-white film. As far as colour film is concerned you can only give it the standard exposure and the standard development. With monochrome film you can vary the final result both by the exposure and the processing afterwards. In this case I was eager to see if I had obtained any good pictures so I developed the short roll of Tri-X first.

The negatives were satisfactory with normal processing so I then developed the other roll, on which I thought the pictures were more interesting. This is always a useful dodge. If you are not sure what development to give your film, chop a couple of inches off the beginning of it, develop that and see how it turns out.

I was lucky with the shark pictures. Some showed the fish on its own, others with divers, and some of the side shots showed how its gill mechanism worked. In all I ended up with half a dozen pictures which pleased me. Others would have come out better if there had been slightly better visibility.

Now, those hectic 60 minutes seem so far away I have to look at the prints and negatives occasionally to convince myself that it really did happen—most of the time I am content to get my excitement from photographing much smaller fishes.

I still get most pleasure out of looking at one of the first pictures I ever took. Well, it wasn't exactly the first one I ever took by a mile of film, but it was the first one that ever came out satisfactorily. It is a shot of a mullet. And I always get a thrill out of remembering how it happened because mullet are such exciting fish to see underwater. They have sleek bodies that glint in the sunlight and blue-grey stripes down their silver flanks. They nuzzle the seabed for their food, or nibble their way up tall strands of string weed and other algae.

The mullet was one of a shoal I met while diving in a remote part of Dorset. After a series of discouraging failures with a cheap camera in a crude case, I had bought a Calypso-Phot amphibious camera and was taking pictures during the day and developing the film each night in a tent in order to see how I was progressing.

The holiday was proving to be a dismal affair because

photographic progress during the first five or six days was nil. I just wasn't taking any worthwhile pictures. Every evening I sat in the tent waiting for it to get dark enough to enable me safely to load my film into a developing tank. Then I got to work with developer, stop bath and fixer and washed the film in a basin at the camp site. Finally, I would look hopefully at the negatives . . . and throw them away. But at least I didn't have to wait until the film came back from the local chemist. Every morning as I set out to take more pictures I knew how the previous day's efforts had turned out.

Processing your own black-and-white films is much easier than you would think—colour is more complicated and best left to the manufacturers or a reliable colour laboratory. All you need for black-and-white film is a developing tank, which is a miniature darkroom in itself, and the various chemicals recommended by the manufacturers of the film you are using. Everything else you need to know is to be found by reading the leaflets that go with the tank and the chemicals.

I would recommend anyone taking up underwater photography to do their own processing. Also I would suggest that unless they are reasonably proficient at land photography they begin by using ex-Government film which they load themselves into cassettes—assuming they are using a 35 mm. camera. This makes the process of learning by taking lots of pictures a much cheaper affair. However, once you begin to get results which please you, don't risk losing a good shot by using cheap film. Switch to fresh, factory-loaded film to ensure that when you get a good photograph the negative is going to be the best you can get.

By the time I met the shoal of mullet I was using fresh, factory-loaded cassettes but I was still plagued with another fault—camera shake. Not one of my pictures was as sharp as it should have been because I was moving the camera during the exposure. In the end I had to use a shutter speed of 1/500th to stop it happening and I now always use this speed when photographing any lively, fast-moving creature. If conditions are so bad that you cannot use a speed as fast as this you should, of course, use a slower setting. But, in this case, you need to take your shot at a time when the fish is stationary or only moving slowly.

However, with the mullet, there was no standing still and smiling for the photographer. They zoomed and swooped around at great speed, swimming off and coming back to have another look at me. Their bodies were sleek and fat, and glinted in the clear water. In all I took 36 exposures of them before I returned to the shore hardly believing I could have been so lucky.

Eventually, unable to wait any longer, I hurried back to my tent. It was still daylight so I put two sleeping bags one inside the other, laid some blankets over the top and dived inside with my film and tank. It was a sweaty, stifling business but I soon had the film loaded. Then the ritual of development was over and I sneaked a look at the negatives. I could hardly believe my good fortune. Some were the best I had produced up to that time.

Of course there was a large element of luck involved in obtaining my favourite shot—a solitary mullet caught in mid-turn. Furthermore, just as it turned a shaft of sunlight lanced down through the waves and lit up its head and back. However, by taking a number of alternative shots, there is more likelihood of catching a natural movement such as this. You must be prepared to have failures when you are trying to anticipate what a lively wild animal is likely to do and will have to press the shutter release at the moment the movement begins.

A similar problem occurs when taking a side view of a fish. It never looks right unless the tail fin is either in line with the body or moving towards the camera. The fish never looks so good if the tail is flicking away from the lens.

Mind you, theories such as this are all very well but just imagine how many times a second a fish will scull with its tail. If you want to capture the right moment you will do so occasionally if you rely on luck, but more frequently if you have a practical technique to help you.

Photographing dragonets raises a similar problem. They are small fish—about the size of teaspoons or slightly bigger—and they trundle about on the seabed like mini-tanks. They dart to a point, pause for a moment, take a mouthful of sand and pump it out through a hole in the back of their neck, then dash off somewhere else. You have to follow them around with your camera. But that's not the only problem. The real one is their eyes.

If you aren't careful you will get a boss-eyed fish because they can swivel them about independently. The answer is to take several photographs. It is good practice and there is no shortage of models if you go to a spot such as the old pier at Swanage.

I have spent hours photographing them there, mostly with a close-up lens so that I had to get the camera within seven inches. It was always difficult but I used to patiently follow them about trying to get pictures of them eating sand. I'm still trying. But I learned a useful fact about fish. They don't like bubbles. I noticed that when I breathed out the dragonets would react by swimming away. So I tried holding my breath or exhaling slowly and gently. This produced better results but I still couldn't get really close until I changed my single hose demand valve for a twin hose model. As soon as I began to exhale out of the back of my neck I found I could get about a foot closer to the fish.

Another technique that developed while photographing dragonets was holding the camera out at arm's length and judging the composition. Press photographers do much the same thing on land. In fact that's where I obtained the idea after seeing them holding their cameras at arm's length above their heads in order to shoot over the top of a crowd. The idea works. All you need is a little practice. With experience it is even possible to take accurately composed photographs with a close-up lens in this manner.

I was certainly glad I had obtained plenty of practice at the technique when I tried to photograph my first John Dory. They are probably the most unusual fish in appearance to be found round Britain's shores. When you look at them head-on they are so thin you can hardly see them. Or you think they are just another strand of the weed in which they often hide. When you look at them sideways-on they have a camouflage pattern over their body and a large dark mark in the centre. They have long spiky fins which give them an exotic appearance and they scull themselves along with rapid movements of their pectoral fins.

Their shape and markings help them to merge into their

habitat so they are often difficult to see. They are also not found in large numbers in British waters so I was particularly interested when several divers saw one in Swanage Bay. In fact, by the end of a week of fruitless searching, I was beginning to think that every diver in the area had seen it with the exception of myself.

Whenever a diver saw the John Dory he would tell me and I would leap into the sea and hunt it. But I seemed unable to line it up in my viewfinder. Eventually I began to stalk through its territory, hiding behind tall clumps of weed or gliding gently across the seabed, holding my breath for as long as I could and then exhaling as slowly and softly as possible so as to disturb the fish as little as possible. But I seemed to be out of luck.

The Dory's luck seemed to run out as well when some divers saw it during a night dive. They transfixed it in the beams of their torches and enticed the John Dory into a plastic bag. It was destined for the preserving jar until the party reached the top of the steps at Swanage pier. There they were met by a friend of mine who told them such an eloquent and heart-rending tale about the crazy underwater photographer who had spent nearly a week trying to find the John Dory that they finally returned it to the sea.

Of course, even with such good fortune and such considerate divers, I still had to find the fish. And I rated my chances of doing that as being pretty slim when I deflated my Fenzy for my last dive of the holiday. I sank down to the sandy bottom. Geoff Harwood was with me. And as we touched the bottom he began to gesticulate towards my fins. I glanced down and then took a longer, incredulous look. The John Dory was right there between my legs.

All three of us looked at each other in great surprise. The fish recovered first and shot off as fast as it could go. We sped in pursuit, taking meter readings and setting cameras as we finned along. Shutters clicked away. Flash lights froze the scene. And the unfortunate fish fled through tall strands of string weed, tangled clumps of wrack and over sandy glades.

Eventually our film was used up. We slowed down laughing so hard that we almost blew our face masks off. And the John Dory quietly vanished, no doubt hardly believing its luck.

As I returned to the shore, still chuckling at being fortunate enough to find the fish at last, I realized that I had been caught napping when I first saw it. I intended to take a meter reading and set my camera when I landed on the seabed. After that I was going to look for suitable subjects.

Now I always set my camera to roughly the correct exposure before I go in the water . . . just in case. Once beneath the surface I take a meter reading and correct the setting, but at least I am ready to snatch any picture that unexpectedly presents itself. You must keep on checking your exposure during a dive because lighting conditions vary due to depth, the sun going behind a cloud or the type of seabed you are swimming over. Sand reflects light. Weed provides a dark background which requires a greater exposure. You must never take anything for granted.

Certainly I should not have taken it for granted that nothing unexpected would turn up when I slid into the clear, calm waters of Kimmeridge Bay to photograph anemones. The coastline was deserted. My buddy and I were alone in the water and we settled down to photograph the tranquil scene. The weed was a medley of muted tints—mostly browns and yellows. In every direction you looked you could see groups of small wrasse darting about or coming up to stare at us for a few moments.

I was determined to photograph anemones. I had a new camera in a prototype housing and had decided to try it out on a simple subject. I never gave a second's thought to the stories the spear fishermen told of finding bass in the Bay. After all, I had seen bass only twice during six years spent trying to photograph this magnificent fish. The first occasion was in the South of France. Three circled round me while I tried to estimate the correct exposure and operate the simple camera in the crude case. It wasn't easy. My right arm was buried up to the elbow in a rubber glove which was clamped round one end of the case and enabled me to put my hand inside to work the camera. My other hand was needed to steady the box. And the new face mask I was using for the first time sprung a leak at the joint with the glass face plate.

As the fish whirled round me and I clumsily tried to follow them the level of water in the mask began to rise. What should I do—clear my mask or try to photograph the fish? I chose the fish and continued taking shots until the water level rose above my eyes. Then I cleared my mask. But by then the bass had swum away.

On the second occasion, near Kimmeridge Bay, I was heavily committed to taking close-ups when a lone bass swam cautiously towards me. I began to tear off the close-up lens and re-focus the camera. The fish came nearer. I changed my mind and put the supplementary lens back on. If it came to within two feet I would stand a chance of getting a super photograph.

But it hesitated. Perhaps it wasn't going to come very close after all. So I changed my mind and once more began to fumble with the close-up lens. The bass swam up so near to me that it was out of focus, gave me a contemptuous glance and swam away.

I should have learned my lesson. But I hadn't. Because I was once more committed to taking close-ups as I began photographing the anemones. I spent half an hour staring through the viewfinder at tiny anemones, trying to find an unusual angle. Finally, almost cross-eyed with concentration, I looked up. An enormous bass was swimming towards me. It looked as big as a whole smoked salmon and it barely spared me a glance. With leisurely arrogance it slowly swam past. A smaller bass kept humble station a few inches from its powerful tail.

As usual I began my struggle to remove the close-up lens and alter the camera settings. It wasn't easy because I could hardly take my eyes off the two magnificent fish. Eventually I managed to grab a shot of their tails as they disappeared from view. Furious with myself I sat on the seabed and cursed. Angry bubbles clattered to the surface. Six years' searching and all I could do was muff it when the chance came. I sucked my air in and out in great gulps, almost beating the "lung" in my excitement and annoyance. I kept swivelling round, staring wildly into the distance in the hope of seeing them again. But it seemed I had seen the last of them.

Dejectedly I returned to the anemones. It had been exciting just to see the bass. And, once my breathing had returned to normal and the adrenalin had washed out of my bloodstream, I was prepared to settle for the mere sight of them.

But, just in case, I set my Nikonos at 1/500th at f5·6—it was loaded with Tri-X—and laid it down on the seabed beside me where I could pick it up quickly. And, this time, I repeatedly glanced up to see if the bass had returned.

After about 20 minutes the bigger of the two came back for another look at the strange creatures which had invaded its territory. It circled round, staring curiously. I began taking shots, waiting until it was close enough to come out big on the negative. Then it swam away.

Soon afterwards the smaller one appeared and took a long look at me. It swam past a couple of times and then it approached from a different direction, gliding near a patch of weed. I know it sounds ridiculous, but it struck me that the picture would be improved if the bass swam through the weed so I sat on the seabed willing the fish to do so. It hesitated then veered to one side and swam through the weed.

But it wasn't as simple as that because photographing bass is similar to trying to take a picture of a silver coin against a white sheet. Flash bounces off the bass's silver flanks. It had to be taken in natural light. And, when the film was developed normally in D.76, the negative showed the bass swimming through the clump of weed . . . exactly as directed.

Most of the time I choose to work in shallow water because the lighting conditions are better. Occasionally, however, I dive deeper in search of photographs that cannot be taken in the shallows. When I rolled into the sea near the Eddystone lighthouse, some seven miles off the shores of Devon, I didn't know what to expect but I hoped I might find some fish I would not normally find inshore.

Steadily I hauled myself down the anchor rope, hand over hand. Twice I paused to clear my ears and check that my companion was following me. Then I reached the bottom and looked around. As I sat there waiting for him to join me the anchor bounded across the seabed towards me. It snagged in a crevice then jerked free, and was dragged along further.

We grabbed the anchor and tried to ram it between some rocks . . . but it was a big boat at the other end. Other divers swam down. With hurried signs I pointed out the predicament. They nodded, gave O.K. signals and swam off. There was obviously only one thing to do. Tell the skipper. So we surfaced and told him. He just nodded and kept on smoking his pipe. We tried again. Nothing but smoke signals.

Well, we had tried to prevent a shipwreck—later we discovered the boat was much further away from the rocks on which the lighthouse was built than appeared to be the case when viewed from water level. Anyway, we decided to go down again and keep an eye on the anchor. It still had a tendency to drag but not as rapidly as before. In fact it progressed across the seabed at a speed that was ideal—slow enough for both photography and anchor watching.

Deeper waters offer considerable attractions for photography. The species of fish that you find are bigger and less afraid of divers. Some are types that do not come close inshore. Also the scene is different. Some weeds are bigger, others are types to be found only at depth.

But deep diving can present a particular hazard to an underwater cameraman. If you take most of your pictures in shallow water it is easy to use up your air more quickly in deep water than you would expect. You must discipline yourself to check your contents' gauge more frequently than usual. You must also remember to adjust your weights for greater depths—I always overweight and, but for a few puffs of air into my Fency, would spend most of my deeper dives crawling on my hands and knees over the seabed because I would be too heavy to fin. In fact, one of my friends who makes a practice of being grossly overweighted with both cameras and lead, quite solemnly tells everyone that it is quicker to climb back up the rock faces to the surface than to fin!

Be that as it may, every photographer must constantly remind himself that the most dangerous creature he is likely to encounter in the sea is . . . himself. Photography can be totally absorbing and, therefore, it is most important that anyone who wishes to take it up seriously should be a proficient diver, or become one as rapidly as possible. Diving and all that goes with it must be absolutely automatic. You should be so competent that checking contents' gauges, exhaling when you surface, checking for approaching boats as you come up and so on are completely automatic. Then, and only then, you can allow yourself to become deeply engrossed in taking pictures.

Most divers graduate to photography after a few seasons

because they want to put their skill to some practical purpose. This is fine. They have already gained sufficient experience. But competent land photographers who take to the sea should be content to hurry slowly at first. I still chuckle at the memory of an extremely good professional cameraman who was given a crash diving course in order to cover the underwater aspects of an assignment. To be fair he did exceptionally well but his success was in no small way due to his instructor who dragged him about the seabed from subject to subject, pointing petrified diver and camera at each one and then giving him a sharp dig in the ribs each time it was necessary to press the shutter release. That photographer had the largest whites to his eyes I have ever seen.

Every underwater photographer must have the best diving equipment he can afford, beginning with a good wet suit. Other divers move around. The photographer spends a lot of time sitting in one place waiting for things to happen. And it gets extremely cold when you are doing nothing. The danger signal is when you get too cold to work your camera easily. That's the time to surface . . . unless you have already used up your film. In shallow water one or other of these things seems to happen before my air supply is exhausted.

Equipment is also important when you are photographing other divers. They must look neat and tidy. Nothing ruins a good silhouette quicker than contents' gauges and other gear poking out at odd angles. If necessary you should tidy up the diver first, either before he enters the water or when he is in the sea. But tell him first. Don't pounce on him in areas where there are reputed to be sharks and begin to shake and tug at him or he will think his last hour has come.

There are several problems associated with photographing other divers. The first one is to avoid finding that all your pictures show divers finning away from the camera. This is just bad planning.

When you are diving with one or more companions you must be swimming ahead all the time so that your shots show them coming towards you. Wait until they pause to look at something, then move on to a rock arch or clump of weeds they will have to swim near. This will give your photograph an attractive foreground.

The more interesting small finds of the 1968 expedition to the wreck of *Liefde*. (See chapter 5)

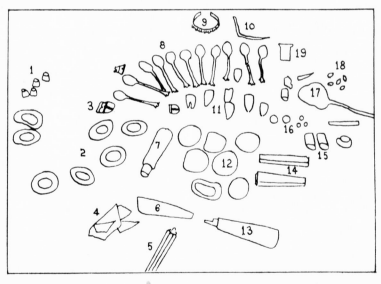

KEY:

1. Thimbles
2. Small circular metal discs, use unknown
3. Buckle
4. Coloured glass fragments
5. Instrument for piercing holes – similar to a knife handle
6. Standard type of knife handle recovered in quantity
7. Ornamented round knife handle
8. Small pewter spoons
9. Ornamented pewter clasp
10. Unidentified piece of metal
11. Clay pipe bowls
12. Lead seals for casks or bottles
13. Knife handle with fragment of blade remaining
14. Horn knife handles
15. Glass bottle corks
16. Two buttons and beads
17. Large pewter spoon
18. Fruit stones
19. Upper part of wrought iron nail

Above: The divers came back telling a great yarn about a "nest of flying saucers" they had found at about 60 feet. What they had found was an ancient wreck containing about forty huge millstones. The wreck, near Atlit in Israel is still there for anyone who wants a huge millstone. Picture by the Undersea Exploration Society of Israel. (See chapter 7)

Below: Are these divers working in what used to be the arsenal of an old fortress besieged by the Crusaders? Avramela and Shuka use an air-lift to probe the secrets of a newly-discovered chamber in the Tower of Flies. (See chapter 7)

Another fault to avoid is getting pictures of divers with black masks. This happens because there isn't enough light to illuminate the interior of their masks. There are several solutions. Use fill-in flash to touch in sufficient light to show their eyes. Choose a diver who is wearing a panoramic mask because this lets in much more light. Or take your picture when the diver is not looking directly at the camera. If he is peering into a cave, or looking at something, the picture looks natural and it doesn't matter that you cannot see his eyes.

The biggest problem, however, is to get them to do what you want them to. You must be particularly patient if you are planning a specific shot. You must get the diver to one side before he enters the water and tell him exactly what you want him to do. Draw a sketch of the type of picture you hope to take or show him a photograph that is similar. The best model is another photographer because he will immediately understand what you want. But if he thinks it might make too good a photograph no doubt he will pretend that he is uncertain of the effect you are seeking!

Mind you, don't be surprised if nothing happens as you had intended no matter how carefully you briefed everyone. I once tried to get a picture of a diver swimming along close to the surface. I explained in great detail to three divers what I wanted them to do. Then they joined me in the water one at a time for me to take their pictures.

The most important thing each diver had to do was to remain about two feet below the surface and give me an O.K. signal. The first one trod water with the down current of a helicopter. Huge clouds of silt rose in the water and visibility dropped to zero. I gave him a reassuring smile, told him I had taken his picture and then moved to a cleaner area for the next diver. He looked at me intensely from white-rimmed pupils and sank out of sight. Third time lucky, I thought. But just to be safe I briefed the third diver in the water before we got down to shooting. He nodded vigorously to indicate that he understood implicitly what he was to do. He formed his forefinger and thumb into a perfect O.K. signal, sank to the required level beneath the surface then flicked his body horizontal and finned off into the distance. I surfaced and watched his bubbles disappear. He must have travelled over 400 yards before he came up, looking puzzled. By then I had given up screaming oaths and curses at the waves. Otherwise he would have looked extremely hurt as well.

Before a particularly helpful underwater photographer thinks that I might be slandering him, however, let me say immediately that I tried a somewhat similar idea near Newton Ferrers in a kelp forest and it worked extremely well without any previous briefing. The moral is always dive with another photographic enthusiast. Just as my buddy at Newton Ferrers did, such a man will not only grasp what you want him to do but probably improve upon the basic idea.

The most essential feature of any picture of divers under-water is that it must have bubbles in it. Without bubbles photographs of divers look lifeless and false. I can only recall one shot I have seen of a diver where the fact that there weren't any bubbles didn't matter. This particular one had an ethereal quality about it that was enhanced by the diver being sus-pended in mid-water. But I'd still like to see a similar photo-graph with bubbles rising in shimmering clusters.

Getting a diver to breathe out when you are taking his picture is far from easy. At least it is in my case because I tend to hold my breath in anticipation when I am about to squeeze the shutter release. As I hold my breath my subjects always seem to do the same thing and we just sit there going blue in the face until one of us can't stand it any more.

If you are really keen on getting good photographs of divers then you should save up your film until you go to the Mediter-ranean or Red Sea. There's nothing so impressive as being able to get five or six divers in one photograph. In addition, as most dives in the warmer and clearer waters tend to be deep ones, there is tremendous scope for pictures of divers holding up the keel of the boat, or rising up the anchor rope in statuesque groups.

There is a great shortage of good photographs of divers, mostly because no one else wants to pair off with a camera-man. Most photographers I know work their way across the seabed slowly as they search for suitable subjects. They see the underwater world with more perceptive eyes than most. They revel in the muted colours of the weed. To them it is not merely a pretty scene.

Their keen eyes will spot algae so small and delicately fashioned that it might be made of lace. They will also see the colours clearly—the plum-reds and the damson-reds, the iridescent greens and the varied tones of browns.

They will know more than most about fish and their habits. They have to. Otherwise they won't know where to find them if they want to photograph them.

This is one of the most fascinating aspects of underwater photography. It not only adds purpose to your diving but also encourages you to take a keener interest in the world beneath the waves.

Maybe the photographer takes longer to move over the seabed. But in swimming over it at his speed he will see far more and obtain much more lasting enjoyment and pleasure from his diving than the tearaways who fin madly from one spot to another, or plunge down into the gloom solely to see the needle of their depth gauge swing past the magic 100 feet mark.

Underwater photography is easier now than it has ever been. Better or improved equipment is available. And films have improved greatly, particularly in the last few years.

Don't be misled by most of the books on the subject. Excellent though they may be, the majority are out of date. They were written before the improvements in equipment and films. Furthermore, there are now many more people taking pictures underwater and their experience has increased the knowledge and information available to anyone who wishes to take up this fascinating hobby.

But if you do decide to immerse yourself in underwater photography, don't forget the golden rule. Fill your viewfinder with the subject—but if it's a shark watch out for camera shake!

DIVING IN THE HOLY
LAND

by Alexander Flinder

Alexander Flinder is the Chairman of the British Sub-Aqua
Club. He is one of this country's most active archaeological
divers and has taken part in many expeditions to the Holy
Land. Much of his underwater survey work has convinced him
that ancient writers when describing places and events were
not, as was once believed, mixing a great deal of romance with
reality, but were in fact accurate reporters.

"—King Herod constructed a harbour
bigger than that at Piraeus,—he dedicated
the city to the province, the harbour to
those who sailed these seas; the honour of
his new creation to Caesar; and Caesaria
was the name that he gave it".
Josephus—*The Jewish War*

THAT was how Josephus finished his long and detailed
description of the building of the mighty harbour at Caesaria
in 12 B.C. One thousand nine hundred and seventy-seven years
later I and four companions were diving amongst the submerged
remains of this long-lost wonder of the ancient world. There
was Joseph Shaw of the University of Philadelphia, fresh from
his exciting underwater discoveries at Kenchreai in Greece;
Chiam Stav, the Chief Instructor at the new Diving Centre
at Caesaria; Elisha Linder, Director of the Undersea Exploration Society of Israel (U.E.S.I.), and Red Granough, B.E.A.
pilot, and member of the Silver Wings Branch of the British
Sub-Aqua Club, who had dropped in to join us for the day.

Although there was this famous description by Josephus,
travellers to Caesaria in later years could find little trace of
the harbour, and indeed, some writers in the 19th century even
suggested that this gigantic structure was merely a figment of

Josephus's imagination. "Beyond all doubt, much of that description is magniloquent Josephian hyperbole," wrote the eminent Reverend W. M. Thompson in his classic, *The Land and the Book*.

It was an aeroplane that came to the rescue of Josephus's reputation, when on one hot summer day in 1958, an Israeli airman was flying over the shores of the Mediterranean. As he gazed down into the blue waters off Caesaria, he was intrigued by the dark shapes that lay beneath the surface of the sea. Could it be a harbour? Aerial photographs taken later revealed with astonishing clarity that the airman's suspicions were right. Those shadows, stretching in a vast semi-circular arc, were none other than the submerged breakwaters of King Herod's harbour.

History had repeated itself, for the ancient ports of Tyre and Sidon were also discovered from the air by the French archaeologist, A. Poidebard, in 1938. Father Poidebard followed up his aerial discovery by detailed underwater investigations carried out by divers. Clearly this was the sort of thing that was needed at Caesaria, and the call was promptly answered by the American industrialist, and underwater researcher, Edwin Link. With his magnificent boat *Sea Diver* and his team of divers, among whom were Stav and Linder, Link was able to map the general outline of the breakwaters, locate the entrance to the harbour, and discover large areas of stonework, with some of the blocks still containing lead embedded in the joints. His most exciting discovery, however, was a tiny bronze medallion located near the harbour entrance. On one side of it were the Greek letters KA for Caesaria, and on the other side an illustration of the entrance to the harbour showing the tremendous statues which had been described by Josephus. When I met Ed Link at the B.S-A.C. Brighton Conference in 1966, I reminded him of this discovery. "That tiny medallion," he remarked, "cost us about 100,000 dollars, but I guess it was worth it."

Linder and his group of divers continued to survey the harbour after Link's departure, and it was at his invitation that Joseph Shaw and I joined him in Israel. As Linder explained, "My country has access to four seas, each entirely different in character—the Mediterranean, the Sea of Galilee, the Dead

Sea and the Red Sea, all steeped in thousands of years of history. There is so much to be discovered, why don't you chaps bring out expeditions from the U.S.A. and Britain, and we will join you?" The prospect sounded exciting, and just to whet our appetites, we were taken on a two-week underwater archaeological tour of Israel.

And that was how we happened to be at a depth of 10 metres, 300 metres off shore at Caesaria. I was sitting on a block of stone measuring approximately 6 feet long, 2 feet wide, and 2 feet deep, and ranged out in front of me in perfect line were similar blocks regularly spaced; I could count fifteen in all. Joe Shaw looked at these blocks, and then peered at me quizzically through his face mask, and I could sense that the same question was puzzling both of us—as the sea level in the Mediterranean had not changed significantly since Roman times, how had King Herod's engineers laid such immaculate stonework at these depths? I have worked on many ancient submerged sites over the years, and this same question keeps cropping up. As far as I know no one has as yet been able to give a satisfactory answer.

The entrance to Caesaria's harbour, which can be seen very clearly on aerial photographs, is flanked on one side by the largest stone blocks that I have ever seen underwater. The gigantic breakwater which curves in a magnificent sweep is mostly heavily overgrown, and buried under many feet of silting, but here and there one can make out the signs of man-made masonry. What an immense task it would be to excavate this vast site. And yet for the student of ancient harbours, and the underwater archaeologist, an extremely important one.

Honor Frost, the authoress of *Under the Mediterranean*, explained why this is so. "All over the Mediterranean," she said, "divers are discovering submerged sites, breakwaters, jetties. It is extremely difficult, however, to date these finds because as yet little is known about the methods of construction used by the ancient peoples when building in the sea. In the case of Caesaria, however, we know, thanks to Josephus, that the construction of the harbour commenced in 22 B.C., and it took twelve years to complete. This was at the time when Palestine was under the rule of the Roman Procurators. The knowledge derived from an excavation could, therefore, be related to a precise date in history, and thus the first part of the jig-saw will have been solved."

Joe Shaw and I spent a few fascinating days at Caesaria getting the feel of the place. One day was spent doing a rough survey and photographing the remains of a fascinating partially submerged building, called the Baths of Cleopatra. This stood on a promontory about a quarter of a mile south of the harbour, and very close to the newly excavated Roman amphitheatre. An oblong pool measuring about 80 feet by 40 feet, it was strewn with the remains of column capitals, and to me it still seemed to retain an aura of Roman exotic splendour.

Within a few minutes of our arrival on the site, Joe gave a shout of astonishment. I rushed over to him to find him pointing to a channel constructed in the ground. What particularly excited Joe was that this channel, which was about 8 inches wide by 12 inches deep, was cut off by a stone slab sitting in slots let into each side of the channel. Joe explained to me that he had only recently come across very similar channels at Kenchreai. Joe and I examined these very carefully, and it seemed clear that they were a means of bringing fresh water into the pool, for at the far end, where the pool faced the sea, and also on its flanks, were other channels with similar damming slabs. These channels, no doubt, acted as outlets. As an architect who has made a particular study of the design of swimming pools, I was fascinated by this example of Roman expertise.

Joe, Chiam and I dived, snorkled, and explored the beaches where the remains of these ancient buildings come right down to the sea. It is here that nature is her own excavator; for unable to withstand the remorseless beating of the waves, the crumbling city daily and changingly reveals itself to the 20th century. Thus the casual beachcomber can pick up Roman and Byzantine coins, pieces of Roman glass, and occasionally a fragment of necklace, or even a brooch.

We could happily have spent the rest of our visit at Caesaria, but there were other sites to be seen, and soon we were on our way northwards to Atlit. Here facing the Mediterranean on a small rocky promontory stand the noble remains of the Pilgrim's Castle. Fortified by the Crusader Templars in 1217, Atlit was one of the principal ports for pilgrims visiting the Holy Land. From the castle we gazed down into the bay with its little islands, and rocky outcrops. Within a short time we were into our wet suits, and snorkling in the comparatively shallow waters. We were to see that what we had thought were rock outcrops were, in fact, the remains of breakwaters and man-made structures. On coming out of the sea I said to Elisha, "Crusader of course?". His reply was "Maybe."

I pressed him further, but all he would say was, "Wait and see, we are doing a survey, and I think we may come up with one or two surprises." Elisha was true to his word, for in the following year his Society produced a report announcing the discovery of a Phoenician harbour at Atlit. There is no reason to doubt this because Phoenician remains have for many years been discovered on land immediately overlooking the harbour site.

It is sometimes difficult for a newcomer to an ancient site, such as Atlit, to comprehend at first glance the vast span of history concentrated in one very small area. There was I, in the 20th century, standing under the Gothic arches of the Crusader dining hall, built nearly 700 years ago, and I was gazing at the remnants of a harbour which was in use about 2,000 years before the Crusaders came to the Holy Land.

Two of the divers of the Undersea Exploration Society of Israel engaged on the Atlit survey went off for a reconnaissance of the areas outside the harbour. Within an hour they were back at base telling a great yarn about a nest of flying saucers that they had discovered at a depth of about 60 feet. They could not keep up this leg pull for very long, however, but the truth of their discovery was just as exciting. They had found a wreck containing about 40 millstones; each of these was about 3 feet in diameter. The wreck is still there for anyone who cares to dive on it.

We completed our tour by visits to Akko (Acre), and then right down south to the Red Sea Port of Eilat. These two ancient towns were to be the sites of my most exciting expeditions in the years to follow. We slept our last night in Israel on Kibbutz Maagan Michael. Joshua Shapira, the second-in-command of the U.E.S.I., was to call for us in the morning. Known to everyone by his nickname of "Shuka", it was a frustrating experience to be in his company with other Israelis; for Shuka is known as a wit, but in those days his English was very limited. Joe Shaw and I had no difficulty in waking up that morning, because at 5.0 a.m. Salome, the Kibbutz's prize cow, began to serenade us right outside our window, and she kept it up until Shuka's arrival at 8.0. "Shuka," pleaded Joe, "why on earth does that goddam cow keep mooing like that?" With a gesture which said, "Don't you understand," Shuka replied, "She sad, she know Joe go."

> "*The end of our voyage from Tyre came when we
> landed at Ptolemais where we greeted the brothers
> and stayed one day with them.*"
> St. Paul—The Acts of the Apostles 21.7

Following my return from Israel in 1965, Elisha Linder and I wrote to each other principally with the object of arranging an expedition to one of the sites that we had already visited. We both felt that we might be able to do some useful work at Akko. This fascinating place is one of the oldest cities in the world, and in the days of the Old Testament, it was known as Accho. It lies on the coast in northern Israel at the tip of a broad crescent bay that sweeps southwards to Haifa, nine miles away. During the period of Roman rule in Palestine it was called Ptolemais, and it was the Crusader capital of Palestine when it was known as St. Jean d'Acre, or Acre. During the 18th century it was ruled by the infamous Jezzar the Butcher, and it was here that Napoleon was defeated and his aspirations in the Middle East ended. Here then were thousands of years of exciting history during which time its port was more or less in continuous use. Clearly, a must for the underwater explorer.

On my return from a long Easter weekend diving with Holborn and London branches of the Club at Newlyn, I found a letter from Elisha waiting for me. It contained an invitation to come and dive at Akko. He explained that in the previous year the construction of a new concrete breakwater had become a matter of urgency because of the persistent demands of local fishermen who were very poorly served by inadequate installations. The proposal was to build the new breakwater on top of the ancient structure, and as this had never been surveyed, the Israeli Department of Antiquities appealed to the U.E.S.I. to carry this out as quickly as possible. As a result the Israeli divers found themselves surveying and photographing underwater whilst new concrete was being poured just a few feet away from them. In spite of this they managed to complete their survey before the ancient break-water was completely covered in and lost for ever.

From this short operation, however, the divers were able to glean something of the importance of the whole harbour area, and Elisha's letter to me contained an invitation from Dr. A. Biran, the Director of the Israeli Government Department of Antiquities, to join them in surveying the harbour.

My advice to anyone who wants to mount an underwater archaeological expedition is to seek the help of Joan du Plat Taylor—and that is exactly what I did myself. Joan, who is often affectionately referred to as the "mother" of British under-water archaeology—certainly it was her drive and keenness that led to the formation of Britain's Committee for Nautical Archaeology—went carefully through my plans and pro-gramme of work, advising about this point and that. I adopted all her suggestions based as they were on the years of ex-perience she has obtained through field work on sites on the shores of the Mediterranean.

I had incidentally, round about this time, been in touch with Dr. E. T. Hall, the Director of the Laboratory for Archaeo-logical Research at the University of Oxford. He had recently returned from Turkey where he had been putting his proton magnetometer to good use. To those readers who are not familiar with this instrument let me explain that it is basically a means of measuring the magnetic field of the earth to a high degree of accuracy in a short period of time. The instrument is, therefore, capable of detecting iron, or steel, varying from iron fastenings on ancient ships to cannons weighing several tons or ships weighing thousands of tons. Furthermore, wrecks con-taining large quantities of amphora can also be detected be-cause of the magnetic content of the fired clay of which these ancient oil or wine jars are made. The proton magnetometer had proved its value on land, but the possibilities for use of the equipment underwater had not been so well studied, and very little practical work had been undertaken in this direction.

With the invitation in my hands I was on the telephone to

Dr. Hall. "How about coming to Akko and doing a complete magnetometer survey of the harbour and the sea areas around it?" I asked. "Accepted," replied Dr. Hall. "When do we start?" With Joan du Plat Taylor's help, the Committee for Nautical Archaeology gave our programme its approval and thus the Anglo-Israeli Archaeological Expedition to Akko, 1966, came into being, and that September saw the beginning of what was to be a stimulating three weeks.

As well as the proton magnetometer survey we planned to search the sea bed for artifacts, and to survey the harbour with particular attention to the Tower of Flies, an ancient structure, the remains of which protruded from the sea, and stood as a sentinel at the entrance to the harbour. Our party from the U.K. consisted of Teddy Hall and myself, two technicians, David Wallington and Phil Wigmore, Jean and Simson Karpadeos, divers, and my wife Trudie, who was the expedition's secretary and recorder. Elisha brought along a full team of expert divers, and Uri Kellner, the U.E.S.I. Treasurer kept a fatherly eye over all of us.

Teddy Hall had sailed over from Cyprus in his boat, the *Blue Bonito*. A 31-foot Bertram Express Cruiser with twin petrol engines it was capable of a speed of over 30 knots. This boat proved ideal for the survey, as its ample deck space was sufficient for the magnetometer and its associated apparatus, and crew. The magnetometer itself was housed in a large box about the size of a television set. The recordings were marked on a continuous roll of paper, so that when there was nothing being detected, the pen produced a comparatively straight vertical line, but immediately an anomaly was recorded the needle would jump about in all manner of fashions. We soon grew to understand the shapes produced by the needle. For example, a cannon ball would produce a long stiletto-like trace, whereas metal spread over a larger area would show up as a much broader pattern with jagged edges. The part of the instrument which did the actual detecting was towed behind the boat so that it floated along on an even plane, a few feet above the sea bed. It looked very much like a small torpedo, and we called it "The Fish".

Teddy Hall decided to set up five survey areas, each oblong in shape. The corners of the areas were located by hand-bearing

compass readings on fixed land marks, and these were marked
by sinkers and flagged buoys. The boat was steered parallel to
two of the corner flags, and a series of lanes were run, each
approximately 30 feet wide. As the boat reached the end of the
lane a mark was made on the travelling paper roll. In this
manner we were able to locate all readings in relation to the
flagged buoys and the lane.

We started off on our first run at a nice steady pace of 5 knots
and at the end of the second lane the needle jumped about like
mad. Chiam Stav, who had been with me at Caesaria was all
ready geared up and jumped in immediately to identify the
expedition's first discovery. We followed his bubbles expectantly, and within a couple of minutes he had surfaced about
50 feet from the boat. He lifted his face mask, and waved to us,
calling out, "Very interesting, but not very old." "What is it?" I
called back impatiently, and back came the reply, "A very nice
iron bedstead, but it's too heavy for me to lift." "Well, at least,"
said Teddy, "it proves that the magnetometer is working."

At first we thought it was a good idea for the boat to carry a
diver who could immediately investigate any anomaly recorded. After the first day, however, we decided that this was
not practical, as it meant having to stop the boat frequently and
this interfered with progress and accuracy of steering. It was
decided, therefore, to drop a buoy overboard whenever an
interesting anomaly was recorded. The buoys were then dived
on subsequently at leisure.

Among the first of the finds recorded by the magnetometer
were three large iron anchors, all of similar design, and each
weighing about 150 kilos. These were probably of late
18th- or early 19th-century origin. Close to the breakwater a
particularly large and mysterious anomaly was recorded.
Teddy said that the reading suggested a three-ton mass of
metal at least, but when we dived on the area we could find
nothing at all. Obviously the anomaly was under the sand, and
its nature still remains a mystery. The magnetometer's finest
discovery came towards the end of the expedition. Each time
the *Blue Bonito* passed over a position between the end of the
breakwater and the Tower of Flies it recorded a significant
anomaly. We sent Shuka and Chia Eddleman down to investigate. Their bubbles circled around over a fairly wide area

for some time, and then after about half an hour both lots of bubbles seemed to rise from one spot. Elisha turned to me and said, "I think they must have found something," and he was right. A quarter of an hour later Shuka and Chia surfaced, each holding a small piece of waterlogged timber, and in one of these pieces was embedded a copper nail. "It's a wreck," shouted Shuka. The words which every underwater archaeologist dreams of hearing.

We had found the remains of a well-constructed 18th-century battleship of the second or third line. Its tonnage would have been about 800 to 1,000 tons, with a length of about 150 feet. The timber, which was of pine, indicated that it was probably of Turkish, or French origin. The planking was lined with sheet copper, and the hundreds of nails and bolts, found protruding from the timber were also all of copper. Unfortunately, there was little time left for the boat to be thoroughly excavated and surveyed, indeed my wife and I had to return to England the day after its discovery. The Israelis, however, were able to carry out some useful preliminary recording, and then covered over the wreck with sand, so that they could return to it sometime in the future to carry out a thorough survey.

One of the things that puzzled us about this wreck was that it did not seem to contain any armament. I was able to solve this mystery, however, when I visited the Map Room of the British Museum on my return. I found a rough map drawn at the time of Napoleon's siege of Acre in 1799. This map, which shows the disposition of the British ships under the command of Sir Sidney Smith indicates, between the end of the breakwater and the Tower of Flies a "Wreck filled with sand". The position of this corresponded very closely with our wreck. It appears that what we had actually discovered was a "blockship", emptied of its armour, filled with sand, and sunk in the entrance of the harbour by Admiral Sir Sidney Smith in his defence of the city.

I have described our work with the magnetometer, and the discovery of the wreck. Now let me tell you about the Tower of Flies. The remains of this Tower are situated at the south-east extremity of the harbour, controlling its entrance and commanding a wide view of the bay of Haifa. Although now a total ruin a lithograph from the 18th century shows it as a lighthouse. A vivid contemporary description of the Moslem defence of Akko against the Crusaders in the 12th century refers to the Tower as a fortress. The structure above sea level appeared to be of typical Crusader construction, the stone blocks measuring in elevation about 18 inches by 9 inches, but immediately below water level the blocks were mostly of a much larger size, averaging 40 inches by 30 inches.

We wanted to find out as much as we could about the origins of the Tower, and the best way to do this was to examine closely and survey the masonry below sea level. This sort of job is one of the less glamorous tasks in underwater archaeology. It means working in shallow water from 6 feet to 25 feet deep. It was very slow, and even exhausting, particularly when the surface was choppy. Imagine trying to take detailed measurements and draw these on to a pad while you are being thrown backwards and forwards by the waves. As the masonry was not laid in regular courses we had to mark nearly every block with a plastic number and carefully measure, and draw each in turn. Little by little we worked our way along from the east end of the Tower into deeper water, where the stonework seemed to disappear into the natural formation of the seabed.

Jean and I had finished a long morning's work, and were snorkeling about on the surface before getting into the dinghy and going back to camp. We were about 30 metres west of the Tower floating lazily on the surface, and basking in the hot sun which by that time of the day was right overhead. As I peered through my mask, my eye was caught by a couple of thin straight lines on the seabed. Jean had also seen these, and we dived down to investigate. What we found was that the lines were actually long slits in the rock into which we could slip our hands. The rock was completely covered by a thick soft layer of seaweed, and cutting this way we pushed our hands further and further along the slits. The slits were about 40 inches apart, and parallel, and as I held on to one of these with my left hand I groped along with my knife and nearly lost it down another slit the same distance on. "Blocks," squealed Jean, out of the corner of her mouth and we were off like a shot, searching for and locating more and more blocks all of which ran parallel to each other. They turned out to be extremely large blocks of

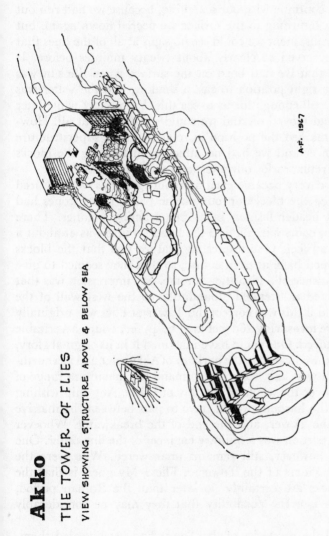

Fig. 11. Alexander Flinder's own drawing of the mysterious Tower of Flies at Akko showing the structure above and below sea.

stone, measuring 40 inches square by 12 feet to 15 feet long. (Fig. 11.)

This was a tremendously exciting find, but unfortunately we could not continue with our searching, because we had run out of air. On returning to the surface we peered down again, but to our astonishment we could see no signs at all of the lines that we had observed so clearly about twenty minutes before. It appeared that we had been on the surface when the sun was just in the right position to cast a shadow, and the water was calm and still enough for us to see this. Yet a short while later the sun had moved on and we could see nothing at all. However, we marked the position in relation to the superstructure of the Tower and we had no difficulty in locating the blocks when we returned for our afternoon surveying session.

Our discovery became even more intriguing as we measured and plotted the blocks on our plastic pads. These stones had been laid header fashion in a very exacting manner. There were seven courses in all, and the lowest course was at about a depth of 29 feet. One interesting feature was that the blocks were stepped back at each course, so that they seemed to give the appearance of a gigantic staircase. My impression was that these formed a "stepped" foundation to the west wall of the Tower and if this was correct the Tower of Flies was originally a structure measuring 160 feet long by 45 feet wide; a veritable fortress indeed. One could have imagined it in its original glory, poised at the entrance to the harbour of Akko, planned in a north-east–south-west axis, so as to command the maximum range of visibility over the whole of the Bay of Haifa. Any ship wishing to enter the harbour would have to pass between the massive walls of the Tower, and the end of the breakwater. Whoever built this bastion was a military engineer of the first order. One question, however, still remains unanswered. Who were the original builders of the Tower of Flies? My guess is that the large blocks are certainly no later than the Roman period, but there is every possibility that they may be considerably earlier.

Not all the mysteries of the Tower had yet revealed themselves, and the next fascinating discovery was to be made by one of our favourite Israeli divers, Avramela—"Little Abraham". A grinning chubby face mounted 6 feet 4 inches above the ground

Was this the port of King Solomon? The Island of Jezirat Faraun may well have been. A combined expedition of British Sub-Aqua Club members and those of the Undersea Exploration Society of Israel started to probe its secrets. *Below*, Israeli diver Shuka carefully cleans away encrusting sand from a buried amphora. The numbered tag on the diver's right marks another find. Photographs by Joseph Galilee. (See chapter 7)

Did they tie this stone around the neck of Saint Feliu and fling him off those cliffs? Kendall McDonald examines the millstone he found underwater close to the town of San Feliu de Guixols on Spain's Costa Brava. Picture by Penny McDonald. (See chapter 9)

over a 50-inch chest, Avramala, who was hardly ever seen in anything more than the briefest of trunks, was undoubtedly the
Biblical Samson reincarnated. Inseparable from Avramala was
Joseph Galili, known to every diver in Israel as Yoske. Israel's
representative on the World Federation (C.M.A.S.), Yoske and
his son, Udi, are a veritable diving club on their own. Yoske,
who has a strong resemblance to Charlie Chaplin, and Avramala, make one of the most skilful and funniest diving teams I
have ever met. A word of warning to anyone who dives with this
pair—learn how to be convulsed with laughter and still keep
your mouthpiece in!

When they were diving on the Tower they noticed that an
area behind the external wall on the south face was filled with
boulders. Working with a "Hookah" supplying them with air
from the surface they removed the boulders one by one. So
engrossed were they by this job, we could not entice them out
of the water, and Avramala had one five-hour session when
we had to take him down bananas, and Coca-Cola, which he
consumed lustily at a depth of 10 feet. The removal of the
boulders revealed a chamber, in which we found a large number
of cannon balls neatly stacked, and perfectly clean. What
appeared to be the remains of a staircase led up to the floor
of the Tower just above water level where it coincided with the
bottom of the staircase on the upper part of the structure. I
think that this chamber must have been an arsenal. The walls
of the chamber were domed, and had been made of some sort of
concrete. I was rather apprehensive, however, about the divers
working in the chamber because the cement to the concrete
walls had been nearly wholly washed away, leaving it honey-
combed and fragile. Happily the sea was perfectly calm, and I
guessed that as long as it stayed this way the equal water
pressures on both sides of the free-standing wall would keep it
reasonably safe for the moment. My fears were not unfounded
however, for when I returned to dive on the Tower in the
following year the walls had completely collapsed.

The finds that we recovered from inside, and around the
harbour were in themselves testimony to Akko's long and
exciting history. Pieces of prehistoric flints, large stone anchors
from the Iron Age, early Arab pottery from about A.D. 700,
iron masonry clamps from the Crusader period, Turkish pipes

9

from the 18th century, cannon balls, lead musket shot and large iron anchors.

Our expedition lasted only seventeen working days, but we had learnt enough to stimulate further research in the area, and as soon as the weather had improved, in the spring of the following year, the U.E.S.I. were back and in a very short time had found two more 18th-century wrecks. From these they were able to recover large cannon, swivel guns, carronades, and a multitude of small arms.

Before we returned home, the group decided to dive on the wreck of the *Sciré*. This was the Italian submarine sunk by the motor torpedo-boat *Islay* in 1942, with the loss of all its 50 crew, and ten frogmen. The *Sciré* took part in the famous frogman attack on Alexandria Harbour, when the battleships *Valiant* and *Queen Elizabeth* were immobilized. Dr. Hall had no difficulty in detecting the submarine, which produced a very strong symmetrical trace on the magnetometer. This vessel, once the proudest submarine in the Italian Navy, now lay silently on its side in an 80-foot grave. To dive on a "dead" submarine is a sad experience, and we said little as the *Blue Bonito* carried us back to harbour.

"And King Solomon made a navy of ships in Ezion-Geber which is beside Eloth on the shore of the Red Sea in the land of Edom. And Hiram sent in the Navy his servants, ship men that have knowledge of the sea with the servants of Solomon. And they came to Ophir, and fetched from thence Gold, 420 talents, and brought it to King Solomon.
First Book of Kings IX, 26–28

My first visit to Eilat on the Red Sea was in 1963, and its magic has drawn me back every year since then. In fact many members of the B.S–A.C. have become familiar with this divers' paradise under the guidance of Willy Halpert, and his colleagues at the Aqua Sport Diving Centre.

Located at the north of the Gulf of Akaba, Eilat is centred in the area that saw the dawn of western civilization. It is a never-forgotten experience at the end of a long drive through the fabulous Negev Desert to have one's first sight of the Red Sea, flanked on its east by the mountains of the Arabian Desert, their peaks orange and purple from the sinking sun, and on the west by the Sinai Peninsula, the "Desert of the Wanderings".

In September 1967, I, together with my son Harvey on his first visit to Israel, and a group from the U.E.S.I. arrived at Eilat. Elisha Linder, Shuka Shapira, Yoske Galili, and Avramala, friends from our previous expeditions, were joining me on a short visit to the tiny island of Jezirat Faraun. About ten miles south of Eilat, a few hundred yards offshore from the Sinai Peninsula, this island, 320 metres long by 150 metres wide, rises out of the sea to a height of 29 metres, and is surmounted by the remains of a medieval castle. Our two days spent in diving, and exploring the island, were in themselves sufficient to whet my appetite, and on arriving back home I started to find out everything I could about the island. It was Miss Olga Tufnell, one of our most learned Middle East archaeologists, who said to me, "If you are going to work on the island, you must read Dr. Benno Rothenburg's book, *God's Wilderness*." Rothenburg visited the island for a short time in 1957, and was completely captivated by it.

During my visit I had made a careful survey of part of the remains of the gigantic wall which surrounded the island. This wall, Rothenburg says, is of a "casemate" construction which is typical of the type of walls found in military forts of the period of King Solomon. He also identified the island as being the Island of Jotabe, which was known to exist in the Gulf of Akaba in Byzantine times, but had not yet been definitely located.

What was really interesting to me, however, was the existence of a perfect little harbour on the island, the entrance to which was flanked by the remains of two large towers. The stretch of sea between the island and the mainland was sheltered, and it looked to me as though these straits could well have been a sheltered anchorage in ancient times. Surprisingly, other than Dr. Rothenburg's description, and the plan prepared by some of his colleagues, not a great deal had been written about the island, and certainly, nobody had ever done any underwater exploration in its vicinity. There were many questions to be asked about the island. For example, when was it first colonized? And did it play any part in King Solomon's enterprises in this area? Why was it so heavily fortified by a wall, which was 12 feet thick, and had been at least 12 feet high? What was its importance during the Byzantine period? And what could we add to our knowledge that during Crusader times it was known as Ile de Graye, and was heavily fought over by the Moslems, and the impetuous Crusader Renaud de Chatillon?

This was the background to the B.S-A.C.–U.E.S.I. underwater survey of Jezirat Faroun in 1968. The B.S-A.C. party was the largest that I had taken to Israel. Alexander de Fé who had prepared so much of the ground work with me was bitterly disappointed in having to withdraw at the eleventh hour for business reasons, and David Young, one of our photographers, also had to drop out. Nevertheless, we were left with a strong, compact party, and we rendezvoused with the Israelis on December 1. My Diving Officer was Dick Harris, of the B.E.A. Silver Wings Branch, one of the first Englishmen to "discover" the diving at Eilat. Brian Lansdown of Hampstead Branch joined us. So did Gerry Munday, the underwater photographer and film maker, and Edward Goldwyn and his wife, Dr. "Chum" Goldwyn. Edward had asked if he could come along to make a television film, and he and "Chum" had by sheer persistence got themselves up to B.S-A.C. Third Class level in time for the expedition.

Of our Israeli colleagues, Elisha was now at Brandies University in the U.S.A., where he was studying for his Doctorate, and specializing in ancient shipping, and Avramala, I was told, was actually wearing a collar and tie in New York. Shuka Shapira had taken over the leadership of the U.E.S.I., and he and Yoske Galili were there to meet us, with Dony and Oded, two of their most experienced divers. Also joining us were some local stalwarts, such as Dov Neuman, Chairman of the Eilat Diving Club, and one of the best conchologists in Israel, and three of Willy Halpert's helpers, Hans from Holland, David from Israel and Edwardo from the Argentine. Jill from South Africa, who was on holiday in Eilat also joined in, and in her bikini she proved to be one of the star turns in Edward's film.

Our expedition was limited to two weeks only, and so we had to confine our objectives to tasks which could be realized in that time. I decided, therefore, that we should concentrate on carrying out a physical search of the sea-bed over as large an area as possible, and in particular the straits between the island and the mainland. Everything that we saw was to be noted, and identified, and accurately located. In addition I would also get as much information as possible about the harbour, and its construction. We had no excavation equipment with us, other than a simple "corer" and we would concentrate solely on observing, and recording. We did, however, take with us an underwater metal detector, which had been designed and made by Dr. E. T. Hall who had accompanied me to Akko in 1966.

The search system that I decided to use was an adaptation of a method invented by Lt.-Commander Grattan of the Royal Navy. Called the "swim line" system it had been used successfully on Syd Wignall's search for the wreck of the *Santa Maria de la Rosa* off the coast of Ireland. Our divers positioned themselves about 10 feet apart on a rope which had been previously prepared and marked. In the centre of the rope was the "swim line leader", and at each end the "end men". The idea was that the line of divers swam about 1–2 feet above the sea-bed in a predetermined direction. In our case we found that we were able to lay a line between the mainland and the island, and so it was fairly easy for the leader to follow the line. The job of the two end men was to see that the line was kept straight. As the line moved slowly forward each of the divers would be closely scanning the sea-bed for artifacts or indeed anything that looked unnatural. Each diver was equipped with a set of plastic numbered tabs, and when he saw anything suspicious he would attach a marker to it and immediately return to the line.

By this method we were able to get in two sweeps in a day. When the line had completed its sweep, two of us would go over its course and closely examine, draw and photograph the finds. We left the markers on those finds that were important. To these we attached buoys and then took sextant bearings on them so that the positions could be transferred accurately to a plan. In this manner we were able to survey 200,000 square metres of seabed, by sweeping in lanes between the mainland and the island. Dick Harris, my Diving Officer, was the organizing genius of all this. His was a full-time job—

arranging for the filling of bottles and their economic use, planning the dives, briefing the divers, and leading every dive. Everything went like clockwork and this was, in my view, an indirect tribute to those who had initiated and developed the B.S-A.C. approach to diving procedure. To see a group of well-trained divers working together calmly and efficiently, is always a delight. We had divers of five nationalities in the group, and yet they were welded together into a team in just a couple of days.

What did we find? Surprisingly rather less than I had anticipated, but the reason for this became apparent as we learnt more about the terrain. Our principal discovery was a large group of broken amphora and sherds scattered over an area of about 600 square yards. These were all from the same age, Late Roman/Byzantine A.D. 300–500. About 50 yards from the island they lay buried in the sand at depths of 25–30 feet. Some were so encrusted with coral as to be nearly unrecognizable. The discovery of these sherds posed a problem. Why did we find this large group of pottery which had lain on the sea-bed for about fifteen hundred years, and yet we found nothing of later periods? Yet we know, for example, that there was a great deal of activity on the island during the Crusader period only eight hundred years ago. Gerry Munday who, among his many talents, is the holder of a mate's ticket and knows the ways of the sea, was the first to hit on the answer, and this was later confirmed by David Friedman, an expert diver and Curator of the small Maritime Museum in Eilat. Their theory, and I am sure that it is right, is that the violent storms which periodically sweep up the Gulf of Aqaba from the south, bring with them a build-up of sand, so that not only is the land covered in regularly, but also the sea-bed in its shallower areas. Thus the straits that we surveyed had been subject to heavy silting and any artifacts were gradually covered in. Anything escaping burial was then subject to the ravages of coral growth and encrustation.

The west side of the island is relatively protected however; and what we had found may have been the last traces of a sea drama enacted during the last days of the Roman Empire. Imagine a merchantman plying its way northwards through the Gulf of Akaba. The ship is heavily laden with a full cargo. The skipper is apprehensive of the darkening clouds behind him and he knows that very shortly he will be in the midst of one of those violent southerly winds that can spring up so rapidly in these seas. Hugging the coast of the Sinai Peninsula he heads for a spot where he knows that he can get some shelter—the island of Faraun, but before he makes port he is engulfed in the storm. His little craft is buffeted violently and continuously and its fragile cargo smashed against the sides of the boat. Eventually he reaches the island and tucks himself into its western shore where he can ride out the storm. The following morning the storm has passed and the crew set about clearing up the mess. Many of the grain and oil containers have been smashed and the sailors toss the bits over the side where they sink slowly down and settle gently on the sea-bed only fifty metres or so from the shore. There they lay through the centuries until recovered by our divers. Well, it could be—I can't think of any better explanation.

But our most significant discovery happened accidentally right at the end of our stay. Edward, Chum and Brian were loading up our vehicle and Gerry was packing up his filming gear. As I was walking along the pebble beach on the mainland, coiling up my surveying tape, I glanced towards the sea and what I saw made me shout involuntarily with surprise. The tide had gone down about a foot or so, and there only a few steps in front of me was revealed the unmistakable oblong shape of a landing stage. This small structure measuring fourteen metres long by six metres wide was made up of stone blocks each about one metre by forty centimetres by thirty centimetres thick. It lay on the coral reef and extended out to its very edge. I said that this was our most significant find because it provided the first evidence of some sort of link between the island and the mainland. I was sure that there *must* have been a ferry operating between the island harbour and the mainland in ancient times, and now we had found the proof.

Our short expedition had proved thoroughly worthwhile, for we had discovered sufficient to justify further and more detailed investigation in the future and we had tried out and learnt a lot about the methods and "disciplines" of underwater searching. In common with the rest of the world, underwater archaeology in the Land of the Bible is just beginning, but even as I write I have beside me a letter from the U.E.S.I. telling of further finds such as a set of figurines from a Late Roman wreck, and beautiful pottery from a medieval Arab merchantman. Something tells me that it won't be long before I am back there again, diving at Ashkelon perhaps, or maybe the Sea of Galilee. . . .

COLOUR ME WHITE!

by Dr. John Lythgoe

"What's the viz?" That's the first question that a surfacing
diver is asked by those of his colleagues who have yet to dive.
The reason for the question is obvious—visibility underwater
is vitally important to diving. Dr. John Lythgoe, a member of
London Branch of the British Sub-Aqua Club, is an expert on
underwater vision. Here he explains how a diver's eyes can
mislead him and how his own diving has helped him to understand some of the reasons for the coloration of fish.

THERE are few beasts that can rival the revolting habits of
the animal that the Swedes call "skorve". It is a kind of sea-
slater looking much like a woodlouse but it can be as big as a
man's fist. Skorve are scavengers on the bottom of the cold
northern lakes and seas and are common in the Baltic.

It is quite usual there to pull up a gill net only to find that the
fish you have caught are nothing but a dead skin stretched like
a bladder around a heaving mass of skorve packed tight inside.
There are reports that the same happened to dead soldiers in
the Russo-Finnish war, but the skorve prefer the rather cold
and muddy life in deeper water and so perhaps the soldiers
escaped.

To the fisherman the skorve is an ubiquitous pest and judging
by the numbers of occupied fishes (some not even dead) they
must swarm over the bottom like guests at a garden party.
Obviously this was something to see—they are common at 120
feet, the water seemed clear and I had an aqualung. Uncomfortably I also had a dry suit and I didn't have a torch. The
first dive was a failure, it was a bright and sunny day on top,
but at 80 feet it was too dark to see and the bottom was so soft
it was hard to tell where the water ended and the mud began.
My dry suit had begun to leak at the neck, the water (I later
found) was 4°C and it was still utterly black. End of dive. One
hundred and twenty feet I decided was too deep in the Baltic.

Next time I went in off the shore and worked gradually
down. This is much more interesting for there are abundant

seaweeds, edible mussels to at least 60 feet and sometimes a fish or two. The middle Baltic is brackish, having a salt content of about 6 or 7 parts per thousand rather than the 35 parts per thousand in the open sea. This allows fishes such as pike and perch to swim in the same waters as the Baltic Herring. The water looks a yellowish-green near the surface and as you go deeper gets bottle-green and finally goes a dim colourless grey. Surprisingly even when I had swum out from the boulder-strewn banks of the fjord on to the monotonous flat mud bottom at 110 feet, there was still enough of the dim grey light to distinguish the wandering crab-like tracks of the skorve on the mud. Indeed there was nothing else in sight.

Naturally enough I put down the better visibility on the second day to clearer water, but several dives later I realized that I could always see further if I went slowly down the slope than if I plunged quickly down from the surface to the mud. It wasn't better clarity at all, but my own eyes which had got used to the dark. It is perfectly well known that it takes several minutes of blundering about in a darkened theatre to get used to the darkness—indeed it takes at least 20 minutes—and the same is true when diving into deep dark water.

The adaptation time of twenty minutes does seem rather slow, but during that time the eye has performed a very real miracle. Sunlight is something like 100,000,000,000 times brighter than the dim glimmer of light that can just be seen in deep water. Indeed so versatile is the eye that slow changes of light intensity of 100 or 1,000-fold can pass unnoticed.

Part of the secret is that the eye has two "sensitivity scales"—one for daytime, the other for night. The huge increase in sensitively at night is gained at the sacrifice of some loss in efficiency in other respects. Colour vision is lost and the world is seen in shades of grey. The ability to see small details is reduced and fewer shades of grey can be seen. This last ability to distinguish contrast does not seem very significant at first glance, but it holds the key to vision underwater—or anywhere else for that matter.

The diver is as ready as anyone else to believe the evidence of his own eyes and like anyone else is often misled. There was not a layer of grey water at the bottom of the Baltic fjord in which I had dived. Measurement would have shown that it had much the same in optical properties as that a bit shallower. But it was too dim down there for the eyes to see colour and the message sent back to the brain was "The water is grey" not "I can't see what colour it is".

Night vision has its disadvantages, but it is either that or blindness. However, the slow change from day to night vision can be side-stepped by a very simple technique still used by flyers and seamen keeping watch at night. The day vision system is chiefly sensitive to yellow-green light, but the night vision system sees blue-green light as the brightest and can not see red light at all. (Red flowers look black at night.) The day and night systems work independently of one another and if red goggles or a red face mask are worn, one can see perfectly well by the day vision system, but the night vision system can detect no light and reacts as though it were suddenly dark. After twenty minutes the night vision has got very sensitive and if the goggles are removed in a dark place the eye is at once as sensitive as it can ever be.

I would have been proud to report that the use of a red face plate enabled me to solve the secret of the skorve's sordid life; but I used a torch like everyone else. I discovered that the skorve live buried in the mud during the daytime, but some at least come out during the night and embark on long safaris across the acres of flat mud. The tracks they leave at night are long and straight and have a look of purpose. In the daytime they heave out of the mud with startling speed if a succulent dead fish is put a yard or two away. (They prefer fresh fish, but will *in extremis* eat newspaper.) I think they must find their food by smell because they sometimes pass right by the morsel but eventually find it. There don't seem to be nearly as many skorve as one might expect from the state of the dead fishes— perhaps one or two to the square yard. But they are exceedingly efficient at homing in on their food and they must be able to detect it from several yards away.

The red face plate technique would be used a lot more than it is were it not for (a) torches, and (b) the terrible fiddle involved. However, one piece of underwater sightseeing is well worth while and that is to reveal the "fire" in the sea produced by the myriads of tiny plantonic animals there. Incidentally the correct word for this fire is "bioluminescence" literally "life light" and not phosphorescence or fluorescence. If you dive to depths where normally there is no visible light and substitute a red face mask for a clear one tens and hundreds of little points of light are visible as they flow past in the tide. Bioluminescence often kindles when the tiny animal hits a life line or is disturbed by the movement of a fish. But once turn on a torch and the whole lot disappears as your dark adapted state is destroyed. Bio-luminescence cannot be seen in fresh water because for some reason the animals do not live there. In the fairy-light world of the deep oceans, fishes and squids have complicated patterns of lights arranged along their bellies and flanks. Chiefly, the colours seem to be blues or greens, but some squids have reds and greens. In some cases a light organ points directly into the eye—at first sight a very ridiculous thing—but it may allow the fish to light up its eye to terrify away intruders and predators.

Several kinds of fish have a dense concentration of light organs on their bellies and it has been suggested that these help as camouflage. Underwater most light comes from directly above and the light from other directions may be too dim to see. Anything directly above will thus show up as a dark silhouette and will be eaten accordingly. The array of bright light will make the fish match the background light in brightness and thus camouflage it. This may seem a bit far-fetched. It seems a bit unlikely to me—but during the war strafing aircraft sometimes mounted forward headlights along their wings and attacked out of the sun. It was said to be highly effective.

At night most divers go to sleep and so we cannot be surprised that little is known about what the fishes do then. Actually it seems to me that it is less the dark than the cold that drives divers out of the water and into the pubs and their beds, but the results, or rather lack of them, are the same. It is perhaps significant that more is known about the night habits of tropical reef fishes than about fishes living in less hospitable waters. However, judging by such things as involuntary eye movements some fish do seem to have a genuine sleep whilst others seem to exist in a permanent state of wakefulness. Many fishes such as parrot fishes, wrasse and trigger fish spend the hours of darkness cosily wedged into some crack or crevice in the rock. Parrot fishes actually secrete a thread-like cocoon of mucus around themselves and pass the night in that. Trigger fish seek out a crack in the rock that fits them exactly even if it means passing the night nose down or flat on their side.

There is a considerable mystery how some of the very common Mediterranean and Atlantic wrasse spend the night. Judging by their bright colours, feeding habits and their very highly organized eye they are especially suited for daylight life and can probably see quite fine detail. Some wrasse, like some trigger fish, are peculiar in having a yellow front window to their eye (the cornea). At about 200 feet this yellow cornea must reduce their sensitivity to light by as much as 90 per cent. The advantages of this yellow filter are not very obvious, although I think it will give them better vision of close bright objects in the sea. However, the loss of sensitivity at night would be serious, and it is little wonder that they are never seen then.

In the aquarium at the London Zoo these little wrasse, the Rainbow Wrasse *(Coris julis)* and the Turkish Wrasse (*Thalassoma pavo*) seem to dig themselves into the sand at the bottom of their tanks and so pass the night. But to my knowledge no one has ever seen a similar thing in the open sea. Indeed several people have tried raking through sand patches at night and have found nothing at all. It seems much more likely that they wedge themselves into crevices in the rocks in the same way as trigger fish. I was once snorkeling over a reef in the Canary Islands, perhaps 400 yards from the shore, when I saw a swarm of Turkish wrasse in the rocks about 20 feet below me. It was about sunset and the light was beginning to fail; but diving down I saw that the fish, behaving exactly like a twittering flock of starlings coming in to roost were wedging themselves into small crevices twenty to a hole, so tightly that a sardine packer would have been proud of them. The most extraordinary thing about the whole incident was that in one of the holes was a very big Moray eel and the fish were packing in round him, whilst he glared out at me in a typically unfriendly manner.

There have now been several attempts to watch the wrasse going to roost in the evening. As the sun dips towards the horizon the wrasse, both Turkish and Rainbow, start to come together in schools of twenty or so, young and mature together and seen to "explore" amongst the rocks and cliffs. But they have never been followed right to their roosts. After a bit it gets too dark to see properly and the whole school seems to vanish.

Speaking personally I wouldn't go to bed with a great thing looking in through the window either!

Very little is know about animals that leave their hiding places and come out at night to feed. Dogfish are supposed to be nocturnal and certainly they are sometimes found apparently asleep on the bottom during the daytime. Sand sharks also seem to lie up in caves and under ledges in the daytime and presumably come out at night. Sometimes people assume an animal is nocturnal, so far as I can see, just because they have big eyes and live near holes. The Soldier Fish (*Myripristis murdjam*) is an example. But in nature they keep station in shoals a foot or two above some coral head where they seek refuge if something frightens them. They may be more active at night, but there is no particular evidence to support this.

In practice it is very difficult to decide whether a fish is nocturnal or diurnal and in any case the truth usually lies somewhere in between. Herrings come to the surface at night and sink during the day, but it seems that they change their depth in a way that keeps the brightness of the light reaching them to a constant, rather dim level. Herrings may seem nocturnal to the fisherman, but that is only because they fish with rather shallow drift nets.

Another very interesting thing about herring is the way that they are nearly invisible even in mid-water with no rocks or weeds to mimic or hide amongst. The trick is done by mirrors and there are many fish in this particular magic circle. They include the bass, barracuda, and horse mackerel. Indeed, almost all the fishes that live in open water have silvery, mirror-like sides. A mirror hung vertically in the water is almost invisible for the light it reflects from behind the diver is almost the same in both colour and brightness as the light directly behind the mirror. The same effect can be seen on a dull and overcast day when the windows of a large building look so exactly like the sky behind that there is the illusion that the building is hollow and that you can see right through it. The mirrored surface of fishes is a much finer piece of optical engineering than it looks for fishes are not flat-sided but have an oval cross section.

An ordinary mirror of this shape would not be invisible underwater, but in fishes each scale has in its surface a mass of tiny reflecting flat crystals set in a way that counteracts the roundness of the fish. The brightest light underwater comes from above and to compensate for this, the back of the fish is darker than the belly, otherwise a bright and very conspicuous band would be visible along the back. So delicate is the arrangement of crystals and colour that the whole fine structure begins to break down minutes after death. Also the camouflage depends on the fish swimming steadily and horizontally with its back directly towards the brightest light. If the fish is maimed or ill it does not swim properly and its camouflage breaks down leaving it an easy mark for predators.

It does not follow that all silvery fishes are hidden for it is the arrangement of the fine reflectors in its scales that are important, and such fishes as the sea bream or sar, although silvery, seem to be easily visible. Often it is not easy to decide whether a particular species is camouflaged or not. I have lost count of the number of times that somebody has looked me full in the face and announced "there are no perfectly camouflaged fishes". Mackerel, for example, certainly show up well when they are being chivvied along by the ground line of a trawl, but another diver-photographer, Peter Scoones, reports a dive into a shoal of mackerel where he could see nothing but water until every few seconds a fish, taking a baited hook, suddenly appeared, as if out of nothingness, thrashing about on the end of the line.

It follows that silvery fishes are very hard to photograph by natural light and sometimes nothing at all shows on the negative. The camouflage only works for the light pattern found naturally under water. A low-power flash of light just sufficient to brighten the fish by about one exposure stop on a camera completely wrecks the camouflage built up over centuries of evolution and the fish stands revealed blatantly silver against the blue sea. Too bright a flash will also bring out the fish but so mirror-like are their flanks that the reflected light burns out the film and a white smudge is all that remains. Pictures of silvery fish melting into the background habitually end up in the photographer's rubbish bin despite their scientific interest. Not so photographs of fishes that mimic their background. Every self-respecting photographer has a picture of a flatfish looking like sand or a scorpion fish looking like a weedy rock.

There are few animals that can rival the octopus in hiding out. Not only can they change their skins through a bewildering range of colours and patterns, but they change the texture of their skins according to the needs of the moment. When they are frightened by a diver or perhaps a predator they flatten out, bleach white within a fraction of a second and develop dark circles round their eyes. Suddenly they will shoot off through the water jet-propelled by water squirted from their siphon. As they settle they simply vanish for they assume the colour of the background and they can throw the surface of their skin into a mass of little projections which mimic the surface of an encrusted rock in texture as well as in colour.

The octopus is one of those animals that naturally attracts legends and tall stories, yet there may be more truth than imagination in much of their folk lore. There are persistent stories since Pliny that octopus drop stones into the mouths of oysters and mussels to wedge them open—this has not been proved but there are quite modern eye-witness reports saying the same thing. The octopus is very often used as a subject for experimental work on behaviour and it seems to me that the scientists who do the work are, in private, just as indefatigable myth-mongers as the ancients. This is not apparent from their learned writings which are as staid and respectable as convention insists. But the experimenters swear that the octopus learns faster than they do and half the time it is the octopus that is learning from the scientists and not the reverse.

Sometimes very complicated electronics are used for studies of nerve and brain. There was an octopus in Naples that used to come half out of the water and squirt a jet of sea-water with devastating accuracy at the most delicate and expensive circuitry in the room. Anyone who has involuntarily flooded his electronic flash with sea-water will know the ruination caused.

It is worth remembering that it is hard to kill an octopus quickly—a spear through it or rough handling with dry hands makes no apparent difference. But such treatment has sentenced it to death for they will die in three or four days even when no damage can be seen. I think it is one of the saddest things of all to see a landed octopus pale and flaccid in death beaten 100 times to make it fit to eat. However, I admit my melancholy vanishes when supper is ready.

On the surface. George Cooke, who built his own submarine at home, returning to shore in the rain after a test dive at Black Park near Slough. A *Sunday Telegraph* picture. *Below: Explorer 1*, with George once again at the controls, seven metres down at Stoney Cove. Picture by Geoff Harwood. (See chapter 10)

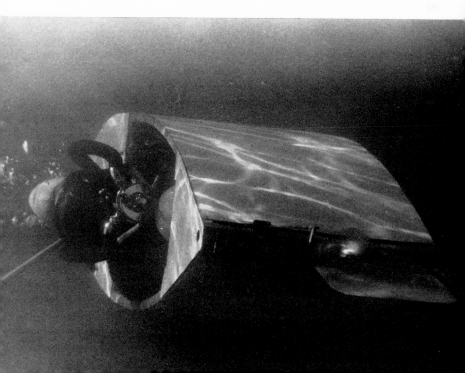

Above : Thunder Rock as seen from the mainland. The diving boats are to the right of the rock engaged in the work of lifting the ingots.
Below : What was going on under the boats. A diver ties a rope to one of the ingots from the wreck. (See chapter 11)

To judge from some books on natural history all fishes are coloured in some drab shade so they can lurk unseen for the better filling of their bellies or preservation of their lives. This is nonsense and a swim over a coral reef leaves the impression that every fish is just as gaudy as nature can paint them. This first impression is a false one for the eye cannot possibly mark all the species present (there may be 500 or 1,000 different kinds on one stretch of reef) and only the brilliant kinds are held in the memory.

At a time when people are beginning to realize how important it is for one diver to be able to see another through the water and when it becomes vital to identify the correct valve in complicated underwater apparatus, one can do worse than study the coral fishes. Consider their problem: a well-stocked reef may have 1,000 different fishes on it and most of these have a different colour and shape for the males, the females and the immature. Some colours, notably the reds, are filtered out by the blue tropical water and cannot be told from black. Other shades such as the mid-greys and blue-greens are almost invisible underwater. Thus with a restricted palette a colour and pattern coding has to be found that will effectively distinguish one fish from another.

In its basic organization the fish's eye is very like our own, although there are naturally enough important changes in detail. We are now beginning to know enough about the practice of vision through the water and the makings of the eye to submit the whole problem of underwater vision to a pretty searching computer analysis. The work has not been in progress long, but one of the answers seems to be that the points of difference between the eyes of the different fishes and man also are much less important than the colour and turbidity of the water itself. Generalizations are always dangerous, especially in biology; but generalization about the colours and shades that are used by fish for camouflage and display are more secure than most.

Fishes like the Sergeant Major can be seen at a very great distance through the water and the bigger and bolder the pattern the better. Oddly enough no one has yet actually tested which colour to paint an object (including black, white and fluorescent) so that it can be seen at the greatest distance through the water, or if someone has done the tests the answer is firmly under military lock and key. Seeing through water and seeing through a slight haze on land are optically very similar problems. On land it is known that a coloured object loses the appearance of colour before it gets too far away to see; I should expect that the same is true underwater. Objects that show up very bright or very dark against their background are those that can be seen furthest off (this has been tested). This is because the contrast is very high to begin with and contrast, whatever the value, decreases at the same rate as the sighting distance increases. The strongest contrast that one can have without actually using artificial lights is a big bold pattern of black and white. This is what the Sergeant Majors have and very effective it is. Bold black-and-white patterns always show up well at a distance and it does not matter what colour the water is, nor what is looking at them (television and lobsters included) nor does it depend on the direction of sight.

I remember being greatly struck by the colours of one of those Scandinavian charts of the different freshwater fishes. There seemed to be so much red splashed around that it looked like a printer's error. But on closer study—I was waiting to be served in one of those superior fish-and-chip shops with the superior languid service—it seemed that the charts did have the correct colours and that there really are a lot of freshwater fishes with red on them. There is for instance the red belly of the stickleback and the char and the red fins of the perch, all of which get brighter in colour at the breeding time. Yet in the ideal blue waters of the Mediterranean or on a coral reef there are no red colours or at least the human eye cannot see them and there is no reason to think that the fishes can do much better. There are many fishes that look grey below 60 feet or so but when shot and brought up to the surface are revealed as bright red. Perhaps the red on freshwater fishes simply doesn't show up in fresh water either—perhaps it could simply be a side effect of increased hormone activity. But in any case you have to discover if red really can be seen in fresh water before taking refuge in the classic "No apparent use" funk-hole of biology.

For some reason which I cannot now remember I felt I could not possibly put off the experiment any longer one time when I was collecting fishes' eyes from Lake Victoria in Africa. The only suitable thing about the lake is that it contains many cichlid fishes with bright red fins and tails. It also contains a few crocodiles which are more of a terrifying prospect than a real hazard. Less terrifying, but a lot more dangerous is the parasite Bilharzia which bores in through the skin and passes part of its life history inside. In the event I escaped the croco-diles and much more surprisingly the Bilharzia too. (Does Bilharzia only live in the surface waters? It would be interesting to know.)

It took only one dive to convince me, at least, that red does show up quite brilliantly in the green waters of Lake Victoria. But there was one little silvery fish with a yellow tail that was almost invisible even at arm's length a fathom beneath the surface. Yellow seems to lose all colour under these conditions and it is true there are very few freshwater fishes with yellow markings.

Why should yellow show up in the clear blue sea when it looks a pale grey in the green of inland waters? And why should red be so conspicuously red in fresh waters when it looks no different from black in the limpid Mediterranean? Many people just deny that it is true and solve the problem that way. Others retort that no one knows what colours fishes can see so why bother.

However, there is an explanation and it applies equally well to fishes as to man and it all hinges on the fact that inshore and inland water is green but clear tropical waters are blue. The kind of ocean water where one diver can see another 100 feet away is much clearer than commercial distilled water—it is even clearer than most double-distilled water. It is blue because of the transmitting properties of the water molecule itself. It has nothing to do with the salt it contains and precious little to do with the colour of the sky. It is blue because the water absorbs the red and orange rays of the spectrum and leaves the blue and green. Of course, pure water has the same properties wherever it is found, but inshore water is not pure at all for it contains large quantities of dissolved yellow substances that are produced by decaying plants. These yellow substances absorb a lot of blue light but allow the rest to pass. Naturally when a yellow substance is mixed with pure water, the blue light is absorbed by the yellow substance and the orange and red absorbed by the water. Only green remains and that is why most inshore water looks green.

The eye can distinguish six distinct colours in the spectrum: red, orange, yellow, green, blue and violet. But there are only three types of light-sensitive cells in the eye (cones) to receive the light, one type most sensitive to blue, one to green and one to red. The intermediate colours are made by "mixing" the sensations from the three cone types. The sensation of yellow is produced when the red- and green-sensitive cones are stimulated, but the blue-sensitive ones are not. The very narrow yellow band in the spectrum looks yellow because the red-sensitive and green-sensitive cones are stimulated in about equal proportions. The same effect of yellow is produced by simply filtering out the blue short wavelength light from a light source. Again the red- and green-sensitive cones are stimulated and the blue-sensitive cones are not affected.

In nature almost all yellows are of the minus-blue type. This goes equally for metallic gold, yellow flowers and yellow fishes. In the ordinary course of events the only yellow produced by a very narrow band of wavelengths is that of sodium street lights. Under these lights the world is seen in shades of yellow and if there are not other lights present, colours all look the same.

Yellow is not the only colour produced by the cut-off method as shown by Fig. 12. Reds and oranges are almost always made in the same way and it is practically certain that any yellow, orange or red paint will be a cut-off colour. For a colour to show up underwater the cut-off must come in a region of the spectrum where light can penetrate the water. For instance, in the green waters indicated in Fig. 12, only light of wavelengths between about 440 and 640 nm. get down to 18 m. Something that looks blue on the surface absorbs all the light in this range of wavelengths and does not reflect anything. In this relevant range blue behaves in the same way as black and cannot be told from it. The same type of thing happens in the Mediterranean, but this time at rather greater depths the colour that resembles black is red. There must be many divers that have been driven to bubbling madness by the red time-marker painted on to the black finish of a very famous underwater camera. The marker literally becomes invisible below about

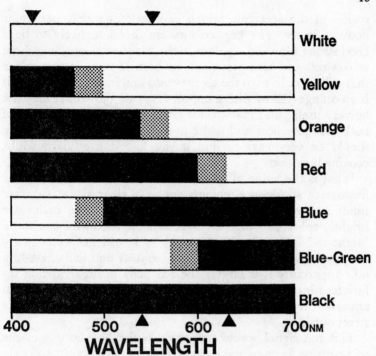

Fig. 12. The colours which result when certain regions of the spectrum are absorbed (black areas) are shown here. The stippled areas are those where the absorption varies rapidly with wavelength. The triangular markers at the top and bottom of the diagram delimit the spectral region where 90 per cent of the daylight incident at the water's surface is absorbed, at 80 m. in oceanic water (top markers) and at 18 m. in coastal water (bottom markers).

120 feet. I suppose it doesn't matter too much because my experience is that the camera in question tends to jam beneath 150 feet anyway.

In this same way something painted blue-green will look no different from something painted white if the water is blue; and a yellow object will look like a white one in green inshore water. The objects that will show up as different in colour to the water background are those where the cut-off comes in the region of the spectrum which can penetrate that particular body of water. The best colours are therefore likely to be a good strong blue and a yellow in the Mediterranean, in inshore waters red and blue-green will be best. If there is any colour that will work in both the clear oceans and in the green lakes, it is an orange-yellow with a cut-off at about 550 nm. It may not be very useful information but given the excellent visibility of both orange-yellow and white in all types of water a fried egg should be very easy to find if you lose it overboard whilst cooking breakfast.

What is the value of all this to a fish? Sometimes, as in the freshwater stickleback, colours act as a clear signal to other fishes in their courtship and breeding. Only the males are brightly coloured with a blue-green circle round the eye and a bright red belly. One male stickleback will get exceedingly stroppy when a rival males comes too near and will chase him off. Apparently it is largely the red belly of his rival that infuriates him. There is even a report of male sticklebacks in an aquarium trying to drive off red post-office vans passing in the street outside.

This red signal would not work in the blue waters of the warmer seas for there red looks no different from black and pale red will look like pale black. Pale black is another name for grey which is very hard to see in any kind of water. Fishes like the red snappers do not look red at all when seen beneath 50 feet or so, indeed they look about the same colour as the water. In the clear blue of tropical seas yellow is a most conspicuous colour and the reason why some sociable fishes like the Angel Fish have bright yellow fins may be to enable them to recognize their kin.

Colour photographs taken without the benefit of flash in even shallow water tend to disappoint the inexperienced for the remembered variety of colours is lost in an over-all cast of blue or green. This is not the fault of the film or even the processing. The camera has in fact recorded the colours in their various proportions quite accurately. The human eye on the other hand having a highly sophisticated design compensates for the low quantities of red and the high quantities of blue by becoming differentially more sensitive to red and less sensitive to blue. The camera film cannot do this automatically and some device such as a filter that reduces the blue, or an extra red-sensitive emulsion must be used. Sadly for underwater photographers their requirements have scant economic importance and it is just not worth the while of photographic manufacturers to make the ideal emulsions that will give results similar to those seen by the human eye.

Fluorescent colours stand out like neon lights under water at least when they are seen close to. This is because the pigments used in them have the property of absorbing short-wave blue light and re-emitting it as longer-wave green, yellow-green, orange or red light. Orange and red fluorescent colours are particularly vivid for they stand out in startling contrast to the surrounding blues and greens. Moreover the eye has got extra sensitive to oranges and reds in an "effort" to detect them in the small quantities that they are naturally present. In a sense then fluorescent hues have actually been made under water and they are quite distinct from anything else in sight. Nevertheless it is a mistake to think that they necessarily show up at a great distance through the water for the water still absorbs the red light they emit and a brilliant red fluorescent diving suit or marker may look a drab blackish-brown at the limits of vision.

The fishes do not possess the ability to make true fluorescent colours or at any rate do not use them despite the brilliance of many tropical forms, although bioluminescence is commonly used by the deep living forms. Fluorescent pigments are found in some corals and sea anemones and once a diver has got his "eye in" for these colours they are easy enough to detect. In Britain the Devonshire Cup Coral is very frequently fluorescent, some being green and some red. There seems to be no other difference between fluorescent red, fluorescent green and non-fluorescent white individuals and no one has been able to think of a convincing reason why it should benefit them to be fluorescent. Perhaps there is no benefit and the fluorescent pigments are simply waste products dumped in the outer layers of the animal where they will be out of the way (that funk-hole again!). My own inclination is to feel that anything so pretty must have a use and that the tiny plankton animals being attracted by light, are lured into the sticky tentacles of the coral polyp and are eaten—a kind of coloured siren call!

It is very important from the practical diving point of view to know which colours show up well underwater. For instance the standard grey of the British compressed air cylinder is about the most invisible colour known to man. I wonder how many people might have been found if only their bottles were painted a conspicuous white. Unhappily, it is not yet possible to paint aqualung cylinders the best colour to show up underwater for the familiar grey with the black-and-white quartering is the colour laid down by the Board of Trade for cylinders containing compressed air. The Continental yellow colour is certainly preferable to our grey especially in the blue Mediterranean waters. In our own green or yellow-green water the yellow cylinders will appear a greyish-white and will be quite difficult to see.

Fluorescent colours are a possibility for good visibility but the best colour again depends on the type of water in which they are used and fluorescent colours are not particularly visible at a distance—certainly no better than white. Nor should it be forgotten that many of the really serious incidents of lost divers happen in deep, dirty water where there is no colour vision anyway and there the brighter the object the better will it be seen. Red and orange appear rather dark to the dark-adapted eye and the best colour would be a blue-green which is a colour not very successfully produced by fluorescent paints.

Of course divers do not always—or even mostly—get lost underwater but arrive unseen at the surface and may have to wait there for an uncomfortably or even dangerously long time before they are seen. White is not the best colour here for it resembles a seagull or the white horses on the sea. The best colour is almost certainly a fluorescent orange and to my mind there is no doubt that divers should wear fluorescent orange hoods. In this I am only following a generally held opinion and I believe fluorescent material for hoods is now available. So far as underwater equipment goes, especially the bottles, the best advice I can give is "Paint it White".

WAS THIS THE STONE THEY USED IN THE KILLING OF SAN FELIU?

by Kendall McDonald

It seemed a simple archaeological find—a millstone jammed in
the cleft of a rock underwater on Spain's Costa Brava. But when
you start to examine the history of the area, you may find that
even such a simple find can stir up the past—and emotions.

"I saw a Roman millstone in Vigueta when we were diving
there this morning." As soon as I had said it, I was uncertain
about it. Had I really seen any such thing? And if I had seen it
why hadn't I said anything about it until now?

I felt exactly the same way as I do sometimes after surfacing
from a dive and trying at once to check how long we've been
down. The mark on the bezel of my diving watch tells me
exactly the time we started the dive and all I've got to do is to
count off the number of minutes to surfacing. It should be
simple, but it seems to turn into a complicated piece of mathe-
matics. If you've had the same experience you'll know exactly
what I'm talking about—if you haven't . . . well, forget it,
you'll never quite understand what I mean.

Anyway, in that little bar off the Ramblas in San Feliu de
Guixols on the Costa Brava of Spain, it was hardly likely that I
was suffering from surfacing problems—unless it was from the
fumes of the brandy we were drinking.

"Have another drink," said Robin Messent, "we'll go and
find it tomorrow." From the way that he said it I was left in no
doubt about the strength he placed on my underwater eye-
sight.

At any other time I'd probably have qualified the statement
by saying that I thought I'd seen something like a millstone,
but the brandy was beginning to talk—and despite my own
doubts—I pressed on. "I'll take you right to it tomorrow

153

morning," I said defiantly. And then we went on drinking and talking about the diving generally. But I was committed and I knew it.

San Feliu has always been a centre for diving on the Costa Brava. It was one of the first places to have an adequate compressor—all gleaming brass and spotless. And now it has a well-maintained decompression chamber too. Many British divers have had their first experiences of Mediterranean diving from the rocks there or from one of the diving boats that leave its busy little harbour every day during the holiday season.

Some of the finest Spanish divers—and spearfishermen—learnt their craft from San Feliu. They and many British divers learnt a lot from people like Pat Harrison, who ran a diving school in the town, and Luis Villa, whose diving boat still leaves the little port each day packed with divers of all nationalities.

I personally owe a lot to San Feliu. It was the ideal place to stay in the early days when good sources of air were few and far between. I owe a lot to Pat Harrison, who gave me back my nerve after it was shattered by something terribly like claustrophobia in a tiny cave 100 feet down off those red cliffs close by the town.

And in even earlier days when such things as aqualungs were unknown there, it was my Spanish friends in the town, headed by Francisco Castello, who taught me about the fish of the Mediterranean—which fish you would find under this kind of rock or that and where the great old groupers lived. But that was long ago and though I have retained my friends, the grouper, alas, has now become a rare, if still splendid, sight.

It was from San Feliu that I went diving for the blood-red coral (before such treasure-hunting was forbidden) and it was on such an expedition that I learnt the importance of wearing a lifejacket and how long you had to wait in the water if the engine on the boat failed—and that you should never go diving without your friends.

It was at San Feliu that I first saw the bends in action and it was after a nightmare drive to Barcelona that I first saw the bends being treated.

Yes, I learned a lot about diving in San Feliu and I learned a lot about people too. I remember the old Murla Hotel (and the new magnificent Murla Park) and the tolerance of Ramon and

Pearl Murla when we would sit up half the night in the bar and when pieces of a demand valve all over a table would make it impossible for Florenzio Planes to clear away the mess as he would obviously have loved to. I remember the huge pinna shells and the oysters and the great fish we had speared and the way everything would be passed across the bar for Ramon's approval. And the way Josef Murla would cook what seemed possible to cook. And the way that nobody complained.

So you will see that San Feliu holds a firm place in my personal history of diving. When in Spain I now stay at the superb Aigua Blava hotel run by the ever-smiling Olympic swimmer and man of the world Xiquet Sabater, but every now and then I go back to San Feliu. And each time the memories come flooding back . . .

From my little Spanish fishing boat *Penelope*, the great rose-red cliffs of San Elmo echoed back the thump-thump of the engine. I headed her through the little channel between the mainland and Freu Island that brings the hotel, swimming pool, and flats of the bay into view. It would be nice to be able to say that I thought the flags of all nations flying from the poolside of Port Salvi impressed me, but in truth I hardly noticed them, I was more concerned with getting around the point and running down the headland between Sa Dolitx Island into the calm of San Telmo Cove and Vigueta Bay. For it was here that my words of the night before would be tested. And, to be honest, I feared they would be found wanting one millstone.

I tried desperately to remember exactly where we had anchored the day before. I had the impression that fairly close in to the sheer cliffs a reef of rock ran outwards underwater to the west. It was not connected to the cliff; a stretch of pure sand lay between it and the mainland. In the end—it would not do under Robin's scornful eye to hesitate too much—I heaved the anchor over in what I thought was about the right place. It wouldn't do either to give the impression that I was by any means convinced that such a millstone existed. But somewhere back in my sub-conscious I felt I had seen something.

I think divers will know what I mean about seeing something and not really doing anything about it. All of us in our early days of diving have seen things, or thought we saw them, and have turned back later and not found them. But this was different. I had the distinct impression that I had seen something—indeed under the influence of brandy a door in my mind had popped open and I had said firmly that I had seen it. But once again the same question nagged at me: why hadn't I said something about it immediately after the dive? Why wait until the evening? Why not alert the other divers, Robin and my wife, Penny, when we were actually down there?

I have no answer. I can only tell you that when I heaved the anchor over and watched the bubbles come up and the dark shape sink down on to the equally dark shape of some underwater rocks, I had little confidence in finding anything—let alone a millstone. Surely if I had seen such a thing underwater I would have investigated it? I mean you just don't swim by a curved shape like a stone motor-tyre and say to yourself— "that's a Roman millstone"—and do nothing about it. Or do you? If what I had said the other night was true, then I had. It sounds absolutely ridiculous—particularly as I have always had a great interest in underwater archaeology. In fact at one time finding an ancient amphora was my greatest ambition.

So you can see that it was without the slightest confidence that I kitted up and led the way down into the 100-foot clarity. The fact that you could see all that way did not increase my unease. But once I saw the reef—it was more like a gigantic city wall of whitish stone—all my doubts vanished. Confidence flooded through me. I swam along the seaward side. And there, as though in a dream, it was.

Imagine a flat car tyre coated in cement. Then imagine it jammed into a cleft in a wall of rock. In the sunshine which streamed down through the water in obvious bars of light, the "tyre" stood out from the green, thin eel-grass which climbed over the rock around the cleft. White and obviously curved, the thing in the cleft was impossible to mistake for anything else but something man-made.

I pointed it out to Robin and Penny with what I hoped was a "there-you-are-I-told-you-so" underwater signal. And then I got hold of my millstone and pulled—and pulled. For some reason I expected it to come clean away in my hands, but heave as I might—even with a flipper braced against the rock either side of it—I could make no impression. Looking closely, despite the murk I had stirred up around it, I could see that the stone was firmly "concreted" to the rock on either side of the cleft. But it wasn't firmly enough attached to the rock to resist chipping with a diving knife. I don't think that I was even then completely certain that this was a millstone until I was able to make sure that my stone had a hole right through the middle. Then it was only a matter of threading a rope through the centre hole and heaving from the boat until it came free with a rush.

When the stone broke surface it lost its pale underwater colour and glowed and gleamed rose-pink from the growths that covered it. Once on the *Penelope*'s deck the millstone gained weight that it had never had underwater and you needed two hands and a good deal of back muscle to move it around.

The stone was about a foot across and about 5 inches deep. Where the handle had been was just a broken-sided hole. It seemed clear that the millstone had been broken away at the handle before entering the water and for this reason I remembered some articles I had been reading about archaeological finds underwater in other parts of the Mediterranean. These reports suggested that ships of ancient times, when faced with head-winds, would often shelter behind suitable headlands and wait for the wind to blow itself out. During these waiting periods the crew would use the calm of the sheltering spot as an opportunity to clean up their ship. Broken equipment and damaged cargo would be heaved overboard and sound cargo repacked to avoid further breakages.

Was that how my stone had got into the water? Or had it broken on land and been used as an anchor until it finally jammed in the cleft some 40 feet below the boat in which we now sat? After waiting for a short while to rest and to let the muck we had stirred up in freeing the millstone settle, I dived again. If this had been an area for clearing up ancient ships, there might well be other remains on the bottom. I examined the area from which we had pulled the stone very carefully, but there was nothing there. Any other dumped gear would be most likely to have sunk into the seabed of sand at the foot of the rock "wall". However, on a nearby rock I did find one small piece of pottery—it looked like part of an amphora—cemented to the almost smooth surface. There was nothing else.

I surfaced to find a boat load of divers circling the *Penelope*. At the helm was Luis Villa. Robin held up the millstone to show him. "Concreto," shouted Villa and grinned. I looked at the millstone and suddenly had doubts. Was it just a piece of modern concrete that had been used as an anchor by one of San Feliu's fishing boats? It couldn't be. Or could it?

Back in harbour, we moored up and heaved the millstone into the back of the car. Then back to the Murla for what I felt was a well-earned drink or two before a three o'clock lunch. Once in the cool front bar we showed the millstone—like everything else we brought up from the sea—to Ramon Murla. He said it was very like the millstones they still used up in the interior of Catalonia. Smaller of course, but the same style.

This I found not very comforting. It came as something of a shock to know that this type of millstone was still used not very far away from where we had made our find. "Someone said that it was modern concrete," I said gloomily. And had another iced beer. My gloom did not last long, however, for a voice from one of the few tables still occupied at that late lunch hour said: "Querns are not my subject, young man, but I think you can take it that there is nothing modern about that. My guess is that it is very, very old indeed." I cheered up no end. Especially when we found that the owner of the voice was an English archaeologist on holiday—but as he said, querns were not his subject.

This was the first time that I was to hear my millstone referred to as a "quern", but experts later were to call it nothing else. But opinions on my quern were not to end there. A local dropping into the bar for a drink regarded the stone for some time in silence and then spoke to Ramon in Catalan. The answer appeared to excite him. "San Feliu!" he exclaimed loudly. Soon a small crowd gathered around the stone, but now I wanted my lunch and I removed the stone to the boot of the car.

If my removal of the stone from the chattering group seemed a bit abrupt, it was because I was also getting a bit uneasy about the attitude taken by the locals who had collected round it. My Spanish is appalling; my Catalan even worse, but it was clear that some of those present regarded the find as something more than just a minor archaeological discovery. They began to look upon it as a religious relic—and someone there who could speak reasonable Spanish said that they were saying that Saint Feliu was martyred by having a millstone tied about his neck and flung from a cliff into the sea. My millstone seemed to have all the right circumstances to make it *the* millstone involved!

Over lunch I raised all the objections possible to this being so. The millstone was found some way out from the nearest cliff and surely no stone of that weight would have floated. The counter to this was that local legend had it that Saint Feliu had floated for a while to prove that he was a worker of miracles, but, to punish the mob for their sin, had finally sunk.

However, my fears about the likely effect of this discovery were groundless. No one raised the matter again and the stone stayed undisturbed in the boot of my car. And, at the end of my holiday, the stone travelled with me back to London. On my return I contacted Joan du Plat Taylor, who was busy forming the Committee for Nautical Archaeology which was dedicated to ensuring that the finds of amateur divers were properly recorded, and that archaeologidal work by such divers was guided away from the looting of wrecks into proper excavation techniques.

I was sure, and still am, that this is the right way for amateur divers to be guided—and if all divers were to follow the Committee's guidance a lot of the wild stories of divers looting precious ancient wrecks would disappear like the expired air a lot of them are.

The Committee have produced a report form for divers to fill in on the discovery of a wreck or other marine antiquity. I filled in the answers to the questions on the form like this:

1. Kendall McDonald, 4 Pytchley Crescent, Upper Norwood, London, S.E.19. LIVingstone 1823. Work: FLEet Street 6000.

2. B.S–A.C. (Bromley Branch).

3. Millstone. Isolated find.

4. San Telmo Cove, San Feliu de Guixols, Costa Brava, Spain (known locally as Vigueta Bay).

5. See chart tracing. Spot marked "A".

6. Well-weeded rock interspersed with large sand areas at 20 feet. Then rock falls steeply for 10 feet. It levels for short (6 feet) strip before falling again to 40 feet where flat sand sea-bed

slopes almost imperceptibly for some distance before falling to 100 feet plus.

7. Depth of find: approx. 37 feet.

8. Millstone was jammed into rock fault in second steep fall described above. Only part of the side of the stone was showing. Top part covered with 4–6 inches of sand with weed growing from it. Stone was so firmly jammed that it required sand to be cleared, growth to rock broken away and then rope reeved through centre hole and "cranked" from boat before it came free.

9. Stone measures 13 inches in diameter. It is roughly circular. Centre hole measures 2¾ inches in diameter. Thickness at exterior approx. 4 inches. Thickness at centre hole approx. 1½ inches.

10. This is a millstone. It is made of sandstone or pumice. Has inclined planes from centre hole to outer edge on both sides. In the outer edge there is another depression that appears to have been a hole (for handle?). One side of this is broken away and appears to have been in that condition for some considerable time.

11. Attached are reports on discoveries in the same area— and there have, of course, been many more by Spanish divers. This isolated find (i.e. the millstone) had one small piece of amphora near it. This small 6-inch wide piece was very thin (¼ inch) and was cemented by growth to a rock about 30 feet away, but there are no traces of anything in the immediate area that I could discover. The shallow depth and many sandy areas would make any further finds a matter of chance. In my opinion the millstone was either used as an anchor, or was thrown overboard while a ship was sheltering from NE. winds which often occur in the area. Waters in this particular area are extremely sheltered and diving conditions (visibility, etc.) are as near perfect as possible. Prevailing wind is from NE. with sometimes abrupt and strong winds from SE.

That was my report. Not a model of accuracy I fear but it was received by the Committee, as is every report from a diver, with great enthusiasm. Could I show them the quern? Yes, I could and did. Sometime later I received the following report from Joan Taylor. The archaeologists had been at work. Their report put mine to shame, but I was glad to have it. And the drawings which came too. It read:

Some of the recoveries from the wreck on Thunder Rock. *Above*, nearly a ton of ingots recovered from the sea. Each ingot is 2 ft. 9½ in. long and 6½ in. wide. *Below*, elephant tusks from the sea. All are discoloured, some nearly blackened by their long stay in the sea. The diving knife is 9 ins. long and gives an idea of the size of these ivory tusks. (See chapter 11)

An artist's impression of the Sealab Project. The support ship, *Elk River*, is anchored in position over Sealab. The artist has, of course, shortened the depth for the purposes of his drawing. Sealab is, in fact, 600 feet below the ship. (See chapter 12)

"Querns have not received a great deal of attention, particularly on the Continent and in the Middle East where there is so much material of a more spectacular nature to study. What little work has been done is difficult to trace and some of it inadequately illustrated. But more attention has been paid to British querns and there are two articles by E. C. Curwen (in *Antiquity*, Vol. XI, No. 43, 1937, and *Antiquity*, Vol XV, No. 57, 1941) giving particulars of the different types of rotary querns found in this country and discussing their probable origins.

"Although most, if not all, the Iron Age querns were made locally, the rotary quern was not invented in Britain, and the model for a local type must be sought in the more advanced lands bordering the Mediterranean. Changes in details of manufacture took place at various stages, but on the whole, people seem to have been conservative about the models they liked or were used to, and it should be possible by tracing certain features in various areas to show the cultural or trade connections between them.

"Probably the most important diagnostic feature is the angle of the grinding surface. Some querns have quite flat, or almost flat, grinding surfaces, while others have their grinding surface inclined at a fairly steep angle towards the centre, so that the lower stone on which they turned would have an upper surface in the form of a low cone. Both types are found in Britain, but very seldom in the same areas. Those with flat grinding surfaces come mainly from the east Midlands and north, and querns with similar grinding surfaces (although not always identical in other features) are also found in Europe north of the Alps, and would seem to have arrived via northern Gaul— although there is not yet enough evidence to show the exact route.

"This quern, however, has a grinding surface with an angle of 16°, and such querns are also found in South-Western and Southern England. There is an illustration in *Antiquity*, Vol. XI, of a quern from Fifield Bavant of very similar type, and it has been suggested in the past that this type may have come to Britain via the Mediterranean. The present find may represent a step on the way, either as a product of the ancestors of immigrants into Britain, or of peoples trading via Spain and Southern

France with Britain. Of course, it should also lead us back to-wards the original source of the type.

"To trace its history, other querns are needed; but for its own source, it would be necessary to know where the raw material was found. It may have been of local manufacture, and the stone have been quarried in the neighbourhood, or it may have been brought from overseas. Without a thin section of the stone an exact identification cannot be made. From surface observa-tion it appears to be a coarse quartzite grit, probably in a cal-careous matrix. When the raw material has been identified the normal procedure is to consult an expert in the geology of the region to discover the whereabouts and extent of the deposits of the rock.

"Apart from the angle of the grinding surface there are other features which may vary and may help in deciding to what type a quern belongs. The central aperture, or feed pipe, through which the grain and the spindle pin pass, may be circular (as in this case) or oval; or circular with small pro-jections at the side to hold the 'rynd'—a wooden bar which connects with the spindle and prevents too much grain passing at a time when the hole is wide (as in this case, where it is $2\frac{1}{2}$ inches in diameter), or it may be narrow, in which case there would by no rynd and the spindle pin probably quite short and often of iron. The top surface may be flat or dished, forming a 'hopper' for the grain (as it is in this instance).

"The encrustation of the quern makes exact description of the surface hazardous, but the hopper appears to have had a rim of about $\frac{1}{2}$ inch wide round the outer edge. The position and depth of the handle hole or holes (some querns have two handles) is also interesting. In this case the handle hole is broken and eroded at the edges, so that its diameter cannot be estimated, and the blocking of concreted pebbles prevent exact measurement of its depth. The concretions would be difficult to remove if the matrix of the rock is calcareous; as the acid used to dissolve the calcareous encrustation would tend to dissolve the quern. However, it is possible to estimate the depth of the handle and to observe that it does not, as in some types, penetrate to the feed pipe or hopper.

"For archaeological purposes, in order to be able to make comparisons with other examples, as many measurements as possible are desirable, in addition to photographs and a section drawing.

"The archaeological description of this quern may be set out as follows:

Material: coarse quartzite grit in a (probably) calcareous matrix.

(a)	Diameter of upper surface (horizontal)	$11\frac{1}{2}$ ins.
(b)	Width of rim	$\frac{1}{2}$–$\frac{3}{4}$ ins.
(c)	Depth of dishing of upper surface (from summit of rim to top of feedpipe)	$1\frac{1}{2}$ ins.
(d)	Diameter of grinding surface (horizontal)	$12\frac{1}{2}$ ins.
(e)	Diameter of feedpipe	$2\frac{1}{2}$ ins.
(f)	Height of feedpipe above base	$1\frac{3}{8}$ ins.
(g)	Height of handle hole above base	$1\frac{3}{8}$ ins.
(h)	Depth of handle hole (as measurable)	3 ins.
(j)	Width of handle hole (broken and eroded)	$2\frac{1}{4}$ ins.
(k)	Height of quern (vertical)	$4\frac{1}{4}$ ins.
(l)	Angle of grinding surface	$16°$

"These measurements are all, of necessity, approximate, owing to encrustation and erosion of the quern during submergence. The break at the handle-hole probably took place in antiquity prior to the deposit of the quern on the sea-bed and may well have been the cause of its being discarded. There is no evidence of any attempt at making a new handle hole to prolong the quern's working life."

The archaeologists would like to know more about querns. So any diver who finds one is asked to supply the following information:

Information required in the identification of quern types (upper stones) . . . raw material, if possible.

The diameter of the upper and lower (grinding) surfaces.

The height of the quern—maximum and minimum if there appears to be an appreciable difference at opposite sides.

The diameter of the central aperture (or feed pipe).

The vertical depth of the feed pipe opening below the upper rim and its height above base (outer edge, thereof).

The height of the handle hole or holes above base and their dimensions—diameter of hole and depth of penetration into the quern, or of groove for handle.

Whether there is a rim round the outer edge of the upper surface and whether the upper surface is dished to form a "hopper".

The angle of the grinding surface, taken from the outer edge, by placing the quern upside down with a horizontal bar across it and taking the angle between that and the grinding surface, if this is in the form of an inverted cone.

The angle of the grinding surface is of great importance, as a major division in quern types lies between those with a flat grinding surface or one inclined to a low angle, of about 5°, and those with an angle of 15–20° or more.

A photograph and a section drawing.

I am sure that divers will help. But the suggestion that my millstone, sorry, quern, was the one which drowned Saint Feliu still worried me. Could I really be in possession of a religious relic? The obvious thing to do was to find out more about the patron saint of the capital of the Costa Brava. To do this, in England, is easier thought of than done. However, I was lucky enough to mention my problem to John Robbins, who is Features Editor of the London *Evening News*. "I know the very man to help you," said John, "he only lives a little way from me in Sevenoaks . . ." And so he put me in touch with Harold Whitehead, who is an Assistant Keeper in charge of the Rare Spanish Books at the British Museum.

Harold Whitehead can not only speak fluent modern Spanish —he can read ancient texts in old Spanish documents with similar ease. And this, after some research, is what he found:

"San Feliu is otherwise known as San Felix Africano. The Apostle of Gerona, he came from Africa with San Cucufate. He is venerated as the principal apostle of Gerona. He suffered many torments—including being thrown into the sea (at Guixols)—and was finally bled to death with hooks.

"There are no precise dates, but it happened at the beginning of the 4th century. His feast day is 1 August and his attributes are given (in J. F. Roig's 'Iconografia de los Santos', Barcelona, 1959) as Martyr's palm, book of the Gospels, millstone and rake.

"A lengthy account of his life is given in Dorca (Francisco), ('Coleccion de noticias para la historia de los Santos Martires de Gerona', Barcelona, 1807?), but I have not been able to find an account of a millstone having been tied to his neck.

"The following is the relevant part of Dorca: 'On the following morning, he (San Felix) was taken to the heathen altars, in order to make obeisance there. Nothing they could do would cause him to submit, so his body was scraped with iron hooks, he was hung head downwards from the hour of terce until darkness, and gave no sign of pain . . . Rufino . . . then ordered him to be tied and thrown into the sea. But his hands were untied by angels, who helped him to walk over the sea towards the land, Rufino ordered him once again to be torn to the bone with iron hooks and thus his life ended.'

"In an appendix, Dorca says: 'With reference to the Saint's having been thrown into the sea, he is sometimes depicted with a millstone round his neck. This idea may have come from the Gospels (St. Matthew, 18, 6; St. Mark, 9, 42), although it is not mentioned in any of the early histories of the Martyr. But since all accounts agree that he was thrown into the sea in order to sink and drown, he is shown in this manner (i.e. with the millstone) in order to emphasize this aspect of his martyrdom. Through this method of representing the Saint, some writers have become accustomed to refer to this particular circumstance, which, however, is of little importance'."

Little importance! Of course it isn't—until you happen to be in possession of a millstone found underwater close to the highest cliffs to the town from which Saint Feliu was taken to be thrown into the sea!

It would be nice to be able to round off this story by producing some conclusive proof one way or the other. But in archaeology and real life it just doesn't happen like that. All I can add is to say that if you want to see the millstone that we found, then you should go to the little museum in the town of San Feliu de Guixols.

You see I took it back to the place that it really belongs.

YOU TOO CAN BUILD A SUBMARINE IN YOUR LIVING ROOM

by George Cooke

A former National Equipment Officer of the British Sub-Aqua
Club, George Cooke was used to dealing with mechanical
things. Then he decided to go one better than the Americans
and build his own submarine—at home. An electronics
engineer, he is President of Reading Branch of the B.S-A.C.

IT WAS a picture in an American magazine that started it all. A
Minisub it was called—a type of submarine which filled with
water and carried divers about.

Diving is a strenuous business at the best of times, I reasoned,
and an underwater car like that would take most of the effort
out of it and allow one to stay down longer and cover more
ground.

The Minisub was made of resinglass. Unfortunately, I had
no suitable space nor conditions for doing such work at home.
But I was determined to build myself a free-flooding or "wet"
sub so the design had to be simplified. After drawing many
basic hulls, the easiest form of construction which would produce a reasonably streamlined craft appeared to be a wooden
frame covered with aluminium sheets. This would not involve
the use of special tools and techniques. The hull shape finally
took the form of a canoe with a pointed bow and stern. It was
designed to carry one diver.

The next problem was to find information on the various
mechanical systems such as trim tanks, motors and controls.
After searching various libraries it became obvious that there
was no information available on the technical aspects of free-
flooding submarine construction. All the design work would
have to be done from basic principles. So many months of
"spare" time were spent in designing the vital components.

Further calculations were required to ensure that the sub would remain the right way up and would respond correctly to the operation of the trim tank pumps, motor switches and steering controls.

The next question was "Where to build it?" My loft workshop was large enough but I should not be able to get the finished article out through the trap door. I had heard of people building aircraft in their lofts and knocking down the end wall to get them out, but that didn't appeal to me. My front room was temporarily empty, awaiting decoration, so that was where I decided to "lay the keel".

The dimensions of the sub were chosen to make the most economical use of the standard 8 ft. × 4 ft. sheets of aluminium. In order to satisfy this requirement the frame had to be nominally eight feet in length with the centre section two feet square. To avoid difficulties in transporting the craft, I decided to make the hull in two equal sections. These were bolted together at the four corners with stainless steel bolts and "penny" washers.

This arrangement meant that I could carry the sub in a Minivan by mounting the lighter, after-section on the roof rack and the forward section, containing the batteries, inside. The frame was constructed of Parana pine, which is very easy to work and is virtually knot-free. The stringers were $1\frac{1}{2}$ in. × 1 in., supported at bow, centre and stern by pieces 2 ft. × 3 in. × 3 in. Simple half-lap joints were used, using waterproof glue and brass screws. The natural curves on the eight stringers were achieved by saw-kerfing the parts where the bend was maximum to a depth of about half an inch and filling the slots with glue. After screwing one end of the stringer to the centre section it could then be bent around the intermediate frame and glued and screwed to the stem post.

This method achieved a natural-looking curve, giving a canoe-like shape. The stem post was fixed so that its narrow edge was leading but the stern post was arranged transversely so that the motor shaft could be mounted to pass through it. Then the finished frame was given three coats of clear household varnish.

The aluminium sheet arrived at my house in the form of two 8 ft. × 4 ft. sheets of 20 s.w.g. Each sheet was then cut in half lengthwise. One of the resulting pieces 8 ft. × 2 ft. was screwed to the foresection and wrapped round the bow, thus covering both sides in a single sheet. The after section sides were covered with two separate pieces 4 ft. × 2 ft. Brass countersunk screws were used to fix the aluminium to the wooden frame. A dab of lanolin under each screw helps to prevent the electrolytic action of water on the junction between the two dissimilar metals from causing corrosion.

The top and bottom covers were cut from aluminium sheet after having marked them out by using the frame itself as a template. The top cover of the forward section was made removable to allow access to the air cylinder, batteries and sliding weight. All the aluminium sheet was cut with a pair of tinsnips. The upper rear half of the frame was left uncovered in order to leave a cockpit space. Before being finally fitted the aluminium sheets were sprayed by means of a home-made spray gun operated by a vacuum cleaner.

The inside was sprayed grey and the outside with a grey undercoat and yellow top coat of cellulose paint. Several coats were needed to acquire the right colour density.

Having constructed the basic hull the next thing to do was to fit the main tank system. The tank was made from the 20 s.w.g. aluminium sheet and consisted of three compartments. The metal was folded so as to produce a box about 23 in. × 8 in. × 8 in. The ends and compartment walls were hand-riveted; each rivet sealed with a sealing compound. The two outer compartments were open at the bottom where a circular hole was cut in each. Into these holes were led the copper air pipes from an air cylinder fitted in the bow. An intermediate cock allows the air to be turned on and off for blowing the tanks.

When the vessel is launched the air trapped in the main tanks gives it buoyancy while on the surface. After a dive, on surfacing, the water is blown out of the tanks to maintain the craft on the surface.

The centre section of the tank is the trim tank. This is used for final buoyancy adjustment under water. Air from a diver's demand valve mounted just in front of the tank is fed into the top of this tank so that the air inside it is always at the pressure of the surrounding water. If this were not done the thin walls of the tank would collapse inward at a relatively shallow depth.

Two pipes enter the bottom of the trim tank. Each pipe leads to a hand-operated pump simply made from one-inch diameter brass tubing and odd pieces of brass rod. Discs cut from cycle inner tube rubber are used for the valve flaps. One pump empties the trim tank of water and the other one fills it, thereby enabling the driver of the sub to adjust its buoyancy to neutral so that it neither rises nor sinks when under water with the power off.

The air supply for the buoyancy system is contained in a 26 cu. ft. cylinder which is clamped in position in the bow. This is enough air for several dives. Because the tanks are small very little air is used, especially in the trim tank. Each tank compartment contains about one-third of a cubic foot thus giving a buoyancy, when full of air, of twenty-one pounds.

The craft will lose buoyancy as it dives deeper for two reasons. Firstly, the air in the trim tank will become denser as the demand valve restores the pressure equilibrium and, secondly, the diver's rubber suit will compress, causing him to displace less water and thereby become heavier. If a dry suit is worn with a suit inflation air supply then this loss of buoyancy can be compensated for. The overall buoyancy change is slight though, and can easily be compensated for by adjusting the trim tank contents by means of the pump which ejects water.

After initial tests it was found that the after section of the sub lay partly under water when surfaced. This was caused by the weight of the driver's head and shoulders. In order to achieve a horizontal position a stern tank was fitted. This has its own vent and blow controls, the same as the main tanks have.

The fitting of the stern tank resulted in a secondary advantage which was not foreseen. It enabled the sub to be driven underwater sooner by keeping some buoyancy in the stern tank until the bow was under, Without this facility it had been difficult to get the bow under when running under power on the surface. In order to make the vessel stable vertically, thus preventing an undesirable rolling motion, it was necessary to build in some permanent buoyancy. This was done by using expanded plastic foam at carefully selected positions. A hard grade of foam is desirable, otherwise it compresses with depth and the buoyancy of the craft decreases rapidly in proportion. Having put in the fixed buoyancy material it was then necessary to counteract its effect by adding weights to the lower part, either inside the battery box or just outside it.

This enabled overall ballast to be adjusted by adding or removing weights. The combination of buoyancy and weight produces the necessary righting moment to prevent the vehicle from turning turtle. If the tendency to remain upright is too strong it will hamper the necessary fore-and-aft tilting of the sub for direction control. The right amount of buoyancy and weight should be arrived at by experiment.

The control system first fitted to *Explorer I* (as my first submarine was called) consisted of a stern rudder and hydroplanes. Although the rudder was effective because it was fitted right behind the propellor, the hydroplanes were ineffective owing to the slow speed of the craft. It was then that I decided to install a sliding weight in the fore section. A special thirteen-pound lead weight was cast and a brass lug was set into it for the attachment of a lever. A hole was left through the centre of the cylindrical weight into which was inserted a tube of resin-bonded fibre of three-quarter-inch bore. This tube fitted over an aluminium tube on which it could slide in a fore-and-aft direction. A vertical lever fitted to the cockpit floor in the manner of a joystick operated the sliding weight via a coupling rod fixed to the brass lug on the weight.

The first trial of *Explorer I* took place at Mytchett Lake in Surrey. The two halves of the submarine were bolted together on the shore of the lake. The batteries were then installed and connected and the watertight lid was screwed down. The air was turned on, the pressure checked and the valves tested. I donned my diving gear and launched the craft with the aid of a fellow diver. At first the sub floated high out of the water, canted to one side, then, as the water leaked through the panel joints, it gradually sank until the deck was about two inches above the waterline. This operation aroused the concern of one small boy among the crowd of onlookers at the lakeside, who shouted, "Hey, Mister, your boat's sinkin'!"

At this stage only the main ballast and buoyancy systems were being tested. While I sat quietly in the sub my friend pushed it out into the centre of the lake by finning.

I anxiously vented the main tanks and the craft began to descend on an even keel—but it remained on the surface until enough water had been admitted to the trim tank to make the vessel slightly heavy. Once under water some water was pumped out of the trim tank and neutral buoyancy was achieved. The sub remained level fore-and-aft but tended to roll to one side or the other.

From this exercise it became obvious that greater lateral stability and more permanent buoyancy were needed. At least the sub went down and returned to the surface again and I now had a good guide as to what was required to stabilize the craft. During the second test of the static system the sub behaved perfectly. Stability was excellent, there was no tendency to roll and the trim tank functioned correctly.

The next few months were spent waterproofing the motor and making and installing the battery box and switch. Once more at the lakeside, this time with many Club members to help, *Explorer I* was launched. For the first time the craft moved under her own power. She travelled at about two knots and crossed the lake on the surface.

The underwater trial was fairly satisfactory. Nevertheless, further modifications were carried out. The propeller was moved farther aft on an extended shaft in order to achieve a cleaner flow of water past it. Also, the balance of the rudder was improved since it had tended to lock on one side or the other and was over-balanced.

The lake where the tests were conducted is far from ideal. Its maximum depth is only four metres and its visibility before being stirred up was only about three metres at the very best. After divers had been finning around or the sub had rested on the bottom the viz. fell often to zero. To increase the hazards still further there were several sections of railway line sticking up vertically out of the water, their ends embedded deeply in the lake bottom. These were in a straight line, spaced about six metres apart, and they delineated the Basingstoke Canal which passes across one end of the lake.

I was always afraid I might ram one of these steel posts but in all the tests that I carried out in their vicinity I only saw one underwater on one occasion and I just managed to avoid striking it. No light at all was reflected from the black mud of the lake bottom and the general lack of visibility made it impossible to refer to a reference datum in order to know in what attitude the sub was.

The addition of a simply-made "angle-of-dangle" meter at least gave some idea of the fore-and-aft inclination of the craft. This indicator was combined with the compass gimbals which are operative in the fore-and-aft direction only.

The height of *Explorer I*, including the driver's head, is only three feet or so but by the time we had left the surface we were nearly on the bottom. This allowed very little time to make trim adjustments. If I took my eyes from the depth gauge for a moment I would find the sub embedded in the ooze. Even after blowing the main tanks it was usually a couple of minutes before the vessel could tear itself away from the incredible suction exerted by the clinging mud. Once free of the bottom, of course, it hurtled, accelerating, towards the surface and erupted in a cloud of spray and bubbles.

On the occasion of the fifth test in the, now, very familiar lake, there was a heavy thunderstorm in progress and *Explorer I* left the shore for the open water with lightning flashing all around while the thunder boomed across the ruffled surface of the usually placid lake. The forked lightning even appeared to be striking at the water's edge. It was like being under enemy fire and it was just as spectacular. In spite of the conditions the test was satisfactorily carried out.

A new switch had been fitted which enabled the craft to travel at two knots normal and three knots fast speed while submerged. The three-bladed aluminium propeller pushed the sub along at a faster speed than I had expected in view of the motor power of only about one-fifth of a horse power.

The sliding weight in the bow section tilted the craft ten degrees up or down and, once neutral buoyancy had been achieved, was sufficient to effect climb or dive while under power. Only if neutrally buoyant will the machine go in the intended direction. For example, if it were trimmed positively buoyant then, even if the bow were pointed downward, the craft could still be ascending. In order to overcome the difficulty of knowing whether one was, in fact, travelling in the expected direction, a rate of ascent/descent meter was designed and constructed. This instrument also indicated the correct angle of attack and showed whether the vessel was correctly ballasted, even when ascending or descending.

The first deep-water trial took place at Stoney Cove, the National Diving site of the B.S.A.C. Although there were depths down to forty-one metres, it was deemed wise not to exceed nine metres owing to the fact that the battery box construction was not sufficiently sound to withstand the pressure at a greater depth. A stronger box was made later. This consideration was justified as things turned out. At one stage in the trials the sub was sinking fast and failing to respond to the trim tank controls.

The only thing to do was to take emergency action and blow the main tanks. This I did—my ears throbbing under the increasing pressure which I was too busy to relieve. At about ten metres the downward plunge was halted and she began to ascend. Slowly, at first—and then ever faster! Once on the surface it became apparent that the fore-and-aft trim was impaired and the sliding weight control was having little effect. As I had suspected—the battery box had shipped several pints of water through a cracked seam. The only other incident in an otherwise very successful demonstration occurred while I was repeatedly descending and surfacing for the benefit of press photographers and television news camera men.

During the manœuvres I had forgotten to check my compass direction and I suddenly found myself at four metres depth heading straight towards a brick wall at three knots. I was so surprised by the sight that I "froze" and was unable to take avoiding action. When the crunch came it was not so bad as I had expected and the only damage sustained by *Explorer I* was that the top of her aluminium bow was slightly dented. The visibility was as good as eighteen metres in the cold waters of the Cove and, for the first time, I was able to see the bottom while travelling.

On one occasion I landed the sub on the bottom and then took off under power while doing a climbing turn. The effect was similar to that of flying because now I was able to see the effect of manœuvring the craft. After correct trim has been achieved, keeping an eye on the depth gauge and inclinometer enables corrections in the vertical plane to be made by pushing or pulling the control lever which moves the sliding weight.

Lateral steering is by reference to the compass and the operation of a lever connected to the rudder.

The trickiest moment occurs when leaving the surface. A submarine only seems to behave correctly when in its natural environment and does not like being part in and part out of the water. Correct trim must be achieved rapidly otherwise the craft may strike bottom in shallow water. Launching and recovery of *Explorer I* can be done by two people—with a bit of a struggle. The operational weight of the craft is about 180 lb. While *en route* to Black Park Lake, near Slough, for a trial in seven metres depth the stern section of the sub parted company with the roof rack and fell onto the pavement outside Eton College! I imagine it was the first time the ancient town had been visited by a submarine!

The aluminium covering was dented and some of the framework smashed. Needless to say, the trial was abandoned. But later the framework was rebuilt and I took the opportunity to make it stronger.

WATERPROOFING

The Batteries

The most important items in a free-flooding submarine that need to be waterproofed are the batteries, the motor and the motor switch. Probably the simplest way of keeping the batteries dry is to enclose them in a wooden box. This requires no special techniques and the construction of a box is within the capacity of most people, using hand tools only.

Waterproof plywood is the logical material to use, and a thickness of eighteen millimetres was used for the battery box in *Explorer I*. Plain, rebated joints were used for the corners and the bottom. A good quality waterproof glue must be used. An aluminium angle frame fitted into the open top of the box can be made to take the screws for fixing the one-inch-thick perspex lid in place with wing nuts. The frame can be glued and screwed into the box. Strips of rubber are then glued to the frame to act as a seal for the perspex lid.

The second box for *Explorer I* was designed for a working depth of fifty metres. It contains two twelve-volt, twenty-five ampere-hour aircraft type batteries with non-spill vents or one twelve-volt car battery. The dimensions of the box are 12 in. high by 12 in. wide by 16 in. long. The strength of a similar box will be reduced for a given depth if the dimensions are increased. The buoyancy of the box, which must be allowed for in the final ballast calculations, will be equal to the weight of water displaced by it minus the weight of the batteries and the box itself.

It is convenient to have an electrical socket at one end to allow the box to be removed by unplugging the leads from the switch and motor. The socket may be glued in with Araldite adhesive. Wandering leads should be soldered to the socket terminals inside for attachment to the battery lugs. It is essential, for safety reasons, to make all internal electrical connexions very firmly. It is possible for lead-acid batteries to give off hydrogen gas which, when combined with the oxygen constituent of the air in the box, can form an explosive mixture. A spark is all that is needed to set it off. Therefore, switches must *never* be mounted in the battery enclosure. After a dive the box should be vented as soon as possible. On no account should the batteries be left closed up for long periods.

When selecting the cables make sure that they are heavy enough to carry the current which your motor will use. The heavier they are, the more power will be available in the motor because resistance losses will be minimized. For the external connexions plastic-covered cables are most suitable. These can be sealed where they enter the watertight compartments by putting a sealing compound around the point of entry.

Only two leads into the box are needed if one speed is required. If an additional faster speed is wanted then four leads will be necessary in order that the batteries may be connected in series instead of in parallel. Plugs and sockets may be simply waterproofed by slipping a rubber sleeve over the joint. Cycle inner tube will do the trick. The batteries should be either clamped or wedged in position in their box to prevent movement when the attitude of the sub changes.

The Motor

The cylindrical form of waterproof housing provides a

better strength-to-weight ratio than any other except the spherical type or others with complex curvature. Tubes are easy to obtain and to work on and resin-bonded paper tube of four and a half inches internal diameter was chosen for the motor housing.

A fixed circular end-plate of Tufnol was glued in and this holds the motor shaft sealing gland. The gland is a simple stuffing box using a brass housing and greased string. The other end of the tube has a flange fitted round it on which rests a quarter-inch-thick "O" ring. A circular lid of quarter-inch perspex is bolted by six 4 BA bolts to the flange and is pulled up against the "O" ring, thus forming a seal. Perspex was chosen so that you can see if any water has got into the motor housing during a dive. The electric cable passes through the perspex disc where it is made watertight by sealing compound. The lid can easily be removed if water does get in or if you need to remove the motor.

The Motor Switch

A simple make and break switch may be used if only one speed is required, preferably one with a rotary action. In *Explorer I* two speeds were decided upon and the most suitable switch for the complicated circuit turned out to be a lathe switch with a rotary action.

A waterproof cylinder was constructed along similar lines to the motor housing. The switch spindle penetrates through a hole in the perspex cover where a brass gland for an "O" ring seal is fitted. The electric cables pass through holes at the bottom of the cylinder where they are sealed with sealing compound. One cable goes to the motor and the other to the battery box.

The enclosed switch is installed just inside the rear hull section on the right. In operation, "off", "slow", or "fast" can be selected. When varnished, the resin-bonded paper tube is quite waterproof. It may be obtained in large sizes and is very easy to work.

The Instruments

Pressure gauges may be waterproofed by setting them in epoxy or polyester resin in a section of metal tube allowing the

Portrait of a deep diver ready for the water. This U.S. Navy picture shows Lt.-Com. Lawrence Raymond, a United States Navy doctor, wearing an electrically-heated suit, Mark VIII diving rig and Kirby Morgan helmet. Assisting him is one of the authors, the Royal Navy Chief Petty Officer D. J. Clark. (See chapter 12)

Ready for a 600 feet deep dive is Lt.-Com. C. F. Lafferty, co-author of chapter 12. Lt.-Com. Lafferty of the Royal Navy is seen here with the other Royal Navy diver on the Sealab Project, Chief Petty Officer D. J. Clark. The diver is dressed in the Wiswell hot water suit, is wearing a Kirby Morgan helmet and Mark VIII diving rig. In his right hand he holds the main umbilical which supplies him with the breathing gas mixture. U.S. Navy photograph. (See chapter 12)

The Sealab divers had to learn to share dark waters with creatures like sealions that were being trained to carry out messenger duties during the project. Here Chief Petty Officer D. J. Clark of the Royal Navy rewards Topo, the sealion, with something to eat during a training session. U.S. Navy picture. (See chapter 12)

resin to hold in place the transparent lid in the form of a perspex disc a quarter of an inch thick.

Compasses for land use can, if suitable, be enclosed in a
cylindrical box turned from perspex. The box should be per-
manently sealed. The most suitable type of compass is the
"card" type consiting of a revolving disc with the compass
points printed or painted on it. This type is much easier to
interpret than the needle type.

Clocks and watches may be similarly waterproofed but the
lid should be removable and sealed by means of an "O" ring.

THE CHOICE OF MOTOR

Explorer I's motor is a second-hand twelve-volt car generator
run as a motor. Ideally, the brushes should be re-positioned in
order to obtain the maximum efficiency but this was not done
and the power obtained was quite adequate.

Starter motors are not suitable on account of their very high
current consumption. The generator draws only fifteen amps at
cruising speed. This means that the batteries must supply
approximately one quarter of a horse power.

Assuming an overall efficiency of sixty per cent, the final
thrust from the propeller is only about one-sixth of a horse
power. Small though it seems, this power is enough to propel
the vessel at two knots.

If required, the speed can be increased to about three knots
by arranging the circuits so that the armature of the motor
only has twenty-four volts across it from the two batteries in
series. This doubles the power available in the armature.

It is important to note that the shunt field winding of the
motor must still only have twelve volts applied to it, otherwise
it will burn out.

Since the current taken from the batteries is now nearly
doubled they will, obviously, be flattened much sooner and the
higher speed is not economical.

The weight of the motor may be reduced by turning off
some of the yoke material on a lathe. As a result, the efficiency
is scarcely affected but it saves a fair amount of weight. This,
in turn, saves having to instal extra buoyancy material to
offset the weight.

12

Instruments

The essential instruments for an underwater craft are the compass, depth gauge and pressure gauge for the ballast air.

A useful device is an angle-of-attack meter since this can indicate whether the overall buoyancy is correct when the sub is travelling.

A voltmeter, preferably push-button or switch-operated, in order not to put a current drain on the battery, is desirable for monitoring the state of charge of the battery.

For maintaining fore-and-aft level whether moving or stationary an inclinometer is necessary. This may be a simple pendulum type or a transparent "U" tube containing liquid and air.

A rate-of-ascent/descent meter would be a luxury but extremely useful. These are not so easy to devise and are best left to your own ingenuity.

In order to make your wet sub do what is expected of it certain basic precautions must be taken:

The position of the centre of gravity of the craft relative to the centre of pressure of the hull is vital. This determines the steering stability. As long as the centre of gravity is forward of the centre of pressure the craft will be stable but steering in both planes will be improved by having as much distance between these two points as is practical. The centre of gravity, when the craft is stationary underwater, will always lie directly under the centre of buoyancy. It is important, therefore, to arrange the variable buoyancy tank over the centre of gravity. By so doing, you will avoid altering the fore-and-aft level of the vessel every time the trim tank is operated. The centre of gravity may be kept well forward by positioning heavy items of equipment, such as batteries, in the bow section.

If, in spite of careful placing of gear, the sub still will not follow its nose properly, the tail fin area may be increased, thus moving the centre of pressure aft.

When the great day comes for you to launch your sub, on which you will, believe me, have spent hundreds of hours designing and constructing it, you will have to adjust the buoyancy.

With the craft in the water half-fill the trim tank and, while sitting in it in shallow water, have somebody pass you lead weights. Place these in the bottom of the hull until the vessel just starts to sink. Remember that the sub's captain, driver, or pilot—call yourself what you like—should be slightly over-weighted so as to feel that he is part of the machine. Otherwise, he will tend to float off the seat. When placing the weights you may have to put some either in the extreme bow or in the tail area in order to achieve horizontal balance.

Your first sortie under the water will soon show what changes you will have to make to get the sub to behave itself. *Explorer I* is so sensitive to buoyancy changes that even the driver's breathing affects the fore-and-aft angle rhythmically. To avoid this, the driver would have to be sitting at the centre of buoyancy which is difficult to arrange in a small sub. At first, I found myself attempting to correct the changes of angle but, after I realized the cause, I ignored them.

Explorer I was not intended to be anything other than an experimental free-flooding submarine. It has fulfilled its pur-pose and much has been learned from it. It was also a lot of fun to build. Testing it was fun too.

Obviously, a streamlined hull is preferable. The simplest way for an amateur to make such a hull is by the use of glass fibre. The techniques are quickly learned and the materials are rela-tively inexpensive.

Alternatively, you could make use of aircraft auxiliary fuel tanks, some of which are made of glass fibre. These are stream-lined and are suitable for a two-seat open wet sub.

Whatever design is used, the production of a wet sub is an ideal Branch project. Second-hand components may be used— the motor for example—and the cost may be quite small. *Explorer I* cost only £35 to make including two aircraft batteries.

If you like problems, and you'll have plenty, then build yourself a submarine. One thing I'll tell you . . . Once you've started to build a sub, you won't stop 'til you're under . . . Dive, dive, dive . . .

ELEPHANT TUSKS FROM THE SEA

by W. E. Butland

W. E. ("Bill") Butland is a chartered civil engineer. He first dived in 1951, joined London Branch of the B.S–A.C., was National Equipment Officer of the Club for three years and on the National Diving Committee. He then founded and was the first Chairman of the North Wales Underwater Archaeological Survey Team. Here he tells the story of what happened when they first brought an elephant tusk up from the sea near Thunder Rock . . .

THEY call it Thunder Rock. At least that's what the Welsh means. The first I knew about it was in April 1965 when John Stubbs, a member of Gwynedd Branch of the British Sub-Aqua Club, was talking to me about the places we might go for a Whitsun weekend dive.

He suggested having a go at Maen Mellt, which is the Welsh for Thunder Rock. I'd never heard of it before, but I'll give any new site at least one dive before condemning it for evermore. He said it was due north of Aberdaron in Caernarvonshire. This at least gave me a clue about which end of the country it was, but it wasn't until I'd consulted a large-scale map that I really found it.

Why dive there anyway? The answer aroused my interest immediately. Dewi Pritchard-Jones, another Gwynedd member, had done some research in the County archives into wrecks—and had found three which had sunk on the same rock —Maen Mellt . . . Thunder Rock.

*　　　*　　　*

The information was thin but intriguing. The first wreck was the 80-ton sloop *Lovely* from Frodsham to Pwllheli with foodstuffs. She was lost in 1802. The second was the sloop *Ann*,

built in Conway in 1788 and lost in 1864. The third was the
Royal Charter, a schooner of 119 tons. She was lost on the 3rd of
March, 1881.

Maen Mellt, Thunder Rock, is nothing more than an isolated
lump of rock some 650 yards off the mainland with nasty
currents around it. In 1964 some of the Gwynedd divers had
snorkelled out to it and dived. The current had swept them
along very fast, but they did however manage to see some odd
items that certainly were not natural.

As they wished to return to the site again an intermittent
watch was kept on the rock to determine the time of slack
water, which was not given by any of the usual sources.

The Branch boats were in use elsewhere that weekend, but
as John reckoned that he knew the time of slack water accurately we decided we would snorkel off a point on the mainland
and drift down with the current. We could then rest on the
rock until it was slack water, dive, and snorkel back again
when the time had changed.

On the Saturday we met up with Hevin Williams and Ron
Cooper. My first look at the Mellt was a shock, it looked a long
way off and although there was no wind the water around the
rock was obviously choppy, and I could see this from over 700
yards away. John briefed us and we tramped off in full gear
and down the cliffs. When I inquired about other landing
spots without cliffs, they said that Porth Iago was nearest but
we might not be able to cross the tide rapidly enough. The
alternative to the west was Whispering Sands about three miles
or Porth Ysgadan, four miles to the east. That did nothing for
my confidence.

With lifejackets fully inflated we leapt in and swam out to
sea. Very soon it was apparent that we were lined up with the
Mellt and we only had to let the current carry us, so we lay
back and chatted. As the barren rock loomed up so did the
cormorants and their smell—cormorants eat fish and the result
requires no imagination! We scrambled ashore, deflated lifejackets and took a breather.

Within five minutes we could see the water becoming
quieter, it was time to go. John and I were to go around the
seaward side and Hevin and Ron the other way and meet in
20 minutes at the far end of the rock for the snorkel back.

Underwater the rock shelved down almost vertically, we passed through the laminaria on to bare rock and at 65 feet there was the bottom, only broken rock and stone with a little weed but no current. The first thing to interest me was a large crab in its hole. He soon came out! We moved slowly onward, then John stopped and picked up something from the bottom. He waved it at me and I thought, "Same to you," but he hung on to it. Further on we swam over a large rock and found on the far side a large anchor. We spread ourselves along it and guessed its length as about 7 feet. A bit farther on there was a drum-like object. Out came the knives and we started chipping. It was mainly wood with some iron around it, a windlass I assumed. Ever tried miming underwater that the thing was a windlass? John nearly drowned laughing when I tried.

John made the next find, a brass rudder hinge. It took quite an effort to lift, so he balanced it on his knees and slowly filled his Fenzy, the lift when fully inflated was just enough to counteract the weight. It was obviously time to ascend as we could feel the current beginning to press against us. Once on the surface we could just make out the others in the distance already heading for shore and we followed.

We struggled all the way back. The 700 yards took us fifty-five minutes, swimming hard all the way. We grounded in the shallows and lay gasping. Hevin and Ron were already there and plied us with questions. The hinge excited most comment until I remembered the curved, pointed thing John had given me to carry home. He suggested it was an ivory tusk. I was not convinced, but a bit of scraping showed it to be a tusk, rather discoloured and dirty. The others had only found one thing of interest and that was a long wooden mast.

Obviously the Mellt had a lot of debris around it, so it was back again the next day. Going around the rock the second time we took a slightly different route and came across another anchor, this time about six foot long. I also found a small pulley wheel, but we could not find the mast. We had landed on the rock and waited for the others, when suddenly Ron shot to the surface just beneath us saying he had got another hinge but had run out of air carrying it back. John leaped in and followed down Hevin's stream of bubbles, relieved him of the hinge and carried it up. This one looked about the same size as the other one, but still had some bits of wood attached to it.

We thought we would have another struggle to get back to the mainland, but a local fisherman appeared and, when he had recovered from the shock of seeing four divers sitting on a rock normally only inhabited by cormorants, he offered us a lift back. It was then that I learnt always to travel in the bow of a lobster fisherman's boat, the month-old dead fish used for bait may be enjoyed by lobsters, but not by me!

Reviewing the two dives we decided that a mass search was required as there was obviously one, if not two wrecks there. We sorted out the neap tides from the tables and John promised to organize some Branch dives on the rock.

When I came back from a few week's holiday, John reported that they had found more tusks, including fifteen underneath four lead blocks. From then on we shipped divers out to the rock in our dinghies at every opportunity. We dived in all directions out from the rock hoping to discover other items of interest.

One day whilst steering compass courses north of the rock I lost my partner, but decided to continue on a little way before returning to the rock. The bottom was sand on top of rock with some stones. It was rather boring until something caught my eye. What were those straight lines and radiused ends? I swam across to one of the shapes and fanned the sand off it. More ingots! A quick scrape showed that lovely shiny white patina of lead. I nearly leaped off the bottom and swam around counting. I made it a total of forty, a veritable lead mine. Just as I was totting up their worth and deciding to keep silent and come back at a later date with John and a few others for a nice quiet salvage job another diver loomed into sight. It was Ron Whittaker. Bang went dreams of lovely loot!

Back on the Mellt the others were struggling to load the original four ingots into the dinghies. On hearing of another forty ingots their faces lit up, then clouded over. There was obviously a lot of money there, but how could we lift them all? Once we reached shore the four salvaged ingots were dropped on the sand. Everyone started guessing their weight. The strongest said they would soon solve that and bent down to pick up one each. Amid much grunting they did lift them, staggered a few yards and then dropped them, gasping something about two hundredweights at least.

I had only asked for a piece of one for chemical analysis, but now we had four ingots on the beach. In pairs we staggered with them, a few yards at a time, up the beach. We finally arrived at the foot of the path up the cliffs, if you can call it a path. It was really a sand slope about 80 feet high and at a 60-degree slope. Great fun to glissade down but murder to climb, even empty handed.

Finally someone suggested using an old door as a sledge, attaching a length of rope and supplying power by means of a car at the top of the slope. We loaded up an ingot and away went the car—so did the rope, in fact it cut through the door! More thinking. Then somebody tied a timber hitch around the ingot itself and this time it worked.

I had already written to Joan du Plat Taylor of the Committee for Nautical Archaeology to find a method of preserving the tusk. She had replied and asked to be kept informed of any other finds. When she heard of our discovery of the 40 ingots she suggested that we did an underwater survey of the area and made proper drawings of the bits and pieces.

When I next visited London I went in to see her. I was told that the C.N.A. were very interested. So far everyone had done surveys in the nice clear, warm waters of the Mediterranean, but nothing here at home. Blithely I agreed to survey the site—little did I realize . . .

John and I were both civil engineers with plenty of surveying experience so we sat down and discussed the methods to use. All the "foreign" water surveys seemed to have used tape grids, but the next storm would obviously carry ours away, if the normal currents did not do so first. The sea-bed was relatively flat so we decided to hammer steel pins into the rock to act as fixed points which were never likely to move, then tie wires tautly between them to give baselines from which we could measure.

By this time we had begun to worry about the fact that the ingots really did not belong to us, so we declared them and the tusks to the local Receiver of Wreck. We asked him to keep the site of the finds as quiet as possible as we were engaged on an archaeological survey—if anything was taken it would upset our reconstruction of the site. This he very kindly did. At the same time he remarked he was glad we had declared the items as he had noticed we were frequently diving on the same site and he was becoming curious.

Gwynedd Branch realized that their own resources were insufficient to do a complete survey so they invited Flintshire College of Technology Special Branch, who were old friends, to join in. Although the survey was of prime importance we did not lose sight of the value of the lead. So the North Wales Underwater Archaeological Survey Team was formed. Although a member of London Branch I was at the time working in Anglesey and soon found myself nominated as Chairman. We made up a Committee and hammered out an agreement to tie up things legally so that we would not have arguments at a later date.

Winter was already upon us. Now we transferred our efforts to research and pool work. And John trained as many divers as possible in surveying techniques. While anyone can be taught surveying we found it was the engineers, carpenters, bricklayers and the like that produced the best results, for their work depended on their being accurate. If it wasn't they got the sack, so this gave them an in-built appreciation of accuracy which is not easy to instil into "arty types".

On the research side Miss Taylor had put us in touch with Mr. Bathe of the Science Museum, London, and he supplied us with useful tables relating rudder hinge and anchor sizes to vessel's tonnage. This enabled us to tie the hinges and probably the anchors to the 119-ton schooner *Royal Charter*. Mr. Bathe also suggested three old books on ship construction which provided us with many useful drawings and tables so that we could do our own identification.

The tusks proved a real headache. None was over one foot eleven inches long nor greater than one and a half inches in diameter. When we found the original one, I assumed it was a sailor's souvenir, but now we had over twenty so it must have been part of a cargo. The fact that a lot of tusks were under the first four ingots meant they must have sunk first. It seemed unlikely that the ingots had been stowed on top of the tusks for fear of damage and if they had fallen out of the bottom of the same ship the ingots would have fallen much faster. I could only assume that they had come from a wreck earlier than any of the three we knew.

A considerable quantity of ivory was imported into this country in the 18th and 19th centuries for carving into various decorative objects. Billiard balls immediately come to mind, but our tusks were too small in diameter for that. As they were less than two feet in length it was suggested that they were African elephant tusks. Indian ones were much longer.

About this time a member reading *Immortal Sails*, the story of Portmadoc (as a port) came across a brief reference to the *Royal Charter*. It described her as a flashy schooner built for a David Morris and recorded that she traded as far as the North African coast. The tusks must have come from the *Royal Charter* —or so we guessed, incorrectly as it turned out.

It was *Lloyd's Register* that destroyed this theory. They said her final voyage was from Dublin to Portmadoc in ballast, i.e. no cargo. It did, however, explain the heap of odd stones that we found near the hinges. An empty vessel obviously requires some form of ballast to keep her at the correct level in the water, so that she sails without making too much leeway, and stones are heavy and cheap. Lloyd's also noted her as lost 7 miles north-east of Bardsey, near enough to the Mellt, but not close enough. An extract from the local weekly of the time noted that she had gone aground on Maen Mellt and, in view of the rough weather, was likely to break up. And so she did.

The real breakthrough on the *Royal Charter* came in a letter from the Registrar-General of Shipping and Seamen, it confirmed what we already knew and added that she had been built in 1858, with one deck. Two masts carried the schooner rig, her bow had a female figurehead, the stern was square, and she was of carvel construction. Her length was 82·6 feet, breadth 22·4 feet and depth 11·4 feet. At last we felt we were getting somewhere and had pinned down one of the wrecks on the Mellt.

The Registrar had also included a list of her masters and all her shareholders. It showed that David Morris had sold his majority holding in 1865 and between then and the time of her loss there had been three more majority holders.

How the *Royal Charter* managed to get on completely the wrong side of the Lleyn Peninsula is somewhat of a puzzle. On the 50 miles from Dublin she was about 12 miles north and 15 miles east of where she should have been. One can only assume she must have been in trouble all the way across the Irish Sea—or the wind must have been a southerly gale and the skipper had decided to run for shelter on the north side of the Lleyn and wait for the storm to pass.

Soon after Easter 1967 we were back again. Many a time one look from the mainland was enough for us to know diving would be impossible as we saw waves going clean over the top of the Mellt which stood 35 feet above low water level. It also made us feel for the poor sailors that had had their ships run on to the rocks.

John's pool training had sorted out the divers that would work on the survey and those we should use for pure searching. The hammering of the pins into the rock and fixing of the p.v.c.-covered wire was relatively easy, even though underwater visibility was low. One day, however, visibility suddenly improved and it became apparent that if we moved one end of the survey a bit it would make things a lot easier. So up came some of the pins and wire. Fibreglass tapes were lashed to the wires to act as baselines. The distances between all the pins were measured and from the resultant triangles we plotted the outline of the wire.

From then on it was cold, hard work. The searchers were detailed off to cover particular areas and told to note any unusual object and report back. But nothing was to be moved under "pain of death". The surveyors each had sketch boards and rules or tapes and they were distributed around the ingots so that they did not get in each other's way.

After each dive the divers were debriefed and a quick look at their boards soon told if they had missed anything vital. After that John and another surveyor, John Smart, went back and plotted the results. Occasionally it was obvious that someone had made a mistake, so a sketch was made on a board and the dimensions requiring checking marked on it. It was then only a matter of seconds for a diver to mark on the missing dimensions on the next dive.

We found that mistakes usually occurred towards the end of a dive. After about 30 minutes divers got noticeably cold and their accuracy fell off. Some of us got so cold that we could not even hold the pencil to write and had to surface, even though we were not out of air. John Smart once likened our survey to doing one on land on hands and knees in the depths of winter with a howling gale and thick fog. He was not far wrong.

One day as divers were crawling out of the water on to the rock someone stuck his head up and said there was a ship's bell wedged in a crack just beneath us. A frantic check produced one diver with air left. Down he went and after a struggle returned with a brass bell about nine inches high. We rubbed it gently hoping to find a name, but no luck. Our metallurgist was given the bell and told to give it an acid bath, this did nothing so then we gave it a light sand blasting. Still nothing. It was a great disappointment.

All the summer when the weather allowed it we were out there and sometimes conditions can only be described as hairy. The rubber dinghies used to get filled with water and the sight of seven divers apparently sitting upright in the water and the top of an outboard going up and down in the waves gave us a laugh if nothing else. Once one diver left his twin set on the bottom of the dinghy and a large wave sucked it out, never to be seen again. After that all divers travelled fully kitted.

Hazards were numerous around the site. Divers would surface and not be able to swim back against the current to the rock and would have to whistle for a dinghy. Loose tapes and wires always seemed to get snarled around a diver just as he had run out of air and was surfacing—we very quickly learnt to tie up anything that was loose. The overfalls caused a few moments' sweat if one surfaced in them. It was just a matter of waiting till the current carried you out of the turmoil, but you felt like the proverbial pea in a referee's whistle while it lasted.

By the end of the season about two-thirds of the ingots had been surveyed and so our attention returned to research work and the problem of raising the ingots.

The chemical analysis of the lead had shown a silver content of 14 ozs. per ton; this was quite high as the silver was usually removed at a very early stage in the smelting of the ore. Presumably we had discovered ingots that had only just been smelted from the ore without refining. Another breakthrough came with the book *The Lead Mining Industry of Wales*. It quoted Flintshire ore as having a silver content of about 14 ozs. per ton.

The *Lovely* had been going from Frodsham to Pwllheli and one of the Flintshire ports could have been a port of call. Food-stuffs are a bulky, but relatively light, cargo so the *Lovely* would have been riding high in the water. This is not good for a sailing vessel as the wind then causes a lot of sideways drift or leeway. Lead would be a very good ballast, but it would have been rather expensive compared with stones. More checking was obviously required.

A search in *Lloyd's Register* recorded the *Lovely* in the 1807 edition but not in 1808, so presumably she was lost in 1807. Now in 1806 and 1807 the price of lead reached £30 to £35 per ton, higher than it had ever been before or was again until 1916. So the demand for lead must have been very great. The letter "E" and a number stamped on the top surface of each ingot puzzled us for a long while until somebody looking through an old trade journal came across an advertisement for Adam Eyton of Holywell, Flintshire. They smelted lead and cast it into sheets and pipes. So the "E" could stand for Eyton. The numbers which ranged between 1 and 100 are still a puzzle. They could hardly indicate purity, for metallurgical analysis in those days was simple. We discovered that lead was then sold by auction so perhaps the numbering was to enable various buyers to ensure that what they had bought was what they got. The only trouble is that we have a number of ingots with the same figures.

Each ingot weighed about 200 lbs. Again confusion—the old Welsh fodder was 2,400 lbs., it contained eight pigs (300 lbs.) or sixteen pieces or sows (150 lbs.), so our ingots did not tie up with any known standard. The National Museum of Wales, the Committee on Ancient Monuments and other authorities think we have found a new standard weight ingot and the first two authorities have bought ingots from the Receiver of Wreck for display.

Anticipating the finish of the survey we discussed lifting the ingots. We could have hired large boats with derricks but this would be expensive and odds were that the skippers would not risk taking their vessels close enough to the Mellt to recover all the ingots. Finally Ron Cooper suggested building a cata-maran pontoon out of oildrums, fitting a deck with a hole in it, then mounting a tripod and winch over it. Ron happens to be a carpenter so he was nominated to build it; it proved to be the perfect answer.

That winter we struggled with our research, but could add very little to the facts we already knew. Most disappointing was the failure to find anything about the *Ann*. Records of that era were very sketchy. Lloyd's had dozens of vessels of that name but none of our known facts fitted even remotely. As for finding details of her loss it was impossible. In those days ships just disappeared and details were not even known, let alone recorded.

As soon as the weather cleared in 1968 we sent a team on to some ship's timbers that had been found sticking out of a sand mound some distance from the ingots. We were hoping for a hull beneath the sand. We probed and dug, but found nothing more. And so we went back to the survey of the ingots.

Once the survey was completed, we started to lift the ingots. First we tried lifting bags. Having filled them with air we got the ingots off the sea bed but as they went up, the water pressure decreased and the air in the bags expanded. The whole lot went faster and faster towards the surface. Two ingots went so fast that when they hit the surface air spilled out of the bags. The 200 lbs. ingots went very rapidly back to the bottom. They only just missed divers and we decided it was too hazardous a method of recovery.

Finally we rigged the tripod and winch and used a pair of tongs on the ingots, so that when the rope tightened so did the tongs on the ingot. The last one was brought ashore on August Bank Holiday Sunday.

The following day we decided to do a drift dive along the axis of the Mellt just for fun. When about 100 yards south-west of the rock somebody spotted another two ingots, so everyone stopped and looked around. There were more copper bars, some timber and a bale of thin copper sheeting! More money!!

We plotted the new finds and then brought up the sheeting. It was for sheathing of ship's timber hulls to stop the warm-water borers. In the corner of some sheets we found the initials "NL", went back to the trade journal and sure enough, there was a firm of copper smelters and rollers called Newton Lyon of Greenfield, Flintshire, only a few miles from Holywell.

Chemical analysis showed the sheeting to be pure copper.

This dated it to pre-1840, since after that date copper zinc alloys were used as they were much cheaper. Being prior to 1840, and close to ingots identical to the others, the sheeting must have come from the *Lovely*. We had also had some copper bolts and bars from close to the Mellt which were similar to the latest ones. An old local historian had told us that he had heard of copper bars being taken from the Mellt many years before at a low tide. He also told the story of local fishermen going out in their boats after the loss of the *Lovely* and harpooning the floating Cheshire cheeses with pitchforks. The first story I can agree with, but the second one I doubted. When I tried floating a piece of Cheshire cheese in water it sank!

The story of the *Lovely*'s last voyage is probably this. At Frodsham she loaded up with foodstuffs from the Cheshire plains. In fact such boats were often called "cheese boats". She sailed round the Wirral and at Bagillt or Greenfield loaded the lead ingots and copper sheeting. The trip westward past the Great Orme, round Anglesey and past Bardsey would require a ship that handled well, so correct ballasting was important. Rounding Anglesey she must have set the wrong course or not allowed sufficiently for leeway, for instead of clearing Bardsey, she hit Maen Mellt, seven miles to the north-east.

It was probably night or very bad visibility when she struck hard on the rock. She stove a large hole in her bows, an anchor fell off the bows and some copper bolts and bars tumbled out. Her sails backed in the wind and the current carried her off as she settled rapidly by the bows. The ingots suddenly tumbled out giving us the main lead ingot area on the bottom. Suddenly lightened the crew may have got her under control again and started for the mainland, but it was too late. She drifted along and suddenly plunged beneath the waves. Over the years she broke up to leave a few waterlogged timbers and a couple of ingots and the copper sheeting as a monument.

The more we dive around the Mellt, the more we find in the way of small items. Part of the brass compass binnacle ring came from the *Royal Charter* area, iron mast straps, the odd tusk and ingot, pulleys and deadeyes are all over the place. A piece of blue glass in the shape of the prism of a ship's navigation lantern is a mystery—why blue? Since the inception of navigation lights white, red and green have been the only colours.

Blue has recently been used for Dracones, those floating plastic sausages for carrying oil, but you do not get them off the Mellt. Another mystery is a "rudder hinge", at least that is what it looks like, except that instead of a circular hole for the pin it is semicircular. No one can give us a definite answer as to what this is.

Because owners of our finds could not be traced the Receiver of Wreck held everything for a year hoping that the owners would claim it. Unclaimed it was auctioned. In October, 1969, $5\frac{1}{2}$ tons of lead and about $\frac{1}{4}$ ton of copper sheeting. We got only about a quarter of the sale price but we hope it will provide another boat for the group.

What have we achieved? A lot of things. Purely as divers we have improved our diving, boat handling and safety techniques. We will now dive on sites that five years ago we classified as impossible and with the salvage money we will be able to get to them as well!

From the archaeologists' viewpoint we have found a new standard type of lead ingot and some perfect examples of copper sheeting for ship's hulls. We have proved that amateur divers can do underwater archaeological surveying in British conditions in currents up to $2\frac{1}{2}$ knots and with visibility as low as 2 feet.

We now have a team of divers who are competent underwater surveyors. We are now teaching other branches our techniques and helping out on small surveys as we wait for the big archaeological find off North Wales so that we can put our Group into full operation.

British Sub-Aqua Club divers have probed the waters all over the world. These pictures by Andrew Losh, a founder member of the London University branch, qualify as the coldest water pictures in this book. They were taken after cutting through the ice around the island of Signy, South Orkneys, in the Antarctic with the six-foot blade of a chain saw! Losh joined the British Antarctic Survey as a diver and general assistant. His pictures show, *top*, the expedition doctor under the ice near an old oil tank used by whalers of long ago, and *above*, the expedition's geologist dredging on the sea bottom. Note the lifelines attached to both divers. This is so that they can find their way back to the hole in the ice through which they dived.

Underwater photographer Geoff Harwood found this cuttlefish sound asleep—or so it seemed—in Swanage Bay, Dorset. But just after he took this remarkable close-up portrait, the cuttlefish objected strongly to such intrusion into his dreams and retreated at high speed.

"It is best to make friends with your subject before taking any photographs at all"—so runs the advice of a famous above-water portrait photographer. Applying that advice below water to a plaice is Geoff Harwood. Picture by Colin Doeg.

DEATH OF AN AQUANAUT

by Lieut.-Commander C. F. Lafferty and Chief Petty Officer D. J. Clark

Two Royal Navy divers were specially selected to join the United States Navy's Sealab III project. Those Royal Navy divers are Lieutenant-Commander C. F. Lafferty and Chief Petty Officer D. J. Clark. Here, first Lafferty and then Clark, tell their stories of the events leading up to the terrible moment when Aquanaut Berry Cannon died 600 feet down . . .

"BERRY's dead, he's dead!"

These chilling words gasped by a shivering, exhausted Aquanaut from 600 feet down in the Pacific Ocean not only brought the operation to a temporary end, but the squeaky, disembodied sound of his voice tragically reminded us of the enormity of the task we had undertaken.

Berry Cannon was the 30-year-old engineer Aquanaut for Team I of the Sealab III operation. He had risked and lost his life on this operation towards which he had been working for many years. We, his friends and diving partners admired and respected him as one of the most outstanding diving engineers in the business. He was that rare combination of a clever engineering mind, skilled and practical electronics engineer and outstandingly capable diver which is almost impossible to replace. His loss made us seriously wonder if our ambitions were worth the risks. Were we justified in risking men's lives or must we admit that the cold and merciless ocean had defeated us?

After much hard thinking we have decided that our goals are worth striving for and that no more fitting memorial could be given to Berry than to complete the task he had started.

If we were attempting to seek glory or publicity, if we were

attempting to break an existing record, if we were attempting
to be the first for the fun of it, then we would be entirely un-
justified in continuing our programme.

But what are we trying to do and why do we think we really
are justified in our attempts to live in the sea? We certainly
would not be the first to reach these depths. George Wookey
dived to 600 feet in 1954 and Hans Keller to 1,000 feet in 1964.
They, however, like many other deep divers, spent so little time
at depth that they could achieve little or no productive work
and to pay for their short trip they had to suffer many hours of
uncomfortable decompression.

In 1964, I and seventeen other men spent periods of up to
one hour at 600 feet in the Mediterranean, but again had to
spend at least 36 hours in the decompression chamber. One
hour's work every 36 hours is a high price to pay for labour.
Captain George Bond, U.S.N., has for several years been working on his theory of "Saturation Diving". He has proved his
theory is practical and safe in the past, but never at such a
depth as we are trying now.

His theory is that a man's body can be compared to a sponge.
When he is under pressure his body soaks up some of the gas he
breathes and when he reduces that pressure his body releases
that extra gas that was forced in by the higher pressure. The gas
must be released slowly however, or else it forms bubbles which
can be trapped in the body. These bubbles expand, as the
pressure decreases and can cause excruciating pain, paralysis or
even death depending on where they occur. It is to prevent
these bubbles from forming that the diver has to be decom-
pressed very slowly. In other words, we are trying to prevent
the diver from getting the "Bends". Dr. Bond argued that if a
diver stayed down so long that his body could not absorb any
more gas (in other words he became saturated with gas) then
his period of decompression would always be the same. For
instance, if he spent 24 hours at 600 feet his body would be
saturated with gas and it would take 7 days to slowly and safely
decompress him. However, if he stayed at 600 feet for 20 days
he could not absorb any more gas than he did in his first 24
hours, and therefore, his decompression would still be 7 days.
Then, for the first time, we can see the ratio of working time to
decompression time being favourable to the diver.

So now we think we have a safe decompression routine for a saturation dive and a diver is safely able to spend long periods on the bottom at great depths. Now we must find out if it is really possible in the real conditions. Perhaps other factors such as cold or physiological changes may prove we are wrong. But if we are right, can our diver work usefully while he is on the bottom? If he can work usefully, is there anything useful he can do? That is what Sealab is all about. And that is what Berry Cannon died trying to find out and that is why we are determined to continue our efforts.

If at the end of Sealab we find that a man can live and produce effective work for long periods at such depths, we will not have progressed very far unless we have some idea of the type of work we can usefully give him. That, too, is what Sealab is all about. We hope to be able to show that we can live and work at 600 feet. for a period of 13 days and we also hope to demonstrate that we can work reasonably efficiently and that the work we can do is of some real value.

These then are basically the objectives behind Sealab III but none of these can be achieved without the right people. The right people for this type of project are difficult to find and unless they are the right sort of people the programme will inevitably fail.

The divers required for a programme like this are a rare brand of men. They have been chosen mainly from the U.S. Navy and Government scientific establishments. However, the United States invited Australia, Canada and Great Britain to send experienced men to take part in the dives. The men for these dives had to be experienced divers and many had to have special outside skills. Among the 54 divers we have, we must have a selection of the most varied skills in any one organization. They vary from the only man to orbit the earth and spend 30 consecutive days under water, Cdr. Scott Carpenter, to veterans of 20 years' diving experience and Ph.D.s in electronics and marine biology. We have doctors, engineers, electronic experts, biologists, photographers, construction and salvage engineers and just plain divers.

Apart from their very obvious qualifications these men are a remarkable breed. They must be physically tough and mentally alert; they must be able to withstand physical hardships and psychological stress; they must be confident in themselves as individuals, but able to live and work in close proximity with other equally determined individualists; and above all they must be able to inspire their team mates to the extent that each man is willing to place his own safety directly in another man's hands.

Most of these qualities cannot be trained into a man. He must possess them already, but the training he's given can be designed to demonstrate to that man and to his partners that in fact he does possess them.

The first step in this training is to determine whether these men can withstand the mental and physical effects of spending many days in extremely confined conditions under a pressure of at least 283 pounds per square inch. While doing this we can also establish that the schedule we plan to use for our dives in the sea are in fact safe. We tested all the potential Aquanauts in a large pressure chamber where they were pressurized for many days to an equivalent of at least 600 feet and were given an arduous series of physiological, psychological and manual dexterity tests.

These tests taught us many useful things. We found that it is an amusing though painful practice to eat Rice Crispies. The rice particles each contain a small vacuum and when the outer layer is punctured the rice particle clings to your tongue, cheeks or teeth. I remember one sleepy man taking his first spoonful of cereal and then to the vast amusement of his team mates he started choking and clawing at his mouth. He complained that he was supposed to eat the Crispies and not vice versa.

We learned too that the diver's ribald sense of humour must be considered. For instance, on one dive one man's body temperature was being continuously monitored by an electric lead to a rectal probe he had to have in place throughout his dive. This poor man was never spoken to: no matter how he tried to conceal his electric cable his so-called team mates spoke to him only by giving him coded diving signals by pulling on his rectal probe.

However, our simulated dives taught us that we can survive, with relative ease, these extended periods under pressure down to a depth of 1,002 feet. It is one thing, however, to do a simulated dive in a warm chamber where if during a dive you get into trouble you can simply stand up on a table and lift your head out of the water, but it is another thing to do the same dive in the sea.

In the sea you are cold, in the dark and a long way from help and very much on your own. We had to build the diver's confidence in himself, his partners and his equipment up to the stage where he can feel confident to cope with these hazards.

We are all, of course, more than used to the unfriendly conditions we will meet underwater, but we are not familiar with the equipment we will eventually be using and testing. There are many problems to be dealt with when we are doing a deep dive. First of all, we must use a different breathing gas than the one we are normally used to. We must have oxygen to survive, but under pressure, too much oxygen will poison us and quickly kill us. However, the air we breathe is four-fifths nitrogen which will itself kill you if you breathe it below about 300 feet. We have found though that helium has little or no adverse effects when used under pressure—so we breathe a mixture of helium and oxygen. To provide the diver with just the right amount of oxygen at 600 feet we use a mixture that contains 98 per cent helium and 2 per cent oxygen.

Though this provides us with sufficient oxygen to live, the helium itself gives us other problems. Helium is a very light, fast-flowing gas and a diver who breathes it inherits a new voice. His voice goes up in pitch by several octaves and in addition, he finds it difficult to form his sounds in the normal way. As a result, the diver sounds like a very indistinct "chipmunk".

We have found that even to the trained ear it is almost impossible to understand a helium diver and many years' research have been put into the development of the helium voice unscramblers we now use. However, even with these we can only understand about half of what the diver says and the unaccustomed ear will have great difficulty understanding anything at all. This communications problem provides many hilarious misunderstandings, but hilarious though they may be a misunderstanding can easily be fatal if a diver is asking for assistance. Add to the diver's squeaky voice the fact that he has a mouthpiece or tight face mask on and probably has a peculiar "Limey" accent and the problem is infinitely compounded.

We spent many months training ourselves to use all the various pieces of equipment and many months using our diving sets. The diver at 600 feet cannot possibly carry enough gas on his back to last him for long. Each breath he takes uses more than 19 times the amount of gas he uses on the surface. So the diver must wear a set which can supply him an infinite amount of gas through a hose attached to a large supply. Helium is very expensive and just to store the amount of gas the divers will require needs a huge supply. To try to conserve the amount of gas the diver will use we use a set which enables us to re-breathe a large proportion of the gas by re-circulating it through a system which cleans out the dangerous carbon dioxide the diver breathes out with every breath. However, this type of set takes a great deal of practice to use safely.

Once all our divers had learned to use all the various parts of their equipment, and our best men had been selected for the various teams, we then had to train them to carry out all the major tasks they would undertake on the bottom. It was our plan to have five separate teams of nine men. Each man was to spend a period of 13 days living on the sea-bed followed by a 7-day decompression period. "Nobby" Clark was selected to be the diving equipment expert in Team 3 and Lafferty was to be the Team Leader of Team 4.

Nobby's team were to undertake a very difficult underwater construction operation. They planned to put together a pre-fabricated building that could be used either for a shelter or to put around a job so that a diver could work in a dry and safe atmosphere. This job involved working as a very close team using large weights and lifting devices. It was impossible, of course, to practise this operation at anything like the depth of Sealab, but it was assembled, modified and re-assembled many times until the whole operation could be done by only two men in the worst conditions.

"Nobby" also spent some time training with the porpoises and seals. One team was going to work with some trained marine mammals to assess whether these highly intelligent and adaptable animals could be usefully employed by man. This training had two initial stages. The first was to coax our intrepid divers to get their feet wet when their surprisingly large workmates were in the same water. The second was to introduce the mammals to the divers and establish a friendly atmosphere.

Most marine mammals will work only for a reward and "Tuffy", the most experienced of our dolphins, could be very touchy. One diver was unable to take his fish out of his bag to reward Tuffy on the successful completion of his task and Tuffy, after waiting a considerable time and making some very gentlemanly hints, ran out of breath and with a flash of his powerful tail drove himself to the surface and the diver into the mud.

On the whole, however, working with the mammals was very rewarding and on occasion awe-inspiring. They were trained to dive on one breath from the surface to depths well below 600 feet and, unerringly, in the complete dark take a life-line to a lost diver. To do this they wore a leather harness to which the line was attached. Once on Sealab II, Tuffy's harness was too tight and was hurting him. When he found the diver he tried to tell him by nuzzling him and rolling over on his back. The diver was slow to understand and eventually Tuffy heaved his chest and snapped the leather straps like paper.

The dolphins seem to understand that we are aliens in their world and are patient with our inability to cope with conditions as well as they can. In pitch black water it is eerie waiting for a black bullet weighing more than you do to crash unexpectedly into you. However, time and again the first you would know would be a gentle nuzzle on your hand skilfully directing you to the harness.

Others of us spent time training in the use of a Muon radiation-meter which we had to use and calibrate in the total dark without the use of any lights. We also learned how to record and photograph fish to attempt to discover which type of fish made which noise. We learned to use various types of new underwater tools and equipment for salvage work; we learned how to use the batteries of underwater cameras; we learned to use the many scientific instruments for the measuring and recording of tides, currents and temperatures. And while we were doing all this we had to learn everything there was to know about the complex Habitat in which we would be living and the diving system which would enable us to get to it.

The Habitat is a 60 feet long steel cylinder equipped to house 9 men and provide them with a safe atmosphere and a modicum of comfort. It has to be supplied with electric power, breathing gas and water from the surface. To do this we are using a specially modified ship, the U.S.S. *Elk River*.

The ship is equipped with two large compression chambers in which the divers are initially compressed to an equivalent of 600 feet. When the divers reach this depth they climb up into a small capsule which is then lifted off the compression chamber and lowered through the centre of the ship to the sea-bed. At the bottom the divers then swim out of the capsule to the Habitat where they set up house for their long stay. When the divers' 13 days on the sea-bed are over, they swim back to the capsule and are lifted back to the ship where they can begin their 7-day decompression in the ship's chambers.

Also on board are two very sophisticated control centres. One contains all the communications and closed circuit television controls and the electronic recording equipment. The other is the medical laboratory where our doctors can continually monitor the atmosphere our divers are breathing and where they can carry out all the medical tests required. Throughout the diver's stay on the bottom, they will have to give regular daily blood samples, they will have electro-cardiograms taken and give regular biological samples. All these, after careful study, will help us determine whether man undergoes any significant biological changes as a result of being exposed to such extreme pressures for so long.

All these preparations and problems, all grossly oversimplified in this story, led up to the point where we prepared for our first dive.

The scene was set in February, 1969, with the *Elk River* firmly secured between a pattern of buoys with the bright yellow Habitat sitting quietly in the water. San Clemente Island, a desolate island 70 miles off the coast of California was shrouded in a faint clean rain. All was ready for the Habitat to be lowered to the bottom when a rainbow appeared framing the Habitat and providing a dubious omen of luck. With a vast ribbon of power cables, gas lines and our hopes hanging heavily from her, the Habitat was gently lowered to the sea floor, 600 long feet away.

All appeared well. The miniature submarine Deepstar "4000" followed her down and jubilantly reported everything was in good order. The yellow Habitat was sitting level on the firm sea-bed with its floodlights casting an eerie gleam and its remotely controlled television cameras moving and tilting like an H. G. Wells's robot.

However, that night we started losing gas out of the Habitat and were having to send more and more gas into it to prevent it from being crushed. It was obvious that a leak had developed and that we were faced with a serious problem. There were only two answers. One was to raise the Habitat from the bottom and the other was to send the divers down to repair the leak. To raise the Habitat at this stage and lift it out of the water again represented many weeks' work and hundreds of thousands of dollars expense. The divers on the other hand might be able to repair the leak, but if they could not, at least we would know the exact location and cause of the leak and would only have wasted another one or two days.

While the divers were compressing to 600 feet, Commander Scott Carpenter and Lafferty were sent down in the Deepstar "4000" to photograph and survey the outside of the Habitat. We hoped to be able to supply the divers with the exact location of the leak and to give the Command some idea of the size of the leak.

We spiralled down slowly through the still, silent world with only the plankton flashing past our ports to show us we were moving. As we approached the bottom the pilot switched on his motors, released some ballast and took control of what, until this moment, had been a wildly gyrating, freefalling sphere. We cruised slowly a few feet above the hard sand, over the frequent rocky outcrops and silently moved towards Sealab. Gradually in the distance a faint yellow glow appeared. The whole scene was unreal, too much like a science fiction movie to be taken seriously. Sealab glowed with a bright unearthly light and a silver stream, streaking and flashing with bubbles stretched into the blackness above.

Cautiously we crept close to the outer edge of the circle of light almost, it appeared, afraid to enter the sphere of influence of this strange apparition. In fact, we were making ourselves fully familiar with the whereabouts of all the electric cables, gas lines and wires and assessing how the current affected us near the Sealab. We crept around the lee side of the Habitat past the television cameras which followed us like the eyes of a wary animal and then down past the diving station.

Bubbles were coming up in streams from the whole length of the Habitat, but we soon discovered that they all emanated from one place and then broke up into several different streams. The leaks were from the penetration where the electric cables entered the hull of the Sealab and the gas was leaking out at such a rate that we would have to repair the source of the leak.

Late that day the first team of divers was ready to go down to the bottom. Bob Barth, the team leader, and probably one of the most experienced saturation divers in the world, was to go to the Habitat with Berry Cannon. They had to make sure the Habitat was sitting level on the sea-bed, lock the Habitat in place on its anchor and then open it up. This in itself was considered by all of us divers to be the most difficult dive of all. It had taken three-quarters of an hour for Barth and Cannon to do it in shallow water. They had to work as a team and know exactly what the other was doing. While opening and levelling the Habitat a mistake could cause it to take on an uncontrollable list and cause a very dangerous situation.

Barth and Cannon entered the water and swam away from the safety of their capsule to the towering Habitat. After five minutes Cannon returned to the capsule and told Blackburn and Reaves, who were in there tending his lines, that he was completely exhausted and needed to rest. Only a couple of minutes later Barth returned on the point of complete collapse. He had to be assisted by the others and was having so much trouble breathing that he used the emergency breathing masks. All four men were shivering uncontrollably. The helium gas they had been in for so long was such a good conductor of heat that, despite the many layers of clothing they wore, they could not keep warm. The helium-induced squeaky voices and the uncontrollable shivers made it impossible to understand them. We brought the four exhausted men back up to the chamber in the ship where they could rest and warm up.

It was here they told us that in the few minutes they had spent in the water they had completely prepared Sealab for entry and all they had left to do was to open the hatch. This amazing feat, however, had left them exhausted and this, combined with the cold and the frightening conditions, had prevented them finishing. They told us that they were so cold that even before getting into the water they were all shivering. When they opened the capsule's hatch steam rose from the almost freezing 40°F water and Blackburn says it was like getting into a warm bath when he got into the water.

It was obvious that we had vastly underestimated the effect of the cold on the divers. We had provided them with a heating system for when they would be diving out of the Habitat but had not, for various highly technical reasons, been able to do this for diving out of the Capsule.

A few hours later Barth and his team said they were ready to once again try to open the hatch to the Sealab. I watched them as they swam over to the Habitat on our remove TV cameras. All seemed well as Bob Barth swam to the hatch and found it was too heavy to move so he moved over to get a crowbar which was provided for just this eventuality. Suddenly he turned around and we saw him pick Berry up out of a cloud of sand. Berry was twitching and jerking and he had lost his mouthpiece. Desperately we watched as Barth repeatedly tried to force the life-saving mouthpiece back between his friend's clenched teeth. Finally he swam with his dying partner back towards the capsule. We had by this time told Blackburn and Reaves that Berry was in trouble and Blackburn jumped into the water and dragged Berry up into the capsule. Frantically in the cramped conditions his friends tried to revive Berry but, after a long period of desperate work we had no trouble understanding John Reaves' broken, distorted words—words which we were all praying he would not say. "Berry's dead, he's dead."

HOW IT ALL HAPPENED—SEALAB III

The Sealab III project is the third in the series of the U.S. Navy's Man-in-the-Sea (M.I.T.S.) programme, which forms part of their Deep Submergence Systems Project (D.S.S.P.).

The initiation of the programme belongs to Capt. George F. Bond, U.S.N. Medical Corps, affectionately known as "Papa Topside", who, while serving as Assistant Officer in Command of the Naval Medical Research Laboratory at New London,

Connecticut, in 1957, was primarily concerned with Submarine Escape, but as a "spare time" project started tests with animals. He exposed the animals to long periods of high pressure with various gas pictures. His work eventually became an official full-time project and was code named "Genesis"—the first step towards "Dominion over the sea" as promised in the first book of the Bible.

Genesis progressed, and in April 1963, at the Experimental Diving Unit (E.D.U.) in Washington, D.C., three U.S.N. Chief Petty Officers Barth, Manning and Lavoie spent six days at a pressure equivalent to 100 feet of sea water. Later that year, Barth, Manning and Navy Doctor Lt. Bull lived at a pressure equivalent to 200 feet for 12 days. On the successful completion of these tests, the laboratory phase of the M.I.T.S. programme was complete.

The first underwater experiment, Sealab I, was soon organized and took place, 26 miles off Bermuda in 193 feet of water. In this experiment four Aquanauts, Barth, Manning, Anderson and Navy Doctor Lt. Anderson, spent from 20 July to 31 July, 1964, successfully working from, and living in the Habitat at this depth. The dive, although cut short by an impending hurricane, was a major success.

A further experiment was quickly organized with no increase in depth, but with different conditions and a larger number of men working on the botton. Sealab II consisted of three teams of ten men, each team to spend fifteen days on the bottom, with Cdr. Scott Carpenter staying for two periods with Teams I and II and a Navy Doctor, Lt. Sonnenburg, also doing two periods with Teams I and III. This experiment was held in 205 feet of water, from 28 August to 14 October, 1965, off La Jolla, California.

During Sealab II, Aquanaut Scott Carpenter spoke to Astronaut Gordon Cooper, whose space craft *Gemini* was circling the earth some 200 miles above him. The Aquanauts also made contact with Jacques Cousteau, in his Conshelf III experiment, which was in 328 feet of water off Nice. Besides living underwater the Sealab II Aquanauts carried out a multitude of physiological experiments and studies and work tasks in Salvage, Oceanography, Geology and Construction. Approximately 400 man hours of useful work was done outside the

Habitat. On completion of the second successful experiment, plans went ahead for the third and most ambitious experiment, Sealab III.

Selection and training of personnel started October 1966, when the Technical Office of D.S.S.P. was founded in San Diego. The training schedule included a series of saturation dives from February 1967 to May 1968, conducted at the E.D.U. in Washington, D.C. Included in these dives was one with five Aquanauts, Lugo, Risk, Conda, Winters and Klechner being saturated to a pressure equivalent to 825 feet of sea water, with an excursion to 1,025 feet by Lugo and Risk in the Wet Chamber section of the Complex. They spent 13 minutes at this depth, and carried out their assigned tasks well.

During this period representatives from the Commonwealth Navies of Australia, Britain and Canada joined the programme, and the "Royal Alien Navy" was founded! Its members—Lt.-Cdr. C. F. Lafferty and C.P.O. D. J. Clark from England, Lt.-Cdr. Lafontaine and P.O. W. P. Lukeman from Canada and Lt. R. R. Sutton from Australia—joining up with the Sealab personnel in Washington in January 1968 to participate in the saturation dive training.

During the five dives from January 1968 (four to 600 feet and one to 825 feet, with excursions to 750 and 1,025 feet), of the 25 men saturated during this period, only three men suffered from the "bends". Two had slight aches in knees, which were treated as "bends" before they fully developed and the third, a subject who had a record of the "bends" in his right knee on his two previous deep dives, possibly a motorcycle accident he was involved in years before had left his right knee susceptible to this ailment. On completion of these dives in Washington in May, all hands returned to San Diego, where the next phase of training, in Aquanaut Equipment, was being run from the Technical Office.

Included in this phase, which continued through until early August, was a month when all the civilian participants from both military and civilian establishments concerned, joined together for a concentrated training effort. By this time Lt.-Cdr. Lafferty and I (C.P.O. Clark) had got ourselves well acquainted with the equipment, and we were appointed to the training staff. This kept us very busy, and also gave us plenty of diving time and practice in the equipment, as we would, in turn, dive with each of the trainees.

The equipment we were primarily concerned with in this phase, consisted of all the associated equipment concerned with the underwater swimming side of the project. It was listed as:

"The body—daily P.T., running and as much diving as possible, the Mk. VIII Breathing Apparatus, Kirby Morgan Helmet, M.D.L. Mask, the Wiswell and Welson hot water heated suits, the divers umbilicals and associated diver communications."

By 1 August all the Sealab personnel had moved up to San Francisco for training with the Sealab Habitat and the support ship, *Elk River*, which housed the Mk. II Deep Diving System. (D.D.S.). The D.D.S. consists of two Deck Decompression Chambers (D.D.C.) situated athwartships, two Personnel Transfer Capsules (P.T.C.) for transferring the Aquanauts from the D.D.C. to the Habitat on the sea bottom. Each D.D.C. and P.T.C. complex are controlled by their own Main Control Console (M.C.C.) from which all communications, and Life Support-monitoring are controlled. Each P.T.C. is lowered by its own winch and has its own cable, which consists of its power and communication lines and is known as the Strength, Power and Communications Cable (S.P.C.C.).

At San Francisco the Naval Shipyard had not completed their tests on any of the systems, thus the training became a tangle of test and training, with the onus being on the testing. A special training group was set up to train Cdr. Scott Carpenter, Phillipe Cousteau, Dr. Joe Macinnis, Dr. Raymond and a Mr. Harrell in the use of the Mk. VIII breathing apparatus. The group consisted of Lt. Cdr. Lafferty as training officer, assisted by Clark and Lukeman. The training and testing progressed steadily and the Sealab Habitat managed to be ready to carry out the scheduled shallow water tests from Friday, 6 September, till Tuesday, 10 September 1968.

During this long weekend the Habitat was lowered into 35 feet of water and each team spent up to a maximum of four hours at a time in the Habitat, combining tests with team training. This training continued around the clock, and those tiring five days were invaluable to all team members and support personnel. During these tests, many problems had come

to light and had to be rectified by the shipyard. Then the training and work detail shifted to the support ship and the Mk. II
D.D.S. Also we had just received the Mk. IX rig from the Experimental Diving Unit, and all the Aquanauts had to be
trained to use this new mixed gas rig. The training during this
period was mainly by teams, in the systems and procedures, as
well as each team's ocean floor programme, which were:

Team One—Opening up and Initial Occupancy procedures
Physiological Studies and Oceanographic
Studies

(The oceanographic studies included lobster transplants,
seeing if lobsters from the Atlantic, caught off Maine on the
East Coast would settle and adapt themselves to the conditions
off San Clemente Island in the Pacific.)

Team Two—Salvage technique and tools
Oceanographic Studies
Team Three—Construction project. (Construct a
small structure of 12 feet diameter
and approximately 6 feet high includ-
ing the domed top section.)
Team Four—Oceanographic Studies
More Physiological Studies
Team Five—Working with Mammals
Oceanographic Studies
Equipment recovery and clean up
Closing down procedure for the Habitat

Teams One and Four remained at San Francisco to carry
on with the testing and their own training whilst Teams Two
and Three went to Port Hueneme, to carry out their associated
salvage and construction programmes in the favourable conditions found off Anacapa Island, which is about 10 miles off
the coast from Port Hueneme, where the Naval Construction
and Engineering Laboratory, which had instituted these programmes, was situated. Team Five also left San Francisco for
Point Mugo, a few miles south of Hueneme where the mammals
that were scheduled for participation in the Sealab project were
housed, for a two-week training period with them.

Lt.-Cdr. Lafontaine, Lukeman and I were included with the

Team Five training, and two weeks of diving with these mammals was an unforgettable experience.

We had several dives with Topo, an intelligent sealion, Rascal and Tuffy, the porpoises. Besides training the mammals for their prescribed tasks, delivering of tools, mail, and finding a lost diver, it was also a useful period for us, the Aquanauts, firstly to get to know these well-trained mammals, and secondly, to learn the art of using them, and not letting them use you. On the first dives, especially with Tuffy, who was used on Sealab II, it was difficult to tell who was training who, as Tuffy would remind us of any incorrect procedures, with a nudge of his snout.

On completion of the team training sessions, all personnel returned to San Francisco for a further concentrated training effort in the Mk. II D.D.S. and the new Mk. IX rig.

It was at this time that all teams were increased to nine men, which all team leaders had been pushing for, since the publication of the proposed Ocean Floor programme, which gave all the alien navy team billets as follows:

Team III—C.P.O. Clark—Mk. VIII specialist
Team IV—Lt.-Cdr. Lafferty—Team Leader
Lt. Sutton—Mk. VIII specialist
Team V — Lt.-Cdr. Lafontaine—Mk. VIII specialist
P.O. Lukeman—Mk. VIII specialist

Due to the increase in team size, the alternates list had been depleted considerably, and it was decided that a further acquaintance course would be run to bolster up the alternates. As the Habitat was leaving for Long Beach, it was decided to run the course there as well, so that we could also complete some of the tests scheduled for the electrically heated swim suits at the same time. I accompanied the Habitat to Long Beach and conducted the course during the last two weeks of October and the first week of November.

The support ship completed her dockyard work and left San Francisco for San Clemente Island about mid-November, where all personnel joined her and prepared the Mk. II D.D.S. and especially the P.T.C.s for their certification dives, as well as the final work up for all hands in preparation for the start of the project.

All was going smoothly till the night of 30 November, when the first stroke of misfortune attacked the project. No. 2 P.T.C. was being lowered to 600 feet, unmanned, when she completely flooded. The result was a two-month delay, as all the interior parts had to be removed, cleaned and repaired. These repairs did not put No. 2 P.T.C. back to its original status, as this would have taken at least six months to complete, but instead most interior components were made to run from batteries, which rather simplified the operation of the P.T.C., but increased its logistic support, because the batteries had to be charged after each capsule operation.

Although the delay was a disappointment to all, as everyone was keyed up and ready to go, it did allow the majority of the personnel to spend Christmas and New Year with their families. After the Christmas recess P.T.C. training recommenced about mid-January in Long Beach and then moved out to San Clemente Island on the 1st of February, with high hopes that we would be able to get underway this time. But within three days of arrival, misfortune struck again, P.T.C. 2 was again involved. This time the capsule was being recovered after a training dive and a CO^2 scrubbing test. The hydraulic fingers, which hold the capsule into its basket, had failed to home properly, and the capsule dropped 15 to 20 feet before the S.P.C. cable took the strain. Many of the outer strands were severed, so much so that the entire cable had to be replaced with a spare from ashore, which took a full working day to complete. Two men had entered the capsule minutes before it fell, to shut the lower hatch, so that the capsule could be lowered and the hydraulic fingers properly secured. For a few agonizing moments there was great concern as to their safety, but they had managed to shut the hatch, and apart from a few bruises both were well.

The minor repairs needed only delayed us a few days, and on their completion, the certification dives, and unmanned hydrostatic dive to 950 feet and a manned hydrostatic dive to 600 feet were carried out. Then as a final checkout for the system and personnel a 100-feet saturation dive, using both D.D.C.s was carried out, lasting three days.

Finally all was ready, final briefings were held and the Habitat left the surface at 16.26 on Saturday, 15 February, 1969, and reached bottom in 610 feet of water at 20.55 the same evening. The submersible "Deep Star," on loan from Westinghouse, was in attendance for the lowering, and kept the Command on the *Elk River* informed of the progress of the Habitat. It was gratifying to hear the report that "the Habitat has settled, looks level and stable with no visible leaks".

During the night, however, the situation changed, and the Habitat began to lose pressure, and with the aid of the closed circuit TV and observation by "Deep Star" the following morning with Cdr. Scott Carpenter and Lt.-Cdr. Lafferty, the leak was found to be from the electrical connectors on the Habitat.

Team One were all ready to enter the D.D.C.s for their pressurization, but because of the leak it was decided that the group consisting of Bob Barth, the team leader, Berry Cannon, electrical engineer, John Reaves, team photographer and Dick Blackburn, equipment specialist, would be pressurized at a faster rate than normally used, at about 4 feet every minute, while the remainder of the team would enter the second D.D.C. and be pressurized at the normally used rate of descent of 40 feet per hour.

Bob Barth and Berry Cannon made their first attempt to enter the Habitat on Sunday evening, 16 February, 1969. They completed all their tasks apart from opening up the Habitat's diving station hatch, this they could not complete due to over-pressurization inside the Habitat and having to abort the dive due to the cold, not only in the water, but also prior to entering the water. Barth reports that on opening the P.T.C. hatch, steam rose off the sea water into the P.T.C.; and the water temperature was about 45°F. After this tremendous effort, they were all brought back to the D.D.C. to be warmed and tested.

To understand what Barth and Cannon had been able to accomplish in their short excursion, it should be realized that during all the training sessions with the Habitat the best time they had managed for this procedure had been about 45 minutes.

After the group had rested, they agreed to make another attempt to enter the Habitat, as the leak was becoming worse by the hour. They made their ill-fated second dive in the early hours of Monday, 17 February. The P.T.C. reached the bottom at about 04.45, and again Bob Barth and Berry Cannon entered the water to try and open the Habitat's diving station hatch. Barth reached the diving station platform and attempted to lift the hatch, but could not, and he moved to the far side of the Habitat to pick up the crowbar, provided for use in this eventuality. As he returned to the platform, he saw that Berry was in trouble, and went to assist him. Berry had lost his face mask and mouthpiece, and was making convulsive movements. Barth attempted to force his open circuit buddy breather into Berry's mouth several times, to no avail.

By this time Barth was beginning to feel the effects of his efforts, and started to move back to the P.T.C. Topside had informed the P.T.C. and Blackburn had entered the water. Between them they managed to get Berry into the P.T.C. and commence emergency resuscitation, but it was no use—Berry was dead. The P.T.C. was retrieved and mated to the D.D.C. and Berry's body brought to the surface while the remainder of the team carried out their $6\frac{1}{2}$-day decompression.

The Habitat was still on the sea-bed in 610 feet of water, and still leaking, and the gas supply aboard the support ship would not last for more than 24 hours at the rate it was being used. To back up the support ship in its efforts to save the Habitat, a U.S. submarine was dispatched from Long Beach, 60 miles away, to provide air for the Habitat.

Lifting the Habitat posed a problem, as the lifting craft available on site, was not designed to lift the extra 9,000 lbs., that the Habitat's mooring clump now held, being flooded. But by hastily constructed safety structures and added counter-weights, the Habitat was saved, reaching surface at about 02.00, Wednesday, 19 February.

Then the Habitat was taken to San Francisco where repairs were being conducted. All personnel returned to San Diego. There, on completion of the official inquiry, we awaited the go-ahead from Washington to get the project underway.

APPENDIX

The British Sub-Aqua Club

For those non-divers who have read this book and would like to find out more about underwater swimming, there follows a complete list of the branches of the British Sub-Aqua Club:

ORDINARY BRANCHES IN THE UNITED KINGDOM, OPEN TO GENERAL PUBLIC

Aberdeen (67): J. B. Gray, 20 Carnory Road, Aberdeen.

Alfreton (302): T. West, 147 Leabrooks, Alfreton, Derbyshire.

Barnsley (95): M. D. Brunt, 28 Longman Road, Barnsley, Yorkshire.

Bath (33): Miss P. A. Molyneux, "Conifers", Hoopers Pool, Southwick, Trowbridge, Wilts.

Bedford (89): Mrs. G. S. Potter, 11 Griffin Street, Rushden, Northants.

Belfast (30): P. A. M. Paice, B.A., 63 Glenholm Park, Belfast, BT8 4IQ.

Bermondsey (42): F. H. White, 14 Brookehouse Road, London, S.E.6.

Birmingham (25): R. M. Leveton, 65 Burford Road, Birmingham 22C.

Blackheath (188): J. Martin, 155 Ampleforth Road, Abbey Wood, London, S.E.2.

Blackpool (4): C. J. Walmsley, 10 Cumberland Avenue, Blackpool.

Bolton (84): G. Diggle, 19 Top O'th Gorses, Darcy Lever, Bolton, Lancs.

Bournemouth (6): R. Smith, 15 Wickfield Avenue, Christchurch, Hants.

Bradford (44): Miss W. G. Walton, Barnsley Cottage, Charlestown, Baildon, Yorks.

Brighton & Worthing (7): J. F. MacMahon, 3 Leigh Road, Broadwater, Worthing.

Bristol (3): K. Hicks, 7 Eaton Close, Fishponds, Bristol, Somerset.

Bromley (26): M. Inch, 8 Alton Close, Bexley, Kent.

Burnley (143): D. Kitson, 55 Newport Street, Nelson, Lancs.

Burton-on-Trent (296): J. A. Stone, 18 Stanley Close, Netherseal, Burton-on-Trent, Staffs.

Cambridge (240): M. J. Wilson, 5 Pettits Close, Fulbourne, Cambs.

Chapleton (256): Mrs. M. Hobson, 106 Potters Gate, High Green, Sheffield.

Chelsea (45): Miss Lilian Stokes, 82 Urmstone Drive, London, S.W.19

Chorley (304): I. Ramsbottom, 76 Wigan Road, Euxton, Chorley, Lancs.

Coventry (58): Mrs. J. McDonagh, "Welcome", Birmingham Road, Warwick.

Crawley (148): Mrs. C. J. Bramson, Wallace Lane, Crawley Down, Sussex.

Croydon (23): R. S. Frankham, 38 Farley Road, Selsdon, Surrey.

Darwen (47): A. Smith, 23 Thornhill Road, Chorley, Lancs.

Deptford (M7) (236): L. S. Surridge, 143 Trundleys Road, Deptford, London, S.E.8.

Derby (72): R. D. Price, 7 Howe Street, Derby.

Doncaster (75): K. Rucastle, "Ke-Bar", 6 Conisburgh Road, Edenthorpe, Doncaster.

Durham City (104): W. Welch, 19 Grange Farm Drive, Whickham, Newcastle-upon-Tyne.

East Anglia (11): M. D. C. Maltby, c/o Anglia Television Ltd., Anglia House, Norwich.

East Cheshire (100): Mrs. S. Hamer, Brooklyn Cottage, Holly Vale, Mill Brow, Marple Bridge, Cheshire.

East Lancs (2): Mrs. P. A. Winterbotham, 5 Wilson Crescent, Ashton-under-Lyne, Lancs.

East London (15): J. H. Simpson, 15 Colvin Gardens, Chingford, London, E.4.

East Yorks (176): J. B. Forrest, 3 Morgan Street, Scarborough, Yorks.

Edinburgh (21): Dr. D. W. Green, 22 Priestfield Avenue, Edinburgh 9, Scotland.

Exeter (62): D. Folland, High Street Studios, Crediton, Devon.

Falmouth (214): J. E. Andrew, Windsor House, 30 Greenbank Terrace, Falmouth, Cornwall.

Folkestone (106): Mrs. J. Windridge, "Rosedene", 38 Price's Avenue, Cliftonville, Margate, Kent.

Furness (61): E. Lowether, 36 Foundry Street, Barrow-in-Furness, Lancs.

Grimsby (37): J. C. Nuthall, 5 Spring Bank, Grimsby, Lincs.

Guildford (53): M. Douglas, Leander, Manor Road, Farnborough, Hants.

Gwynedd (71): Miss I. R. Beamer, 23 Llwyn Onn, Rhos-on-Sea, Colwyn Bay, N. Wales.

Halifax (48): Mrs. J. M. Cowan, Middle Hallershelf Farm, Luddenden Foot, Nr. Halifax.

Hampstead (179); K. A. White, 125 Highfield Way, Chorleywood, Rickmansworth, Herts.

Harlow (141): E. T. Goss, Janan, High Field Place, Epping, Essex.

Harrogate (39): S. Clarke, 21 Castle Close, Killinghall, Nr. Harrogate, Yorks.

High Wycombe (293): Mrs. D. S. Hutchinson, 16 Rayners Avenue, Loudwater, High Wycombe, Bucks.

Holborn (130): Miss E. J. Bryan, Flat 1, 88 Church Road, Lowther Parade, Barnes, London, S.W.13.

Hounslow (55): R. C. S. Grove, 30 Forest Road, Kew, Surrey.

Huddersfield (18): K. Flinders, 15 Red Doles Road, Fartown, Huddersfield, Yorks.

Hull (14): Eric Rose, 3 Kilvin Drive, Hull Bridge Park, Beverley, East Yorks.

Ilford (49): Mrs. T. Lightfoot, 5 Macclesfield House, Dagnam Park Drive, Harold Hill, Romford, Essex.

Ilfracombe (86): N. Hutchinson, 27 Heanton Street, Braunton, N. Devon.

Ipswich (32): A. R. Todd, 66 Beechcroft Road, Ipswich, Suffolk.

Isle of Man (76): Mrs. J. P. Colby, Bay View Central Promenade, Douglas, I.O.M.

Keighley (117): B. Stubbs, 2 Reservoir Place, Mountain Queensbury, Bradford, Yorks.

Kingston (17): J. Stanton, 5 Minerva Road, Kingston-upon-Thames, Surrey.

Leamington & Warwick (217): Mrs. K. I. Herbert, 17 Cowdray Close, Leamington Spa, Warwicks.

Leeds (115): B.S-A.C. Sec., 65 Hall Lane, Leeds 12, Yorks.

Leicester Club Del Mar (312): J. M. Collard, 3 Churchill Drive, Leicester Forest East, Leicester.

Leicester U.W. Exploration (321): Mrs. M. Mitchell, 191 Wicklow Drive, Leicester.

Lincoln (109): A. C. Temperton, 29 Minster Drive, Cathedral View, Cherry Willingham, Lincoln.

London (1): Miss R. J. Cracknall, 376 Wickham Road, Shirley, Croydon, Surrey.

Lunesdale (138): A. Hargreaves, 5 Quermore Drive, Glasson Rock, Lancaster.

Luton (105): J. Austin, 9A Marsh Road, Luton, Beds.

Matlock (121): P. A. Morley, 18 Warner Street, Mickleover, Derby.

Medway (59): M. J. Varney-Burgh, 76 Townley Road, Bexley Heath, Kent.

Merseyside (5): W. M. Smith, 17 Davenham Road, Formby, Lancs.

Mexborough (41): G. Calderbank, 6 Woodside Avenue, Wath-on-Dearne, Nr. Rotherham, Yorks.

Newham (168): T. F. Barwick, 2 Markhams, Stanford-le-Hope, Essex.

Newport & Cardiff (35): Mrs. V. Barlow, 30 High Street, Newport, Mon.

North East Essex (54): G. K. L. Cousins, 6 Sparrow Close, Sille Hedingham, Nr. Halstead, Essex.

North Oxfordshire (74): T. T. Winkleff, 10 Park Road, Banbury, Oxon.

Northampton (13): Mrs. A. P. Shepherdson, 126 Beech Avenue, Northampton.

North Gloucestershire (80): D. Rockett, 10 Cherry Avenue, Charlton Kings, Cheltenham, Glos.

North Staffs (12): W. J. B. White, Hilltop, 9 Liverpool Road E., Church Lawton, Stoke-on-Trent.

North Warwickshire (315): R. Veasey, 89 Heather Road, Coventry, CV3 2DD.

Nottingham (16): D. J. Townsend, "Nerys", Church Road, Boughton, Nr. Newark, Notts.

Oxford (34): Miss A. Symons, Bramblefinch, Boults Lane, Old Marston, Oxford.

Pennine (323): Mrs. J. V. Greenwood, 5 Hebden Terrace, Midgehole, Hebden Bridge, Yorks.

Penzance (116): R. H. Trethowan, 26 William Street, Camborne, Cornwall.

Perth (218): G. Leishman, 9 Kinnard Bank, Perth, Scotland.

Peterborough (297): Miss L. Coates, 9 Elmfield Road, Peterborough, Northants.

Plymouth Sound (164): G. Jensen, 34 Fairview Avenue, Laira, Plymouth.
Pontefract (190): Mrs. P. Hudson, 30 Baden Powell Crescent, Pontefract, Yorks.
Reading (28): G. Vance, 131 Overdown Road, Tilehurst, Reading, Berks.
Redditch (248): P. L. Batty, 98 Harport Road, Redditch, Worcs.
Rhondda (282); E. G. Thomas, 47 Mikado Street, Penycraig, Tonypandy, Rhondda, Glam.
St. Albans (311): V. R. Jones, 15 Alma Road, St. Albans, Herts.
Sandgate (303): Mr. J. Devereese, 3 Edward Road, Folkestone, Kent.
Scarborough (83): The Secretary, Scarborough Branch British Sub-Aqua Club, 25 St. Mary's Street, Scarborough, Yorks.
Sheffield (36): M. G. Plater, 32 Beechwood Road, Dronfield, Sheffield, Yorks.
Solihull (264): A. C. Holmes, 75A Alcester Road South, King's Heath, Birmingham.
Southampton (139): M. Elliott, 1A Forest Meadow, Crawte Avenue, Farley, Hants.
Southend (22): T. R. Hall, Rustana, Lancaster Road, Rayleigh, Essex.
Southport (278): R. Olive, 77 Cornwall Way, Ainsdale, Southport, Lancs.
Southsea (9): H. G. Yelf, 1 Havelock Court, Havelock Road, Southsea, Hants.
Swansea (99): C. D. Withey, 48 Meol Emrys, Swansea, Glam.
Swindon (6): J. E. Hamilton, 11 Springfield Road, Swindon Old Town, Wilts.
Tamworth (137): E. S. George, 13 Borough Road, Tamworth, Staffs.
Taunton (10): A. C. Charlton, "Lorien", 11 Stoke Road, Taunton, Somerset.
Tees-Side (43): J. A. Sturrock, 13 Blackfriars, Yarm-on-Tees, Yorks.
Thornton Heath (210): P. Mann, 30 Springfield Road, Thornton Heath, Surrey.
Thurso (119): D. Mackay, 4 Sigurd Road, Thurso, Caithness.
Torbay (3): E. A. Collins, 20 Sherwell Lane, Torquay, Devon.
Tunbridge Wells (149): Miss L. Gamlyn, Swan Hotel Garage, London Road, Tunbridge Wells, Kent.
Tyneside (114): C. B. Settle, 67 Edwins Avenue, Forest Hall, Newcastle-upon-Tyne 12.

Wakefield (77): S. Webb, 14 St. Richards Road, Otley, Yorks.
West Bromwich (151): F. J. Collier, 198 Frederick Road, Aston, Birmingham 6.
West Cumberland (94): E. C. Carnhall, 71 Gosforth Road, Seascale, Cumberland.
West Lancs (153): N. Wall, 35 Finsbury Avenue, Blackpool S.S., Lancs.
Westminster (159): L. Zanelli, 81 Long Lane, London, N.3.
York (50): K. C. Cousins, 26 Bridge Road, Bishopthorpe, York.

SPEARFISHING BRANCHES
Spearfishing only no Breathing
Apparatus used

Home Counties (285): D. M. C. Rosemeyer, 87 Cambridge Road, New Malden, Surrey.
Ipswich Universal Divers (291): A. J. Beckerleg, 101 Claygate Lane, Ipswich, Suffolk.
Southsea Bubbles (295): Mrs. R. C. Pearce, 26 Stockheath Road, Leigh Park, Havant, Hants.
Spearfishing Club of G.B. Plymouth (286): M. J. R. Eccleston, 44 Glenfield Way, Glenholt Park, Crownhill, Plymouth, Devon.
Sussex Spearfishing Club (289): J. P. Weedon, The Sussex Spearfishing Club, "The Cricketers", The Green, Southwick, Sussex.
Weymouth Associated Divers (269): R. J. Ford, 8 Reforne Close, Easton, Portland, Dorset.

ORDINARY BRANCHES
OVERSEAS

Barbados (310): Mrs. S. K. Hendy, "Barhill", Elizabeth Drive, Pine Gardens, Bridgetown, Barbados.
Blantyre (243): W. A. L. Apps, P.O. Box 393, Blantyre, Malawi, Central Africa.
B.S-A.C. de Panama (262): Mr. K. H. Willis, Sn., P.O. Box 62, Coco Solo, Canal Zone, Panama, U.S.A.
Durban Assoc. Divers (200): The Secretary, Associated Divers, P.O. Box 3396, Durban, South Africa.
Indianapolis-1st U.S.A. (154): T. T. Haver, 6001 Compton, Indianapolis 20, Indiana, U.S.A.
Jamaica (51): The Secretary, Jamaica Sub-Aqua Club, P.O. Box 215, Mona, Kingston 7, Jamaica, W.I.

Limasol, Cyprus (258): S.A.C. Woodward, M., A.R.I.C. (N.E.), R.A.F. Episkopi, B.F.P.O. 53

Montego Bay, Jamaica (192): Miss D. Titterington, c/o Montego Bay High School for Girls, Union Street, Montego Bay, Jamaica, W.I.

Napier N.Z. Pacific Divers (244): Mrs. C. A. Hammond, 3 Surrey Street, Taradale, New Zealand.

Nee Soon (228): Q/Pte. Dennis, J., 32 Coy. R.A.M.C., B.M.H., c/o G.P.O., Singapore.

New Jersey (220): F. A. Vogel, 1557 Deer Run Drive, Manasquan, N.J. 08736, U.S.A.

Rhode Island (284): Mrs. W. S. R. Russell, 7 Sylvan Terrace, Newport, Rhode Island, Zp Code 02843, U.S.A.

Salisbury-Rhodesia (63): The Secretary, Salisbury R. Branch, B.S-A.C., P.O. Box 3532, Salisbury, Rhodesia.

Trinidad (129): A. Oliver, c/o Myerson Mouldings Ltd., n O. Box 111, Port of Spain, B.W.I.

SPECIAL BRANCHES
—HOME & OVERSEAS

Membership confined to those who are members of the other organizations listed

Aberdeen University (214): R. B. Smith, Wavel House, Hill Head Halls of Residence, Don Street, Aberdeen, Scotland.

Aquatic Group (180): Mrs. D. R. Shiers, 11 Epping Way, London, E.4.

Aston University (341): K. B. Higgs, 65 Wootton Crescent, St. Annes, Bristol.

B.E.A. Silver Wings (146): Miss S. E. Savage, 21A Northdown Close, Ruislip, Middlesex.

Berlin Inf. Brig. Group (203): 23802231 Sgt. Oates, W. J., 247 Prov. Coy. R.M.P., B.F.P.O. 45.

Borough Polytechnic (186): D. F. W. Hewes, 79 Tarnwood Park, Court Road, London, S.W.9.

Boston & Horncastle School (215): Secretary, Sub-Aqua Club, Boston & Horncastle Grammar School, Boston, Lincs.

B.P. Meadhurst (181): R. Tunesi, 12 Napier Road, Ashford Common, Middlesex.

Bradford City Police (195): R. Holt, Central Police Office, York House, Upper Piccadilly, Bradford 1.

Bristol Aeroplane (88): N. Besant, 3 Bromley Drive, Downend, Nr. Bristol.

Bristol University (276): P. G. Baker, 9 Nugent Hill, Cotham, Bristol 6.

Cambridge University (52): C. J. Wakefield, Trinity Hall, Cambridge.

Carnegie College (287): K. S. Watson, Fairfax Hall, C.L.C.C. Backetts Park, Leeds 6.

Chelsea & Sir John Cass Colleges (123): F. J. Perkins, 50 Stafford Street, Heath, Hayes, Cannock, Staffordshire.

City University (70): British Sub-Aqua Club, City University Union, St. John Street, London, E.C.1.

29 Commando Light Regiment R.A. (268): Capt. J. A. Cook, R.A.P.C., 29 Commando Light Regt. R.A., Dieppe Barracks, F.A.F.B. (F.E.), B.F.P.O. 164.

Croydon Technical College (187): M. K. Todd, 23 Hillcrest Road, Orpington, Kent

De Havilland-Bolton (101): F. J. Lloyd, 26 Crescent Avenue, Ashton-in-Makerfield, Wigan, Lancashire.

Dhekelia (120): 22234578 W.O.II Holmes, A. R. G., Garrison Admin. Unit, Dhekelia, B.F.P.O. 53.

Ebbw Vale Swimming Club (263): Brian Druce, 57 Stonebridge Road, Rassau, Beaufort, Monmouthshire.

Ekon (234): E. E. Hutchings, 8 Fairview Drive, Watford, Herts.

Episcopi J.S. (150): Flt. Lt. S. J. Blower, Families Clinic, Tsiros Estate, Limasol, Cyprus, B.F.P.O. 53.

Eton College (279): E. G. Lock, c/o R. H. Parry, Eton College, Windsor, Berks.

Exeter University (246): M. D. Bailey, Brendon House, Birks' Grange, New North Road, Exeter, Devon.

Exul (320): Miss E. P. Owen, 3/4 Balfour Place, London, W.1.

Famagusta Services (267): Major H. M. Caines, 9th Signal Regt., B.F.P.O. 53.

Farelf (152): W.O.I E. A. Kavanagh, c/o 40 Command Workshop, c/o G.P.O., Singapore.

Fifty-Nine Club (292): Miss M. P. Bailey, 90 Mildred Avenue, Hayes, Middlesex.

Flint College (167); P. Bennett, Craiglea, 2 Millview Road, Shotton, Nr. Chester.

1st Bn. The Sherwood Foresters (257): The Secretary, L.A.D., R.E.M.E., 1 Foresters, B.F.P.O. 17.

Ford Motors (227): M. Wakeling, 51 Windermere Avenue, Elm Park, Hornchurch, Essex.

4th Divisional Engineers (313); Lt. B. N. Wilks, R.E., 44 F.D., S.P., S.Q.N., R.E., B.F.P.O. 16

Granada Aquanauts (253): P. B. Schofield, 17 King Street South, Rochdale, Lancashire.

H.M.S. Caledonia (184): Sub/Lt. N. T. H. Richards, H.M.S. Caledonia, Rosyth, Fife, Scotland.

H.M.S. Mauritius (322): Porrel C. Cordwell, Senior Rates Mess, H.M.S. Mauritius, B.F.P.O. 161.

Hull University (245): The Secretary, B.S-A.C., c/o The Union, University of Hull, East Yorkshire.

Ilford Films (177): T. W. Blake, 21 Carter Close, Collier Row, Romford, Essex.

Imperial College (64): The Secretary, I.C. Underwater Club, Imperial College Union, Prince Consort Road, London, S.W.7.

Joint H.Q. Rheindalen (277): The Secretary, B.S-A.C.,' 2 Headquarters, British Army of the Rhine, B.F.P.O. 40.

Junior Sappers (309); C.S.M.I. Dolphin, D., Jnr. Ldrs. Regt., Royal Engineers, Old Park Barracks, Dover, Kent.

Lathol Special (306): P. Schofield, Swimming and Sub-Aqua Section, Billet Lane, Stanford-Le-Hope, Essex.

Leeds University Union (124): The Secretary, Leeds University Union Sub-Aqua Club, c/o Leeds University Union, Leeds.

Liverpool University (280): The Secretary, Liverpool University Sub-Aqua Club, University Sports Centre, Bedford Street North, Liverpool 3.

London Fire Brigade (250): B. Keane, 12 Maple Court, Winton Way, London, S.W.16.

London Hospitals (254): M. J. Osborne, St. Thomas's House, Lambeth Palace Road, London, S.E.1.

London Inter-Varsity Club (208): Miss B. E. Speyer, 4 Chestnut Avenue, Hampton, Middx.

London Scouts (20): W. Best, 57 Henry Wise House, 53 Vauxhall Bridge Road, London, S.W.1.

London University (69): J. D. Harrison, Sec. Sub-Aqua Club, University of London Union, Malet Street, London, W.C.1.

Loughborough College (165): The Secretary, (B.S-A.C.) Loughborough College Branch, c/o Mr. Millard, 74 Holt Drive, Loughborough, Leicestershire.

Loughborough University (238): A. L. Guest, Loughborough University of Technology, Loughborough, Leicestershire.

Marconi Basildon (219): S. J. Fawkes, c/o The Chairman, Basildon Marconi Branch B.S-A.C., c/o The Marconi Co. Ltd., Christopher Martin Road, Basildon, Essex.

N.A.C.S-A.C. (Naval Air Command Sub-Aqua Club) (66): R. W. Crocker, 51 Mongleath Avenue, Falmouth, Cornwall.

Newcastle University (249): Miss P. M. King, c/o Dove Marine Laboratory, Cullercoats, Northumberland.

New Cross Institute (102): P. R. Hudson, 47A Lewisham Hill, S.E.13.

Otis Special (301); P. McGivern, 45 Sandon Road, Walton, Liverpool 9.

Oxford University (169): David Squire, University College, Oxford, OXL 4BH.

Penang Swimming Club (225): The Secretary, Penang Swimming Club, 517 Tanjong Bungah, Penang, Malaysia.

R.A.A.F. Butterworth (230): A316260 Cpl. Wall, L. K., 478 Matra, R.A.A.F. Butterworth, Via Penang P.O., Malaya.

R.A.F. Akrotiri (107): 3508827 Sq. Ldr. Vincent, R. J., Strike Wing, H.Q., R.A.F. Akrotiri, B.F.P.O. 53.

R.A.F. Benson (156): M. A. Leese, 1 Chipmunk Road, R.A.F. Benson, Oxon.

R.A.F. Binbrook (224): Secretary, Sub-Aqua Club, R.A.F. Binbrook, Lincoln.

R.A.F. Brize Norton (318): The Secretary, Sub-Aqua Club, R.A.F. Brize Norton, Oxon.

R.A.F. Changi (265): The Secretary, Changi Sub-Aqua Club, R.A.F. Changi, c/o G.P.O., Singapore.

R.A.F. College (193): Flt. Cd. C. J. Long, Junior Mess, R.A.F. College, Cranwell, Sleaford, Lincolnshire.

R.A.F. Debden (274): Mrs. S. Cass, 94 Debden Drive, Debden, Saffron Walden, Essex.

R.A.F. El Adem (201): The Secretary, R.A.F. El Adem Sub-Aqua Club, B.F.P.O. 56.

R.A.F. Finningley (211): Officer-in-Charge, Sub-Aqua Club, R.A.F. Finningley, Doncaster, Yorkshire.

R.A.F. Gan (126): Officer-in-Charge, Sub-Aqua Club, Officers' Mess, R.A.F. Gan, B.F.P.O. 180.

R.A.F. Gibraltar (317): Flt. Lt. S. Brayshaw, Officer in Charge, Sub-Aqua Club, R.A.F. Gibraltar.

R.A.F. Gutersloh (221); K0689105 Cpl. McGaw, A. M., 4 Sqn., R.A.F. Gutersloh, B.F.P.O. 47.

R.A.F. Halton (247); Cpl. Steward, G., 87 Longecroft Avenue, R.A.F. Halton, Nr. Aylesbury, Bucks.

R.A.F. Leconfield (307); The Secretary, R.A.F. Leconfield Sub-Aqua Club, Station Post Office, R.A.F. Leaconfield, Beverley, Yorks.

R.A.F. Leeming (298): 1937745 S.A.C. Todd, D. C., G.R.S.F., R.A.F. Leeming, Northallerton, Yorks.

R.A.F. Lyneham (231): Flt. Lt. Warren, T. N., 15 Hungerford Road, Calne, Wilts.

R.A.F. Malta (213); Sgt. L. Magee, B.E.M., 44, A.M.Q., 2 Site, R.A.F. Luqa, B.F.P.O. 51.

R.A.F. Marham (171); Fg. Off. A. Curtis, R.A.F. Marham, Nr. Kings Lynn, Norfolk.

R.A.F. Muharraq (242); Sgt. D. J. Wood, Sgts. Mess, R.A.F. Muharraq, Bahrain, B.F.P.O. 63.

R.A.F. Newton (255); Secretary, Sub-Aqua Club, R.A.F. Newton, Nottinghamshire.

R.A.F. Nicosia (216); Cpl. R. A. Sharp, E.S.S., R.A.F. Nicosia, B.F.P.O. 53.

R.A.F. North Luffenham (273): T4275075 Cpl. Llewell, R. G., R.A.F. North Luffenham, Oakham, Rutland.

R.A.F. Northumbria (324): D. A. Hewitt, Sgts. Mess, R.A.F. Acklington, Morpeth, Northumberland.

R.A.F. St. Athan (281): 3508585 Flt. Lt. Martin, J. A., Officers' Mess, R.A.F. St. Athan, Glamorgan, Wales.

R.A.F. St. Mawgan (288): M1945024 S.A.C. Robinson, J., c/o H. & R., R.A.F., St. Mawgan, Newquay, Cornwall.

R.A.F. Scampton (189): Secretary, Sub-Aqua Club, R.A.F. Scampton, Lincoln.

R.A.F. Seletar (98): Secretary, Sub-Aqua Club, R.A.F. Seletar, c/o G.P.O., Singapore.

R.A.F. Sharjah (270): Lt. A. P. Byles, R.C.T., c/o 90 Squadron R.C.T., B.F.P.O. 64.

R.A.F. Stafford (252): P4266869 S.A.C. Beamish, W., c/o Transportation, No. 16 M.U., Stafford.

R.A.F. Tengah (134): The Secretary, Tengah Sub-Aqua Club, c/o Station Post Office, R.A.F. Tengah, Singapore.

R.A.F. Topcliffe (319): X4273693 Sgt. Anning, T. V., Aircrew Cadets Mess, R.A.F. Topcliffe, Thirsk, Yorks.

R.A.F. Valley (308): 608372 Flt. Lt. Longdon, D. C., Officers' Mess, R.A.F. Valley, Anglesey, North Wales.

R.A.F. Wattisham (299): E0588914 Sgt. Maguire, J. J., M.S.S., R.A.F. Wattisham, Ipswich, Suffolk.

R.A.F. Wildenrath (207): Mrs. J. V. Edington, c/o D1948463 S.A.C. Edington, J. M., A.S.F., R.A.F. Wildenrath, B.F.P.O. 42.

R.A.F. Wittering (305): Secretary, Sub-Aqua Club, c/o R.A.F. Wittering, Peterborough.

R.A.F. Wyton (161): Secretary, B.S-A.C., Sgts. Mess, R.A.F. Wyton, Huntingdon.

R.M.A. Sandhurst (202): The Secretary, Sub-Aqua Club, R.M.A. Sandhurst.

R.S.A.S.R.G. (91): P. M. Brosniham, 4 Gilson Way, Salisbury, Rhodesia.

Ruislip & Northwood Swimming Club (206): Dr. S. Laing, 10 Burwell Avenue, Greenford, Middx.

Second Division Signal Regt. (290): L/Cpl. M. Goatley, 'B' Troop, 3 Sqn., 2 Division Sig. Regt., B.F.P.O. 22.

Selo Brentwood (237): J. W. Sweetingham, 72 Fernbank Avenue, Elm Park, Hornchurch, Essex.

Seremban Garrison (259): Capt. T. M. Pleyman, Seremban Garrison Sub-Aqua Club, 17 Div./Malaya Dist. Pro. Coy R.M.P., c/o G.P.O. Seremban, Malaysia.

7th Signal Regt. (266): 483934 2/Lt. Hughes, B. J., c/o Officers Mess, 7th Signal Regt., B.F.P.O. 15.

South Shields Volunteer Lifeguard (222): R. D. Osborne, 205 Stanhope Road, South Shields, Co. Durham.

S.T.C. Basildon (204): Miss M. South, 14 Beehive Lane, Basildon, Essex.

St. Andrews University (300): Miss R. L. Briggs, 12 Kilymont Road, St. Andrews, Fife, Scotland.

St. John's Singapore (223): J. Haddy, 131 Queen's Avenue, Singapore 27.

Steel Weld Grantham (209): K. R. Mayes, 44 Belvoir Gardens, Gt. Gonerby, Grantham, Lincs.

Sunderland Technical College (275): D. Proctor, No. 1 Caravan, Castletown, Sunderland, Co. Durham.

Tidworth Garrison (294): Capt. B. C. Trueman, Para. Sqn. Royal Armoured Corps, Tidworth, Hants.

University of Surrey (316): R. W. Boaden, 93 Sullivan Court, London, S.W.6.

Walton, Liverpool Technical College (260): Miss P. L. Hassell, Flat 6, Larcherly Road, Fairfield, Liverpool 7.

Woolwich R.I. (62): T. H. Simms, 347 Old Farm Avenue, Sidcup, Kent.

Wycliffe College (68): C. Ellis, No. 7 Queen's Road, Stonehouse, Glos.

Zoology Dept. U.C. Swansea (239): Dr. J. Moyse, Zoology Dept., University College of Swansea, Glamorgan, Wales.

If you do not find a branch conveniently situated in that list and you still want to learn to dive, then please write to:

The Director, The British Sub-Aqua Club, 160 Great Portland Street, London, W1N 5TB.

INDEX